The Politics of Recession

For people in my life
Eileen, Anna, Lucy, Dawn, Tommy, Nahid, Harry, Poppy,
Emma, Christopher, Alexander

The Politics of Recession

Maurice Mullard

Reader in Public and Social Policy, University of Hull, UK

Edward Elgar

Cheltenham, UK • Northampton, MA, USA

Published by
Edward Elgar Publishing Limited
The Lypiatts
15 Lansdown Road
Cheltenham
Glos GL50 2JA
UK

Edward Elgar Publishing, Inc.
William Pratt House
9 Dewey Court
Northampton
Massachusetts 01060
USA

A catalogue record for this book
is available from the British Library

Library of Congress Control Number: 2011932863

ISBN 978 1 84844 871 1 (cased)

Typeset by Servis Filmsetting Ltd, Stockport, Cheshire
Printed and bound by MPG Books Group, UK

Contents

Preface

The recession that started in 2008 was not a global recession. The economies of China, India and the emerging economies of East Asia and Brazil experienced continuing economic growth. In 2011 China became the second largest economy and the forecast is that China will overtake the USA by 2050. After 200 years of global dominance, the economies of the West have to face the challenges of the emerging new economies which are at present out-producing, out-exporting and out-growing some of the advanced economies. While global growth depended on 800 million consumers living in the advanced economies, there are now 2 billion new consumers emerging in China and India. The new global economy therefore offers both challenges and opportunities for the advanced economies. The response of the UK and other European countries of reducing spending on education and infrastructure in response to public sector deficits might deal with short-term concerns but will hinder future competitiveness. Equally, while the financial crisis has confirmed the need for a global solution of global financial reforms that are universal and comprehensive, the tendency has increasingly become one of national and domestic policy making. While Basle III is an attempt to outline a definition of capital requirement that is universal, financial institutions are using their governments as a form of lobbying to seek concessions. A process that is influenced by national priorities is therefore likely to create regulatory arbitrage, with financial entities moving to those countries that offer lower regulatory standards.

The interim Vickers Report published in April 2011, the Dodd-Frank Act in the USA of July 2010 and Basle III represent initiatives to deal with the financial crisis. The common themes of the proposed reforms include responding to the high leverage by financial institutions, the growth of derivatives in deregulated markets and the concern of too big to fail. Policy reform proposals include higher capital requirements, increased transparency by putting derivatives on exchanges and clearing platforms, posting collateral and developing living wills for large banks that would allow liquidation in an orderly fashion in case of bank failures.

All of these reforms represent relevant responses in the crisis of 2007. However, with financial institutions now being global entities the issue of too big to fail would still persist. Governments would not allow the Royal Bank of Scotland, Goldman Sachs or JP Morgan Chase to go into bankruptcy for fear that such an event would be catastrophic for both the financial sector and the real economy. Since the recession, the banks that have survived have become even more concentrated. The top five banks in the USA have assets which are equivalent to 65 per cent of US GDP while in the UK and other European countries the large banks have assets which are three times the size of GDP. There is no way that US policy makers would allow Goldman Sachs with assets worth 950 billion dollars to go into liquidation. This process creates a fear factor and also a dependency relationship between governments and the financial sector.

The financial crisis exhibited major tensions between capitalism and democracy. A capitalism that is defined by the ethic of one dollar, one vote, and a democracy run on the basis of one person, one vote, has generated major issues of inequalities of incomes, but also inequalities in the access to the policy process. Based on the ethic of one dollar, one vote, those on high incomes have quick and ready access to the policy process and the corridors of government where they shape policy at the formulation stage. On the basis of one person, one vote, in the democratic process the majority influence policy making during elections. In contemporary democracy the multitude becomes the quiet audience sitting in the auditorium watching the political actors on the stage and being asked to clap in between acts. Democracy that is limited to election times is, according to Barber (1984), thin democracy as opposed to the commitment of thick democracy and the culture of involvement.

Secondly, the conventional wisdom that has dominated economic thinking during the past three decades of commitment to the free market and rational expectations theory has created a climate in which markets reign supreme; markets are the equivalent to the law of gravity and therefore the outcomes are seen as the natural outcomes of markets rather than political choices. The study of economics, research in economics and publications can no longer be assumed to be independent and impartial when independent Think Tanks' Boards of Trustees are continually seeking new funding to secure new professorships and new research grants and therefore becoming dependent on financial contributions, and those same contributors have their own ideologies and political priorities, which in turn undermine the concept of independent impartial research. There is, therefore, the legitimate concern of how the present research agenda within independent Think Tanks and how the idea of impartial economics reinforces the particular interests of those contributors who favour free unfettered and deregulated markets (Ferguson 2011a; Turner 2010).

interests and ideology often interact in ways so subtle that is difficult to disentangle them, the influence of interests achieved through an unconsciously accepted ideology. The financial sector dominates non-academic employment of professional economists who, however rigorously independent in their judgements on specific issues, will, because only human, tend implicitly to support or at least not aggressively challenge the conventional wisdom which is in the interests of their industry. Regulators need to hire industry experts to regulate effectively; but industry experts are almost bound to share the industry's implicit assumptions. (Turner 2010, p. 9)

The financial crisis has confirmed the absence of a public interest. Fragmentation and struggles of who gets what had undermined the principle of the notion of the public interest. In the advanced economies the period since the mid-1980s has been characterized by growing income inequalities and the concentrations of income towards the top 1 per cent of earners and even more concentrated towards the top 0.01 per cent of earners. Income inequality in 2011 is similar in magnitude to levels of inequality in 1929. This process has distorted policy making but is also undermining the democratic process. The rule by a small elite amidst growing poverty and income inequalities does not allow for the possibilities of hope and societal change.

The financial crisis has exhibited the absence of a public interest at a number of levels. Policy makers depend on financial contributions as do political parties. Those with money have the ability to hire accountants, lawyers and tax advisors that ensure policy is shaped in order to serve their narrow particular interests rather than universal public interests. The process of deregulation and forms of economic thinking that favoured the commitment to unfettered markets created a context that put handcuffs on regulators. The problem of revolving doors, of moving between an appointment as a regulator to an appointment with the private sector as an advisor, or to be hired as a lobbyist, means that elected politicians and regulators know that as they step down from government appointments they will eventually retire as millionaires:

> The appropriate comparison is perhaps with a powerful magnetic field. When The Force is with them – when, that is, Congressmen and women, their staffs, presidential aides, and federal regulators can be sure of walking out of their offices to become multimillionaires when they retire or step down – expecting them to act consistently in the public interest is idle, even if all representatives were elected on 100% public funding. (Ferguson 2011b, p. 27)

The Credit Rating Agencies (CRAs) rated $4.3 trillion worth of asset backed securities as triple-A and then downgraded 87 per cent of those securities to below investment grade within a period of 24 months. Due to their business model of the issuer pays the CRAs were reluctant to walk away from a rating. The ethics of IBGYBG – I'll be gone, you'll be gone – implied that analysts at the CRAs and the issuers of bonds had to focus on the short term of getting an issue rated, getting the fees, improving their personal incomes and not thinking about the long-term consequences.

Thirdly, financial institutions sold securities to their clients, even when the entities themselves were betting that these same securities would default. The client was treated as the sophisticated investor who knew what level of risk they wanted to absorb. However, clients trusted their banks to sell them something that was good for them.

The financial crisis has also resulted in the breakdown of trust. People had trust in the institutions of government, in their banks and professionals who they thought were there to advise them on what is good for them. The financial crisis showed a breakdown in the trust in mortgage brokers who were being paid high fees by originators of loans to channel borrowers towards high interest rate mortgages. Issuers of bonds were concerned with securitization of bonds, getting a rating and selling these to investors. Investment banks were concerned with minimizing their own exposure and getting rid of high-risk assets so that in selling bonds to investors as a long-term investment the banks themselves were betting that these same bonds would default. The CEOs of the 14 major banks earned incomes of $2.6 billion between 1997 and 2007. The top five CEOs earned $2 billion (Johnson 2011). The Credit Rating Agencies through fees in the rating of asset backed securities, increased their incomes from 3 billion to 6 billion dollars annually, while the CEOs of the CRAs were earning salaries similar to the CEOs of the investment banks.

Since World War II there have been approximately 125 financial crises, with a crisis occurring on average once every three years. One major consequence of the latest financial crisis has been the surge in leveraging in the private sector by both households and private sector entities. The climate of a long period of short-term interests resulted in high borrowing by households and private sector companies (Rheinhart and Rogoff 2009). Deleveraging means a loss of output and increases in unemployment. With the declines in house prices and in equities households are repairing their finances paying off debt and increasing savings. In 2008 and 2009 global GDP shrank by 2 per cent, the GDP in the USA declined by 4.5 per cent and the UK by 6 per cent. The majority of governments in the advanced economies are making decisions about public finances in the context of a smaller economy. The crisis in the financial system has major costs for employment and for social provision, including health and education. There are major declines in GDP which then take years to repair. Despite the frequent occurrence of financial crises, governments have opted to deregulate the finance industry when the natural response would have been to seek tighter regulation. This confirms a process of 'cognitive policy capture', with governments and policy makers co-opting the expertise of finance to define and shape policy (Johnson 2011). Advocates of free markets have consistently pointed out that it was always better for market participants to regulate themselves. The repeal of the Banking Act of 1933 and the implementation of the Commodity Futures Modernization Act of 2000 created the context for the growth of the over-the-counter (OTC) derivatives markets. This unregulated market grew to notional amounts of $640 trillion between 1997 and 2007, which was equivalent to 10 times global GDP. There is no evidence that the derivatives markets contributed to the growth of global GDP. The growing economies of India and China and the emerging economies did not utilize the OTC markets. Adair Turner (2011), the Chairman of the FSA, pointed out that most of what happened in the financial markets was economically and socially useless, since the majority of transactions were purely speculative about future prices.

The argument developed in this book points to a structural explanation of the financial crisis. The concept of social structures connects with concerns about relationships of power and influence, the role of ideology and inequalities. The financial crisis was a crisis of economic ideas. Rational expectations and efficient markets theories that had become the intellectual paradigm in policy making provided institutions of government with philosophies and ready-made policy options. The economists who produced these models were well aware of the limitations of their models and yet failed to point these out to the policy practitioners.

The increases in house prices after 1997 – house prices were rising at an average of 10 per cent per year – provided households with the opportunity to exchange the savings and equities in their homes for liquid cash, which they could then utilize for personal consumption. The increases in house prices provided a context of dissaving and increased consumption, as households looked at their homes as their portfolios and as ATM machines. Households took $2.3 trillion of equity out of their homes for increased debt. However, it would be misleading to attribute the financial crisis to the housing bubble or the defaults with the sub-prime mortgages. The total write-offs within sub-prime mortgages were between $500 billion and $1 trillion, which should have been absorbed within a global economy of $65 trillion. The total costs to the government in bailing out the financial sector was $14 trillion.

The OTC derivatives markets and the processes of securitization contributed to the financial crisis because of their complexity, their opaqueness and the lack of market prices, since most of these swaps were private, customized and unique bonds. Derivatives amplified uncertainty and eventually caused a bank run on the investment banks when the REPO markets asked for high collateral and higher haircuts in accepting asset-backed securities. The crisis at Bear Stearns Lehman Brothers and AIG reflected the uncertainty. In the case of AIG the insurance company sold some $80 billion of credit default swaps (CDS) for a premium of $8 billion. Since AIG did not have to post daily collateral, there was no attempt to calculate daily prices movements of the derivatives markets The CDS was not statutory insurance. The CDS reflected daily changes in the market. The absence of collateralized debt obligation (CDO) transactions made it difficult to price these instruments, therefore when Goldman Sachs asked for increased collateral from AIG, AIG disputed the amount. The attempt to put the OTC market on transparent futures exchanges and on central clearing platforms has met with resistance for broker dealers and from end users. The opaqueness of the system has generated fees for the brokers and also reduced the costs for end users. The derivatives market proved to be highly fragile during the financial crisis and the need for higher capital requirements and posting collateral would at least start to internalize the risks posed in the OTC markets.

The costs of the present financial meltdown have been high in terms of increases in unemployment shrinking GDP, falling revenues, and major increases in government debt ratios which have overspilled into debates about reducing public expenditure on education, health and social security spending. All these reductions will impact the quality of life of the elderly, the sick, the unemployed and young people in education. None of these groups caused the financial crisis but now seem to be paying the price for it.

It remains to be seen whether new economic thinking will emerge to replace the paradigm of market liberalism that has dominated thinking for the past three decades. There has always been a plurality of theoretical models of how economies work; the issue is not the absence of alternatives but rather the attempt to explain how these alternatives are marginalized. The financial crisis, therefore, teaches the lesson that that there are political choices and alternatives, as opposed to theories of inevitability of outcomes. The claim made by rational expectations theorists that their economics had solved the problem of stabilization has proven to be misleading during the present recession. The paradigm of free markets did not predict the present financial crisis nor did it provide for the possibility for crisis. Furthermore, free market advocates have offered little policy choice for dealing with the crisis (Summers 2011). Those who seek to break out of the present orthodoxy need to reclaim the ethics of Keynes and start to kick up a fuss. Free unfettered markets work in some sectors, but it cannot be assumed that market completion is the only solution and the only alternative. Markets do produce the dynamic for change for social progress but there needs to be a return to the classical political economy of Adam Smith, Ricardo and Keynes: a political economy that tried to explain how economies worked but left issues of income distributions as contestable issues of political choices, as opposed to the recent ideology that suggested there are no alternatives but to accept the outcomes of markets.

During the writing of the book I broke my leg in two places in the Lake District, which meant the research had to stop as most of the time I had to lie down with my leg in heavy plaster. I need therefore to thank Felicity Plester and the team at Edward Elgar who have continued to support me in writing this book. In writing this book I have many debts to my wife Eileen who has been patient and supportive, and my children who never complained about me talking about the book during the past two years. I want to thank colleagues and friends who read chapters and who listened patiently to some of my arguments in developing this book. However, in the end, I take full responsibility for what I have written.

REFERENCES

Barber, B. (1984) *Strong Democracy: Participatory Democracy for a New Age.* Berkeley and Los Angeles, CA: University of California Press.

Ferguson, C. (2011a) 'The Corruption in Academic Economics', INET Interview, 14 April. Available at: inteconomics.org

Ferguson, T. (2011b) 'Legislators Never Bowl Alone: Big Money, Mass Media, and the Polarization of Congress', INET Conference, Bretton Woods, April.

Johnson, S. (2011) Presentation at the Bretton Woods New Economic Thinking INET Conference, Bretton Woods, April.

Rheinhart, C. and K. Rogoff (2009) *This Time is Different: Eight Centuries of Financial Folly.* Princeton, NJ and Oxford: Princeton University Press.

Summers, L. (2011) 'A Conversation with Martin Wolf', INET Conference, Bretton Woods, April.

Turner, A. (2010) 'Economics, Conventional Wisdom and Public Policy', Turner Institute for New Economic Thinking Inaugural Conference, Cambridge, April.

Turner, A. (2011) Keynote Speech at the INET Conference, Bretton Woods, April.

1. Introduction: the absence of public interest

The recent uprisings in the Middle East have confirmed that autocratic forms of capitalism are, in the long term, not sustainable. An economy dominated by an elite few, with growing income inequalities and no sense of hope for the multitudes, turn protests into revolution. In the advanced economies since the mid-1980s there have been major shifts in the distribution of incomes towards the top 1 per cent of earners, while for the majority of people disposable income has stagnated. The concentration of incomes has produced distortions in the policy process and has also distorted democracy, with those on high incomes through political contributions and the ability to access the policy makers shaping and defining policy choices to reflect particular narrow vested interests, thus undermining the concept of the public interest.

The financial crisis of 2007 has confirmed the absence of a public interest at a number of levels. Firstly, it can no longer be assumed that policy makers seek election as a public service. Money in politics, financial contributions to key policy makers and political parties, together with the presence of strong lobbying at the stage of policy formulation, means that policy is often being shaped and defined to serve particular narrow vested interests as opposed to the public interest. Secondly, regulators who have the role of being the guardians of the public interest undermined their own status as gatekeepers. The Credit Rating Agencies (CRAs) designated as national regulators and trusted with the role of rating securities, undermined their role because of a conflict of interests between the issuer pay models and the ethics of their analysts. The CRAs downgraded $4.3 trillion worth of securities from triple-A to below investment grade. The CRAs contributed to the financial crisis by rating multiples of asset based securities as triple-A. Thirdly, banking institutions sold securities to investors while at the same time the financial entities were themselves taking out insurance that these same securities would default.

The financial crisis points to a model of multiple interests and fragmentation, a framework that explores conflicts of interests and contestability over resources and who gets what explains the causes and consequences of the present recession. The processes of securitization and

1

the growth of over-the-counter derivatives generated fees for the financial sector. Brokers, lawyers and issuers of securities all gained fees and high levels of compensation without thinking of the long-term consequences. Monopolies and asymmetries of knowledge reflected issues of power and influence.

Power and influence are not static. Between 1950 and 1974 labour movements were in ascendance because of full employment and increases in social provision. There was a narrowing of income inequalities. The period after 1979 represents a shift of influence towards high income earners and concentrations of incomes towards the top 1 per cent of earners with 99 per cent of the population receiving income increases of 0.6 per cent per annum. Since 1980 the top 1 per cent of earners have appropriated 65 per cent of GDP growth (Stiglitz 2010)

The recession of 2007 has to be located in social structures of growing income inequalities, with households exchanging equities in their homes for higher mortgages to compensate for stagnant incomes. Households were able to purchase consumer goods using their homes as an ATM machine. Power and influence in the shaping and making of policy generated a deregulated financial sector, while the ideology of free markets that dominated the thinking of institutions legitimized growing inequalities and unemployment as being the natural outcomes of markets.

The growth of income inequalities during the past three decades and the concentration of income within the top 1 per cent of earners have created a process for increased lobbying and political contributions to policy makers. Money in politics 'pollutes' the regulatory system (Ferguson and Johnson 2010). The concentration of power in the financial markets, where three banks in the UK have assets worth three times UK GDP (Haldane 2010) and five banks in the USA have assets equivalent to 65 per cent of US GDP (Johnson 2009), means that the financial sector plays an increasingly dominant part in the domestic economy. In the USA and the UK the financial sector has grown from 15 per cent to 40 per cent of corporate profits and as a ratio of GDP expanded from 5 to 9 per cent during the period 1990–2007.

The title of this book is *The Politics of Recession*. Implicit in that title are two related arguments. First, the approach challenges the argument that recessions are inevitable; that they are inescapable and somehow an inherent part of the market economy. Embedded within the thesis of inevitability runs the theme that recessions are exogenous and that they are experienced as an external event, where the role of government is limited to providing a series of policy initiatives to regenerate stability and economic prosperity. Attempts to regulate financial markets always represent fighting the last war because regulators can only catch a glimpse of rapid change. Secondly, the discourse of policy responses embeds the perspective of policy design serving the public interest, that in the context of austerity there has to be equal sacrifice and the recession is described as being a shared experience. However, recessions are political in the sense that these events are not shared experiences. They do not become part of a collective memory or shared culture or history. Recessions create winners and losers. The politics of recession therefore points to the view that recessions are not inevitable and they represent the outcomes of the policy process. Recessions are therefore not an exogenous event but are endogenous, and the study of recessions must therefore involve the study of the policy processes that contribute to them.

On her visit to the LSE in 2010 Queen Elizabeth II was not completely right to enquire with economists as to why they had been unable to predict the financial meltdown, since that question implied that the crisis was the result of the failure of economic models to predict the recession. However, the crisis was also a crisis of politics, of political institutions and social structures that reflected issues of power, influence and ideologies. Political scientists in their studies of the institutions of government and how these entities were guided by a liberal market philosophy did not make recommendations on the possibility that deregulated regulators were also contributing to the financial crisis. Equally, students of politics have been aware of the role of money in politics and how interest groups in finance were shaping the policy process that undermined regulatory processes. Money is increasingly influencing the policy process. Financial deregulation reflected the relationship between economic theories that pointed to liberalization of financial markets and the finance industry that benefitted from the process of deregulation.

During the years of the Great Depression of 1929, UK unemployment rates reached 25 per cent of the labour force. However, the experience of high unemployment was mainly concentrated in the traditional staple industries of coal mining, textiles and ship building. The new consumer goods industries of white goods, chemicals, car making and aeroplane manufacturing were thriving in the new industrial landscapes of the Midlands and the South of England. Keynes in making his case to the MacMillan Committee pointed out that governments, through a series of infrastructure projects, could reduce unemployment by 500,000 in the context of unemployment of 1.4 million. The cost of his programme was around £100 million, approximately 2 per cent of GDP. Skidelsky and Kennedy (2010) argued that Keynes was 'kicking up a fuss' against the orthodoxy of classical economics thinking that had dominated the Treasury view for the previous 200 years.

The Thatcher government policy choice to deal with inflation through high interest rates and reductions in public expenditure contributed to the recession of 1981 which resulted in a sharp rise in unemployment to over 3 million. At the time Lord Kaldor pointed out that any government could reduce inflation to zero by increasing unemployment (Kaldor 1980) The unemployment rate was explained away as being a labour market shake-out in the over manned nationalized industries. Between 1979 and 1996 the UK lost some 2.5 million jobs in manufacturing. In addition manufacturing output as a ratio of GDP also declined from 23 per cent to 18 per cent. Throughout the years of the Thatcher government, unemployment remained at around 2 million. This has to be compared with the period 1950–1970 when the unemployment rate averaged 250,000.

White (2010) has located the present financial crisis within two explanatory perspectives. These he called broadly 'the school of what is different' and 'the school of what is the same'. White suggested that the explanations that fall within 'the school of what is different' provided a comfort zone for policy makers because they could focus on financial innovations including residential mortgage backed securities (RMBS), CDOs and CDSs and look for ways in which these instruments can be reformed. Policy makers are at present debating on how to make the over-the-counter (OTC) derivatives safer on trading platforms and through central clearing, arguing that the problem with these instruments was opaqueness and lack of transparency. Within this category it is also observed that investment banks became too reliant on REPO markets and short-term lending so the argument is for increased capital requirements and better liquidity:

> The 'school of what is different' focuses on the developments in financial markets that were new this time around. Such innovations as CDSs, structured products, SIVs and conduits, extensions of the originate to distribute model and the role of rating agencies, would all become centers of attention. This school of thought is relatively comforting to all those involved in the governance of the economic and financial system. New developments always have unanticipated side effects, and it would be unrealistic to expect those in charge to anticipate all of them in advance. (White 2010, p. 3)

Explanations that fall within the category 'what is the same' draw parallels with other financial crises and the history of global financial crises, pointing out that these crises have patterns of repetition in that they tend to start off in the financial sector and they usually include high levels of leverage by banks, stock markets and housing bubbles. They also point to the role of government, which has been to recapitalize financial markets, stabilize the economy and return to normality:

> The school of 'what is the same' begins by noting that boom–bust cycles have been characteristic of liberalized economic and financial systems from time

immemorial. Moreover, while each one is different . . . in fundamental ways they all look the same. What is less 'comforting' about this school of thought is that it charges all those responsible for the governance of the economic and financial system with having missed obvious historical parallels. (White 2010, p. 3)

The IMF (2008) has catalogued 122 recessions in the world economy since World War II. The UK has experienced seven recessions since 1948 and the USA eight recessions during the same period. In the majority of cases the causes of recession have started in the financial sector with bubbles emerging in asset prices and in housing. Minsky (1976) and Kindleberger and Aliber (2005) have both provided explanatory framework for understanding bubbles and recessions.

Minsky (1976) has provided a cyclical explanation to explore the relationship between the previous recession and a subsequent climate of stability which then results in the fading of previous memories and which in turn leads to complacency about the past, euphoria about the future and then back to instability:

> As the subjective repercussions of the debt-deflation wear off, as disinvestment occurs, and as financial positions are rebuilt during the stagnant phase, a recovery and expansion begins. Such a recovery starts with the strong memories of the penalty extracted because of exposed liability positions during the debt-deflation . . . However, success breeds daring, and over time the memory of the past disaster is eroded. Stability is destabilizing in that more adventuresome financing of investment pays off . . . Thus an expansion will, at an accelerating rate, feed into the boom. (Minsky 1976, p. 125)

The financial crisis that started in 2007 continues to be an economic, a political and a social crisis. The increases in unemployment in the UK and the USA represent economic, political and social challenges. The crisis in public finances and the reductions in public expenditure on health, social security and housing will impact those who had nothing to do with the causes of the crisis. Whereas public finance looked to be in good shape prior to 2007, since the bubble burst the sudden sharp falls in revenues to the government together with the shrinkage in GDP have created structural deficits in the public finances. In addition, the crisis in finance has also provided the opportunity for governments to redefine the boundaries between public and private provision. The UK coalition government strategy to reduce public expenditure by £82 billion by the end of the Parliament is founded on the argument that the public sector is crowding out the private sector and that a more vigorous, entrepreneurial and deregulated private sector will generate future economic prosperity.

The institutions of government are guided by philosophies and ideas that shape policy frameworks (Turner 2010). Policy practitioners develop relationships with theorists who provide ideas and ideals. Policy theorists have the ideas and but not the power to turn their ideas into policy. Policy practitioners are highly immersed in the policy process and seek the ideas that help policy making. Ideology plays a role in providing a framework of how to think about a problem. The 'approach' of free markets provide easy and ready to use tools for policy makers. Ideology therefore plays a role within institutions. Government organizations are not empty vessels they are guided by ideas and ideals.

> For it is striking in the pre-crisis years how dominant and how overconfident, at least in the arena of financial economics, was a simplified version of equilibrium theory which saw market completion as the cure to all problems . . . Institutions such as the IMF, in its Global Financial Stability Reviews, set out a confident story of a self-equilibrating system. Thus, for instance, the April 2006 GFSR, only 18 months before the crisis broke, recorded that: 'There is a growing recognition that the dispersion of credit risks to a broader and more diverse group of investors . . . has helped make the banking and wider financial system more resilient. The improved reliance may be seen in fewer bank failures and more consistent credit provision.' (Turner 2010, p. 4)

During that same speech Turner (2010) went on to argue that when he became the chair of the FSA he felt that he had become the high priest of the free market ideology that guided the FSA. The role of the FSA, as was made clear in policy statements, was to provide policy guidelines that ensured better working of the market. The FSA was not able to evaluate whether all financial instruments were socially relevant but only had to ensure that those instruments were transparent and accountable. The FSA accepted the concept of risk dispersion as generated by securitization and that the process of securitization was facilitating the process of market completion. Rational expectations and efficient markets theories provide the tools of analysis and were therefore part of the DNA at the FSA. Turner suggests these were the guidelines that also influenced the policy thinking within the IMF, where even in April 2007 the IMF was able to argue that securitization was contributing to market completion:

> And in regulators such as the FSA, the assumption[s] that financial innovation and increased market liquidity were valuable because they complete markets and improve price discovery were not just accepted, they were part of the institutional DNA, part of the belief system. The belief system did not, of course, exclude the possibility of market intervention. But it did determine assumptions about the appropriate nature and limits of intervention. And here, I suspect, lies the greatest challenge for new economic thinking. For while the simplified pre-crisis conventional wisdom appeared to provide a complete set of answers resting on a unified intellectual system and methodology, really good economic

thinking will provide multiple partial insights, based on varied analytical approaches. (Turner 2010, p. 9)

In the aftermath of the Great Depression and in response to the Pecora Hearings Senator Glass and Congressman Steagill were able to push through the so-called Glass-Steagill Banking Act of 1933 (Perino 2010). The provisions put in place the Federal Deposit Insurance Corporation (FDIC) to provide safeguards for individual savers and their deposits with the commercial banks and to prevent future bank runs. The period 1940 to 1980 became known as the Quiet Period for the financial sector (Gorton 2009). The repeal of Glass-Steagill in 1999 removed the divide between commercial and investment banks. The Quiet Period of banking had also become associated with a sort of complacency, the run on the banks was now past history. Commercial banks put policy makers under pressure to remove their restrictions and allow them to compete in the world of investment banking. The so-called shadow banking sector had grown to a $8 trillion business which was now the same size as the regulated commercial sector. The difference was that commercial banks still had the deposits of individual savers as part of their assets. The investment banks had to rely on mutual funds to provide short-term overnight funding. The investment banks had to post collateral and mark their assets to market. Commercial banks could point to the fact that their assets were long-term assets and not prone to mark to market fluctuations.

Soon after Glass-Steagill was repealed the US Congress also passed the Commodity Futures Modernization Act (CFMA) of 2000, facilitating a framework for all OTC derivatives to be traded in non-regulated markets. The legislators passed provisions so that the OTC market was outside the jurisdiction of state regulators. The OTC derivatives market grew to a notional amount of $640 trillion during the period 2000–2007, while the CDS market expanded to $65 trillion (BIS Report 2009; *Financial Times* 17 March 2011). This growth has to be put in the context of global GDP of $65 trillion, so that the OTC market in 2007 was 10 times the size of global income and the CDS market five times as big as the US economy (FCIC 2011).

Alan Greenspan's ideological commitment to free unfettered markets had a major influence on the thinking of the Federal Reserve. President Reagan had asked Greenspan to replace the outgoing Chairman Paul Volcker because Volcker was described as being a pragmatist and not committed to the deregulation of financial markets. By contrast, Greenspan was committed to the concept of free markets. Reflecting on the role of derivatives in the US economy, Alan Greenspan, as Chairman of the Federal Reserve at a conference organized by Futures Industry Association in March 1999, was able to argue that:

By far the most significant event in finance during the past decade has been the extraordinary development and expansion of financial derivatives . . .The fact that OTC markets function quite effectively without the benefits of [CFTC Regulation] provide a strong argument for development of a less burdensome regime for exchange trade financial derivatives. (quoted in FCIC 2011, p. 48)

On 23 October 2008, when over 90 per cent of asset backed securities previously rated as triple-A were downgraded to below investment grade Alan Greenspan provided testimony to the Oversight and Government Reform Committee. In his testimony Greenspan admitted that in 1999 he had made a mistake in his assumptions about markets and his long-held views that financial market participants would regulate themselves because of self-interest and that this was always preferable to government intervention:

I made a mistake in presuming that the self interest of organizations, specifically banks and others, were such that they best capable of protecting their own shareholders and their equity in the firm. . . . So the problem here is something which looked to be a very solid edifice, and indeed a critical pillar to market competition and freedom markets. did break down . . . (quoted in Wessel 2010, pp. 65–6)

To which, Henry Waxman the Chairman of the committee responded:

'In other words you found that your view of the world, your ideology was not right. It was not working.'
    'Precisely,' Greenspan replied. 'That's precisely the reason I was shocked because I had been going for forty years or more with considerable evidence that it was working exceptionally well . . .'. (Wessel 2010, p. 66)

The financial crisis was also a crisis of economic ideas at both the intellectual and at the practical level. Economic models founded on the concept of rational individualism and the representative agent as developed by the Rational Expectations School and the Efficient Market Theorists had become the conventional wisdom within key financial institutions including central banks, but also global institutions such as the IMF (Turner 2010). The concepts of rationality and efficient markets, though both highly contestable concepts, became the essential building blocks in the modelling of the financial sector. The theory of rationality was an important pillar in model building because it assumed that all humans in aggregate behaved in a similar way, in that rational agents would recognize that markets were outside the normal range and would bring them back within the accepted range. This was the idea of a random walk of prices fluctuating on Wall Street representing a diversity of views and yet within that diversity prices would always remain close to the intrinsic value of that bond.

Competition between market participants ensured that stock prices moved around their intrinsic values. The increase in house prices between 1997 and 2007 reflected the intrinsic value of housing. Housing was therefore not over priced but reflected the pressures of demand, of high wages, of limited land spaces and growing demographic pressures. Households behaved rationally in exchanging their 30-year fixed rate mortgages for adjustable rate mortgages that reflected changing market conditions; brokers selling housing with high sub-prime mortgages behaved rationally in extracting higher fees; bankers securitizing mortgages behaved rationally. Stock prices and forward options were all calculated on the basis of rational agents making predictable decisions to buy or sell assets on the basis of expected future dividends earnings. The Black Scholes model of option pricing became the yardstick of calculating stock pricing. The OTC derivatives market developed on the assumptions established by the rational expectations hypothesis (REH) and the efficient markets hypothesis (EMH). The recent work by Colander (2009) and Lawson (2010) has criticized the models generated by Fama and Black and Scholes, firstly because of the unrealistic assumptions of the models and also the failure of these economists to point to the limitations of their models, even as these models became the basic tools of analysis in financial markets:

> Many of the financial economists who developed the theoretical models upon which the modern financial structure is built were well aware of the strong and highly unrealistic restrictions imposed on their models to assure stability. Yet, financial economists gave little warning to the public about the fragility of their models; even as they saw individuals and businesses build a financial system based on their work. There are a number of possible explanations for this failure to warn the public. One is a 'lack of understanding' explanation – the researchers did not know the models were fragile. We find this explanation highly unlikely; financial engineers are extremely bright, and it is almost inconceivable that such bright individuals did not understand the limitations of the models. A second, more likely, explanation is that they did not consider it their job to warn the public. If that is the cause of their failure, we believe that it involves a misunderstanding of the role of the economist, and involves an ethical breakdown. In our view, economists, as with all scientists, *have an ethical responsibility to communicate the limitations of their models and the potential misuses of their research.* (Colander et al. 2008, pp. 3–4, original emphasis)

Economics had to be mathematical and publication in economic journals depended on the elegance of the mathematics rather on how well the model explained reality. Lawson (2010) has suggested that in explaining social material it is not always appropriate to use mathematical models. Social material cannot always be explained through mathematical models. You cannot use a hammer to measure a piece of glass or a violin bow to beat the drum in an orchestra. Each tool has a specific context.

> Like all tools they are appropriate to some uses and conditions and not to others. Though a hammer has various uses it is not particularly relevant to cutting the grass. I want to suggest that mathematical methods of the sort economists typically employ may not be particularly, or very often, well-suited for the illumination of social material, given the nature of the latter. The reasonable way forward, I thus argue, is explicitly to design explanatory approaches to be appropriate to the sorts of contexts and materials with which economists must actually deal. (Lawson 2010, p. 8)

Economists cannot repeat what happens in a physics laboratory that seeks to isolate both the intrinsic and extrinsic aspects of the observed variable. Variables used in economic models are assumed to be independent of each other, and it is also assumed that, through regression analysis, the weighting and explanatory potential of each separate variable can be measured accurately. Each variable is measured in isolation, as in physics. However, laboratory type closures are rare events in the social context:

> Instead of existing in isolation, almost all social phenomena are in fact constituted in relation to each other. It is easy enough in modern capitalism to see the internal relationality of markets and money and firms and governments and households, etc; all depend on and presuppose each other. It would be futile and meaningless to seek to isolate any one from the influence of the others. But human individuals as social beings are likewise formed in relation to others. All slot into positions, where all positions are constituted in relation to other positions. Thus employer and employee presuppose each other, as do teacher and student, landlord/lady and tenant, parent and child, gendered man and woman, and so on. We all slot into, and are molded through the occupancy of, a multitude of such positions, deriving real interests from them, and drawing upon whatever powers or rights and obligations are associated with those positions. So social reality is an interdependent network, it is an internally related totality, not a set of phenomena each existing in relative isolation. (Lawson 2010, p. 8)

Economic theory is not neutral. Those who construct economic models make assumptions on a set of held beliefs about how economies work. The assumption that markets are neutral and are Pareto efficient, meaning that any attempt to redistribute income and make some better off will make some worse off, is in itself ideological. Market liberalism expunges context. The rational individual has no history, no place or culture. Data carries no time break, no possibility of changes of government, of changes in institutions, or reforms that might influence or contaminate the data. Data speaks for itself and does not need to be located in histories. In the rational deductive model either the theory comes first and then the data is squeezed to fit the theory, or the data is allowed to speak for itself but only within the frameworks of statistical analysis.

The discourses of neutral markets and capitalism as starting points are both embedded in ideology (Foley 2010). Friedman and Hayek are both good examples of having an ideology and using their ideology as an economic argument. Hayek's *Road to Serfdom* and Friedman's *Free to Choose* were both political arguments advocating an unfettered market economy. Keynes was equally being political when he argued that his main concern was full employment and that government should intervene, even through the process of socializing investment, to ensure that investment matched savings. Once the threat of unemployment was removed as a market discipline it was therefore likely that this would alter the relationships between capital and labour (Foley 2010). The debate between Keynesians and market liberals is therefore implicitly a debate about the distribution of income and about power. The argument of the neutral market shifts the power towards increased income inequality. The concern about full employment shifts the focus towards government and income redistribution Markets are not neutral they are social constructs.

> Since the time of Adam Smith, his Invisible Hand has become the cliché metaphor for the *stability* of markets. The Hand 'guides' prices and outputs into equilibrium. Market fundamentalist (or laissez faire) doctrines presume that the economy is structured in such manner that this is always true. But the structure within which market interactions work themselves out is a creation of lawyers and politicians and, as all human creations, comes with no guarantee of serving us well for all time. (Leijonhufvud 2010, p. 1)

According to market fundamentalists the cause of the financial crisis was the government. Taylor (2010) put the blame on the Federal Reserve's loose monetary policy of low interest rates which eventually fed into the housing bubble, while Wallison (2011) connected the crisis with government housing policy encouraging home ownership among people who were a high credit risk.

Equally, economists who start from a Keynesian perspective, advocating full employment, are ideological in the sense that they see that we live in capitalist economy as opposed to the market economy and capitalism creates inequality. Although there are many variants of Keynesian thinking, Keynesians would point to concepts introduced by Keynes which a made departure from classical thinking. Keynes introduced the concepts of uncertainty as opposed to risk, the concept of animal spirits and market sentiment. Keynesians put an emphasis on the context of institutions and conventions that create a framework for certainty.

THE STRUCTURE OF THE BOOK

Chapter 2 deals with the anatomy of the present recession. The focus is the dynamics of house prices and the growing derivatives markets. The sub-prime mortgages represented a trigger effect and the chapter shows that attempts to put the blame on the housing bubble would be misleading. While home ownership did increase from 64 to 69 per cent in the USA, home ownership remained stable in the UK, Spain and Ireland, and yet in each of these countries there was a housing price bubble similar to that of the USA. Different housing policies with different structures of housing subsidies still ended up with rapid increases in house prices. The question is, therefore, why was there a global increase in house prices and why were property prices outstripping growth in disposable income. Some commentators in the USA have blamed the Clinton and Bush administration for putting pressures on the CRAs to increase home ownership among communities with high risks of default. There is no evidence that the CRAs actually downgraded their standards. Equally, the evidence shows that US households remortgaged about $2.3 trillion worth of housing assets. This would suggest that existing home owners were converting their equities into liquid cash that allowed them to increase personal consumption. The default in housing estimated at a maximum of $1 trillion has to be put in the context that some investment banks are involved in transactions worth $1 trillion a day. So $1 trillion of defaulting mortgages could have been absorbed within a global economy worth about $65 trillion. The housing bubble should not have resulted in a global financial crisis. Housing was a trigger effect compared to issues of structural fragilities of financial markets. The breakdown in the historical correlation between house prices and disposable incomes shows that while house prices were for long periods approximately 3.5 times disposable incomes, after 1997 this had increased to 4.5 times disposable incomes. The breakdown between house prices and incomes suggested that the increases in house prices were not sustainable in the long term.

Chapter 3 is a review of various explanations and locates these explanations as a series of contestable issues. The first area of contestability is located in the role of government and the question of whether governments contributed to the financial crisis or whether the response of the government did actually stabilize financial markets and thus avoided a depression similar to the Great Depression of 1929. Market fundamentalists have suggested that governments contributed to the crisis through a loose monetary policy – a monetary glut – that resulted in low interests rates which in turn contributed to the housing boom. Pragmatists represented the policy makers who had to deal with the crisis as it was unfolding and did not have the benefit of time or hindsight. While the policy responses were piecemeal and disjointed, they did stabilize the financial markets and avoided a major collapse in the wider economy. The second area of contestability relates to issues of ideas and ideals. Explanations in this category included structuralists who sought to locate the recession within social structures in what Rajan (2010) called fault lines. Institutionalists analysed the process of deregulation and how the climate of deregulation had put handcuffs on regulators and created a climate of reluctance to regulate.

Chapter 4 is concerned with the OTC derivatives markets, the process of securitization and the question whether derivatives did contribute to the financial crisis? The central argument of the chapter is the lack of transparency in the OTC market; the opaqueness and complexity of instruments created uncertainty. The interconnected process meant that buyers and sellers of derivatives could not be sure whether counter parties could meet their obligations. The instruments created resulted in greater uncertainty so that when some mortgage backed securities (MBS) started to default with no clear connections of counter party risks, a number of mutual funds that had previously accepted MBS as collateral were now asking for more collateral and higher haircuts which eventually led to the collapse of Bear Sterns. The near collapse of AIG showed the CDS market was not a conventional form of insurance. AIG was not posting daily collateral for the selling of CDS. AIG had insured $80 billion of CDS for a premium of $8 billion. When Goldman Sachs asked AIG to meet the CDS exposure of $1.8 billion AIG disputed the claim. There were no transactions at the time of CDS bonds. The market was frozen and therefore the prices were being determined through mathematical models. Marking to market was highly removed from statutory insurance. The posting of collateral would have provided signals of the real costs of insurance, but not trading derivatives on exchanges and clearing platforms created arbitrary prices that were disputed between counter parties. The near collapse of Bear Stearns, the rescue of AIG and the bankruptcy of Lehman Brothers altered the landscapes of financial markets.

Chapter 5 explores the credit rating agencies' issuer pay business models and how this connected with the financial crisis. The CRAs moved to the issuer pay model during the 1970s. The three major CRAs – Moody's, Standard & Poor's and Fitch Ratings – were defined as Nationally Recognized Statistical Rating Organizations (NRSRO) by the Securities and Exchange Commission during the 1990s. Regulators therefore used the ratings by the CRAs to approve the investment portfolio of pension fund municipalities and government. These entities were restricted to investing in only triple-A rated bonds. Investors assumed that the ratings given by the CRAs were accurate. Investors did not do their own due diligence. The securitization of mortgages proved a bonanza for the CRAs as their incomes increased from $3 billion to $6 billion a year. CEOs of the CRAs were receiving salaries similar to the CEOs of investment banks. The testimonies given by analysts at Moody's and Standard & Poor's to various enquiries confirmed that there were major discrepancies between the ethics of the analysts and the business models of the CRA. The pressure on the analyst was to rate a bond even when they were unhappy with what was contained in a structured security. Analysts argued that they could not walk away from a rating. There was concern about the models being used and whether these were out of date. Analysts were questioned when they failed to rate an issue. Issuers complained to the CRAs if an analyst was proving too difficult and the analyst was removed from the issuing process. The term IBGYBG (I'll be gone, you'll be gone) was first used between an issuer and an analyst, the issuer was telling the analyst not to take the analysis too seriously since in the long term they would both be gone and at least for the moment it was better to improve on their compensation packages.

Chapter 6 deals with the economics and social issues created by Keynes and other Keynesians who believed that Keynes represented a departure from classical economics, and looks at what the nature of that break implied for economic policy making. Minsky (1976) has argued that attempts to synthesize Keynes are misleading, since concepts such as uncertainty, conventions, or animals spirits could not be located within market liberal thinking. The IS/LM model of Hicks and Hansen and the argument of sticky prices were not Keynesian arguments. Keynes provided a theory of capitalism and not of markets. Keynes was not dealing with market failure but a capitalism that was cyclical and therefore could not guarantee full employment.

Chapter 7 argues the case that the financial crisis needs to be located in processes of social structure, in issues of power and influence, growing income inequalities and the influence of ideology in the policy process. The study of structures of government provides a framework for analysing the relationships between policy makers, lobbyists and financial donations and how these processes shape and define policy making. The shift towards a deregulated environment in financial markets reflected two decades of attempts to repeal Glass-Steagill which was finally achieved in 1999. The shift towards a deregulated environment enabled the growth of the counter derivatives. Secondly the growth in income inequalities allowed for an increased concentration of income towards the top 1 per cent of earners which enabled the process for increases in financial donations for narrow vested interests. Ideology in terms of how economies work was dominated by the conventional wisdom outlined in rational expectations theory and efficient markets theories. These concepts dominated the thinking of institutions involved in the policy process.

Chapter 8 outlines a history of UK economic policy since 1945. It breaks the period into three phases. The Butskellite consensus between

1945 and 1970 represented a dual commitment to full employment and increased public provision. Inflation was to be controlled through incomes policy, which therefore required compromises between government and the trade unions on price controls in exchange for trade union moderation on wages. This was a period of narrowing income inequalities with wages rising in line with increases in productivity. The second phase – between 1970 and 1979 – included the Heath government followed by the Callaghan government. Ted Heath had promised a Quiet Revolution in 1970 on trade union reform and phasing out subsidies on the nationalized industries. The increase in unemployment to over 1 million resulted in a series of U-turns on public expenditure. The British public were not yet ready to accept high unemployment. The Labour Government of 1974 represented a watershed in the sense that with rising unemployment, the government reduced public expenditure, which effectively confirmed the break with Keynesian thinking. The third phase, starting in 1979, saw the Thatcher Revolution, and this chapter explains how economic policy since 1979 has changed the UK economic landscape. The decline in UK manufacturing, continuing high rates of unemployment, the retreat of trade union influence and shifts in income distribution towards the top 1 per cent of earners have all changed expectations of government.

Chapter 9 is a study of the Financial Crisis Inquiry Commission (FCIC) which was chaired by Phil Angelides and which eventually reported in January 2011. The chapter seeks to draw parallels with the Pecora Commission that had been established by President Hoover to investigate the Great Depression of 1929. Pecora was the chief counsel to the investigation and during 10 days of examination in January 1933 had provided the framework for the President Roosevelt series of financial reforms in 1933, including the Banking Act of 1933. The FCIC enquiry was the most detailed enquiry into understanding the financial crisis, lasting 12 months and involving 12 major public hearings with thousands of documents and a series of interviews accumulated by the commission. In the final report of January 2011 the commission report broke down between the six Democrat Commissioners signing the majority report, and the Republican Commissioners submitting two separate dissenting documents. The majority report pointed to the failures of deregulation in the derivatives markets, failures by regulators and credit rating agencies. The majority report pointed to the high-risk strategies adopted by investment banks, the system of compensation, and how structured products created incentives based on the short-term interests of mortgage brokers, lawyers and issuers of securities without thinking of the long-term implications.

Recessions produce different geographies of inequality. Policy choices are central to understanding how issues of power and influence become embedded in the policy process. The present financial crisis reflects a continuing shift of influence towards those at the very top of the income scale. During the past 30 years, wages for the majority of the population have remained relatively stagnant. Improvements in living standards can be explained through the increased participation of women in the labour market with husbands and wives now both working to sustain a certain living standard of living. Secondly the increases in house prices after 1990 provided households with the opportunity to improve their consumption by surrendering the savings in their homes to improve personal consumption.

REFERENCES

BIS (2009) *Annual Report 2008/09*. Basel: Bank for International Settlements.
Colander, D., H. Föllmer, M. Goldberg, A. Hass, K. Juselius, A. Kirman, T. Lux and B. Sloth (2008) 'The Financial Crisis and the Systemic Failure of Academic Economics', unpublished mimeo.
Colander, D., H. Föllmer, A. Hass, K. Juselius, A. Kirman, T. Lux and B. Sloth (2009) 'Mathematics, Methods, and Modern Economics', *Real-world Economics Review*, **50**(8): 118–121.
FCIC (2011) *The Financial Crisis Inquiry: Final Report*. Washington, DC: U.S. Government Printing Office.
Ferguson, T. and R. Johnson (2010) 'When Wolves Cry "Wolf": Systematic Financial Crises and the Myth of the Danaid Jar', INET Inaugural Conference, April.
Foley, D. (2010) 'Mathematical Formalism and Political-Economic Content'. Available at: http://ineteconomics.org/video/conference-kings/mathematical-formalism-and-political-economic-content-duncan-foley
Friedman, M. and R. Friedman (1980) *Free to Choose: A Personal Statement*. London: Harcourt.
Gorton, G. (2009) 'Slapped in the Face by the Invisible Hand: Banking and the Panic of 2007', presentation for the Federal Reserve Bank of Atlanta's 2009 Financial Markets Conference: Financial Innovation and Crisis, 11–13 May.
Haldane, A.G. (2010) 'The Debt Overhang', speech given at a Professional Liverpool Dinner, 27 January.
Hayek, F. (1944) *Road to Serfdom*. London: Routledge.
IMF (2008) 'What Happens During Recessions, Crunches and Busts?', IMF Working Paper by S. Classens, M. Kose and M. Terrones, WP/08/274, Washington, DC.
Johnson, S. (2009) 'The Quiet Coup', *The Atlantic Monthly*, May.
Kaldor, (Lord) N. (1980) *Memorandum on Monetary Policy*. London: HMSO.
Kindleberger, C. and R. Aliber (2005) *Manias, Panics and Crashes: A History of Financial Crisis*. London: Palgrave Macmillan.
Lawson, T. (2010) 'Economics and Science', *The Transatlantic: Journal of Economics and Philosophy*, **1**: 8–13. Available at: http://thetransatlantic.org/2010/03/10/economics-science/

Leijonhufvud, A. (2010) 'Instabilities', paper presented at the INET Conference, King's College, 8–11 April.

Minsky, H.P. (1976) *John Maynard Keynes*. London: McGraw Hill.

Perino, M. (2010) *The Hellhound of Wall Street: How Ferdinand Pecora's Investigation of the Great Crash Forever Changed American Finance*. New York: The Penguin Press.

Rajan, R. (2010) *Fault Lines: How Hidden Fractures Still Threaten the World Economy*. Oxford and Princeton, NJ: Princeton University Press.

Skidelsky, R. and M. Kennedy (2010) 'Future Generations Will Curse Us for Cutting in a Slump', *The Financial Times*, 27 July.

Stiglitz J (2010) *Free Fall: America, Free markets and the Sinking of the World Economy*. London: W.W. Norton and Company.

Taylor, J. (2010) 'The Financial Crisis and the Policy Responses: An Empirical Analysis of What Went Wrong', paper presented to the Financial Crisis Inquiry Commission, Washington, DC, 2 September.

Turner, A. (2010) 'Economics, conventional wisdom and public policy', Institute for New Economic Thinking Inaugural Conference, Cambridge, April.

Wallison, P. (2011) 'Dissenting Statement, Peter P. Wallison, 24 December 2010', *The Financial Crisis Inquiry Report*. New York: Public Affairs.

Wessel, D. (2010) *In Fed We Trust: Ben Bernanke's War on the Great Panic*. New York: Three Rivers Press.

White, W. (2010) 'Remarks by William White to be delivered at the INET Conference Session 1 "Anatomy of Crisis – the Living History of the Last Thirty Years: Economic Theory, Politics and Policy?"', King's College, Cambridge, UK, 9 April.

2.   Anatomy of financial crisis

INTRODUCTION

Politics has been described as being the 'art of the possible' with the emphasis on art, which would suggest that policy making is more about judgement than science. The art of the possible would also point to the power of persuasion in term of how the government makes its case and also reflects what is possible and the process of compromise. Policy making becomes the study of constraints and autonomy. Constraints can be described as events that, at least in the short term, seem to be beyond the control of government. However, policy makers need to be seen as giving direction to policy rather than responding to events. In dealing with the recent financial crisis, policy makers needed to show that they had the institutional capacities to respond and to stabilize a very uncertain financial context. Institutions of the financial industry, including investment banks, were not transparent about their losses, levels of leverage and financial exposure. Very often key regulators found they did not have the legal authority to intervene. Government responses appeared to be piecemeal and disjointed, yet during those times of turbulence, policy conviction was needed to restore confidence in a climate of uncertainty.

The art of the possible represents a dynamic between the dual processes of events that are perceived to be outside the immediate control of government and political autonomy that describes the process of political choices that defines the spaces and the room to manoeuvre. Governments are neither prisoners of events nor do they have complete autonomy; there are constraints to policy choices, at least in the immediacy of the moment when government needs to respond and needs to show that it can respond in situations that are far from calm and without the benefit of hindsight. However, governments have political choices in the sense there are always policy alternatives available, and the choice of alternatives reflects political priorities and the proximity of ideology.

During the financial crisis that started in July 2007 the priority of government has been to stabilize financial markets. Governments, through a series of interventions, had to show commitment to dealing with the crisis of confidence. Globally, according to IMF estimates (IMF 2010) the cost of the bail-outs of the financial sector has amounted to $16 trillion. This has to be put in a context of global GDP of $65 trillion, so the bail-out costs have amounted to some 25 per cent of global GDP. This has to be compared to losses in the sub-prime mortgages of $500 billion, which would suggest that attempts to attribute the financial crisis to lending in sub-prime mortgages would be misleading. Lending in the mortgage market might have been a trigger event but it was the structure of financial markets and the process of securitization that created uncertainty. The responses of governments have been described as being inevitable. Governments did not have a choice. They could not allow for the financial sector to be liquidated.

Equally, in seeking to repair public finances, the response of governments has been to seek reductions in public expenditure on pensions, social security and health provision, assuming there is an inevitable connection between the 'bail-out' of the financial sector and reducing public expenditure. The issue of inevitability raises the question of moral hazard in the sense of: did bankers and financial institutions take on risk knowing that governments would come to their rescue? AIG, the largest insurer in the USA, became involved in credit default swaps (CDS) insuring collateralized debt obligations (CDOs) on behalf of financial institutions. AIGFP sold $80 billion of CDS insurance for annual premiums of $7 billion. AIG did not have to post collateral; the insurance fees AIG received boosted the profits of AIG. When the housing market started to collapse, the CDO buyers, including Goldman Sachs, asked AIG to post collateral. AIG was unable to meet its obligations. Eventually, AIG had to seek the help of the Federal Reserve. The US government could not allow AIG to go bankrupt and bought out all its CDS contracts. The counter parties, including Goldman Sachs, had to be paid in full for their CDS exposure:

> AIG was saved from collapse when the American people came to the rescue with an $85 billion bailout . . . the taxpayers were propping up the hollow shell of AIG by stuffing it with money, and the rest of Wall Street came by and looted the corpse. We still don't know why or how the decision to rescue AIG was made, or who made the decision to offer AIG's trading partners 100 cents on the dollar in the so-called counterparty payments. In the case of AIG, nobody got a haircut. Instead, they were given a piggy bank full of taxpayer dollars. (Towns 2010, p. 2)

The AIG rescue reflected an issue of justice that has continued to recur during the financial crisis. The responses of government have met resentment and resistance. In the AIG case, this resentment focused on the government providing the funding to bail out AIG and then on the way the insurance firm seemed to be using the same taxpayers' funds to pay $12 billion for their obligations on the credit default swaps to

Goldman Sachs. While the majority of people were seeing their homes and retirement funds losing value it seemed inequitable that Goldman Sachs needed to be made whole. Equally, in the case of the acquisition of Merrill Lynch by Bank of America, the government had to pay Bank of America an additional $29 billion to ensure that the takeover would be consummated after Bank of America hinted that it would not continue with the takeover. The government seemed to be held captive by the financial sector.

George Soros, Chairman of Soros Fund Management, writing in *The Financial Times* on 29 January 2009 suggested that the watershed of the financial crisis was the day the US Federal Reserve Bank and the US Treasury made the decision that allowed Lehman Brothers to go into bankruptcy. Soros argues that that decision was a game changer:

> On Monday September 15 [2008] Lehman Brothers, the US investment bank, was allowed to go into bankruptcy without proper preparation. It was a game changing event with catastrophic consequences. For a start the price of credit default swaps, a form of insurance against companies defaulting on debt, went through the roof as investors took cover. AIG the insurance giant . . . was faced with imminent default. The next day Hank Paulson, then US Treasury secretary, had to reverse himself and come to the rescue of AIG. (Soros 2009, p. 10)

There is an ongoing debate as to the question whether the US government was unwilling or unable to support Lehman Brothers, compared to the rescue and merger of Bear Stearns with JP Morgan in March 2008. Fuld (FCIC 2011) who had been CEO of Lehman, in his testimony and evidence to the FCIC, argued the case that Lehman did have the necessary collateral and strength of balance sheet to warrant bridging finance from the Federal Reserve until they had found a partner that secured Lehman's future. By contrast, officials from the Federal Reserve made the point that they did not have the authority to allow them to intervene in Lehman's rescue. Some commentators (McDonald 2009; Sorkin 2009) have pointed to Secretary to the Treasury Hank Paulson's reluctance to come to the rescue of Lehman Brothers because of President Bush's ideological commitment to free markets in addition to the bail-out of Bear Stearns that had already been perceived by Republican lawmakers as one bail-out too many so that there would not be much support for yet another bail-out. Paulson was very much aware that President Bush was wedded to the ideology of markets and therefore unhappy about further intervention. There was a major worry that Republican lawmakers would block requests for additional funding. In outlining his Troubled Asset Relief Program (TARP), Paulson made the case that the money will be mainly used to purchase toxic assets held by US Banks. Paulson did not want to follow the UK Government approach, which was to take equity in UK banks in exchange for injecting government capital. In the United States this was seen as a form of nationalization of the banking sector. It was eventually Ben Bernanke who persuaded Paulson that the purchase of toxic assets was not sufficient and that the government needed to use the TARP funds to take shares in the banking sector (Wessel 2010).

However, in their evidence to the FCIC in May 2010, representatives from the Federal Reserve argued the case that the Federal Reserve did not have the authority to provide funding for Lehman since the investment bank did not have sufficient collateral to provide guarantees that Lehman could pay back their loans. Even under Section 13(3), the bank could not provide the necessary funding, especially after the merger talks with Barclays had collapsed. Lehman did not have a partner similar to the Bear Stearns rescue.

> The Federal Reserve fully understood that the failure of Lehman would shake the financial system and the economy. However, the only tool available to the Federal Reserve to address the situation was its ability to provide short-term liquidity against adequate collateral; and, as I noted, Lehman already had access to our emergency credit facilities. It was clear, though, that Lehman needed both substantial capital and an open-ended guarantee of its obligations to open for business on Monday, September 15. At that time, neither the Federal Reserve nor any other agency had the authority to provide capital or an unsecured guarantee, and thus no means of preventing Lehman's failure existed. (Bernanke 2010, p. 3)

The concern about Lehman's rescue illustrates the degree of uncertainty that surrounded the financial markets starting in July 2007. While Greenspan and Bernanke argued that the early warnings in the housing markets were just blips that the economy could deal with, as defaults in mortgages increased and house prices fell during June 2006, by July 2007 these blips had become a major economic crisis and by 2008 the concern was a repeat of the Great Depression of 1929. Therefore, the question about the present economic crisis is why did market participants and policy makers get it so wrong?

ANATOMY OF RECESSION

The rescue of Bear Stearns and AIG, the bankruptcy of Lehman and the takeover of Country Wide and Merrill Lynch by Bank of America were all major landmarks of government's responses to the financial crisis. During one week in September 2008 the geography of the US financial sector had been completely altered. Morgan Stanley and Goldman Sachs became bank holding companies open to greater supervision and regulation by the government. Brunnermeier (2010) Geanakoplos (2010) and Gourinchas (2010) have provided a series of stages and landmarks to the financial crisis. These stages include the following.

First, like all previous recessions, the crisis that started in financial markets spilled over into the real economy. The near collapse of Bear Stearns in March 2008, the bankruptcy of Lehman in September 2008, and the rescue of AIG reflected a collapse of confidence, with investors asking financial institutions to redeem their exposures, which in turn dried up liquidity and the day-to-day borrowing that necessitated transactions. Overnight lending between banks became more expensive. Investors retreated from financial products to the safety of money.

Secondly, there were the day-to-day declines in equity prices, with all the major indexes showing losses of around 40 per cent during a six-month period between June and December 2008, together with declines of house prices of around 30 per cent. These two components contributed to major declines in household net worth from around $67 trillion to $54 trillion. Households' real worth declined by 15 per cent and savings in pension plans suffered. The consumers' response was to repair their losses by increased savings. Increased savings in turn meant lower consumption, which in turn resulted in companies reducing inventories and unemployment.

Thirdly, as consumers retreated and unemployment increased this only left the government as the major agent that could influence demand. The response of governments through their central banks was to reduce interest rates. In the advanced economies central banks reduced interest rates to an equivalent of 0.5 per cent. In addition governments also attempted to stimulate demand through public expenditure either through tax reductions or through direct expenditures on infrastructure. It is estimated that government spending on stimulus packages averaged around 2 per cent of GDP.

The fourth stage became the condition of the public finances. The UK national to debt to GDP ratio stood at 40 per cent of GDP prior to 2007. In 2009 the national debt had increased to 70 per cent of GDP. Additional public expenditure on unemployment benefits, together with losses in tax revenues, both contributed to an expanding deficit. In the USA national debt is also likely to increase to $10 trillion in the next decade. According to the IMF, the advanced economies have increased their deficits to over 70 per cent of GDP. In December 2009 governments could breathe a sigh of relief as economies were no longer falling off a cliff; GDP figures started to indicate a move towards growth rather than decline. The US reported a growth of 4.5 percent for the last quarter of 2009 while the UK was able to confirm a growth of 0.5 per cent. The Great Recession of 2009 was not a global recession. The emerging economies including the BRIC groups of countries all experienced steady growth in 2008 and 2009. China was still able to predict a growth of 8.9 per cent for 2009 and India grew by 7 per cent. By contrast the economies in the euro zone all experienced economic declines of around 4 per cent of GDP in 2008, Japan around 5 per cent of GDP and USA a fall of 6.4 per cent of GDP.

In the fourth quarter of 2008 the US GDP had declined by 3.8 per cent; the sharpest fall in one quarter to be recorded since 1982 when the then Chair of the Federal Reserve Paul Volcker increased interest rates in his battle to strangle the inflation beast (Dodd (2010). However, the major differences between 1982 and 2008 was that the government then had the ability to reduce interest rates to stimulate growth, while with the present recession the Fed had already reduced interest rates to 0.5 per cent which gave the present government fewer options. Between 2007 and 2008 total GDP had contracted by 6.4 per cent. Household net worth fell by more than $13 trillion during the period 2007–2008 as house prices declined by 30 per cent and retirement assets fell by a further 20 per cent (Bosworth and Smart 2009). Furthermore, since the beginning of the crisis in June 2007 to March 2010 some 8 million people have lost their jobs, with unemployment rising from 4 per cent in 2007 to 9.8 per cent in 2008, the highest jump in the unemployment rate since World War Two. The Federal Reserve forecast (Bernanke 2010) for the US economy published in July 2010 indicated that expected growth for 2011 and 2012 would be between 3 and 4 per cent and that by 2012 unemployment would still be at around 7.8 per cent.

> In all likelihood, a significant amount of time will be required to restore the nearly eight and a half million jobs that were lost over 2008 and 2009. Moreover, nearly half of the unemployed have been out of work for longer than six months. Long-term unemployment not only imposes exceptional near-term hardships on workers and their families, it also erodes skills and may have long-lasting effects on workers' employment and earnings prospects. (Bernanke 2010)

In the UK the financial crisis had a major impact on public finances with debt to GDP ratios increasing from 40 per cent of GDP in 2008 to 70 per cent of GDP in 2010. Losses in tax revenues and a contraction of 5 per cent in GDP provided the context for the UK coalition government to seek major reductions in public expenditure of approximately £80 billion in an attempt to reshape public finances to a changed economic context. Public expenditure plans as outlined by the outgoing Labour Government were criticized as being overly optimistic in the context of shrinking GDP.

Furthermore, the coalition government seemed to be returning to a pre-Keynesian macro economy strategy that said growth would come from the private sector and all forms of public spending were crowding out private investment.

The study of household net wealth is important for the macro economy because consumption and consumer confidence tends to depend on households' perceptions of their net worth. While house and equity prices were rising, households felt they were better off, and savings declined as households were defining their worth in terms of rising house prices. The increase in house prices suggested that people had to save less, which meant more income left for consumption. Households held on to the assumption that their homes represented their savings portfolio for future retirement. Household savings during the late 1990s to 2007 declined from 6 per cent to below 1 per cent. In 2010 that process had been reversed so that while in 2005 US and UK were savings around 1.5 per cent of GDP, by 2009 savings increased to 5 per cent of GDP as households attempted to repair their lost savings. Furthermore, increases in unemployment have also resulted in declines in household incomes. Total household debt in 2010 in the USA amounted to $2.46 trillion in consumer debt, with $864 billion in credit card debt. Households are carrying an average of $16,000 in consumer debt.

RESPONDING TO THE CRISIS

One of the many lessons emerging from the financial crisis has been the different policy responses and concerns emerging from the United States, the UK and the euro zone. In Europe and the UK the focus has become the deteriorating public finances and the EU governments' pledges to make reductions in public expenditure their policy priority. In the UK the coalition government elected in May 2010 planned to reduce public expenditure by £80 billion with the aim of reducing the budget deficit from a present 9 per cent to approximately 1 per cent in 2015. Many of the reductions are aimed at reducing public sector costs, with increases in the retirement age and in pension contributions, and reducing child benefits and other social security payments, including housing benefits. The US government has provided direct finances worth $700 billion and a stimulus package amounting to another $700 billion for the purchase of toxic assets, in addition to funding the rescue of AIG, which is estimated to have added about $1 trillion to government debt. It is now estimated that the US annual debt is likely to rise from 4 per cent of GDP to 9 per cent of GDP, while the national debt is forecast to expand to 80 per cent of GDP.

In the UK, prior to the financial collapse, the national debt ratio to GDP was around 40 per cent with the public sector borrowing requirement (PSBR) at 3 per cent of GDP. The UK government bail-out of Northern Rock, RBS and Lloyds bank, government guarantees on loans and deteriorating tax revenues have contributed to an increase of the PSBR to 12 per cent of GDP, and an estimated national debt ratio to GDP of 90 per cent. The question that needs to be asked is why have public finances in the UK become the central political issue. The Governor of the Bank of England has been criticized for politicizing the role of the Governor of the central bank by intervening in the public expenditure debate, showing more sympathy to the Conservative Party view of the need for debt reductions and also advising the leaders of the Liberal Party after the elections of May 2010. These events have made the Governor seem to be acting in a politically partisan way in siding with the Conservative Party, with some prominent members of the Monetary Policy Committee (MPC) suggesting that the Governor should now resign:

> Adam Posen, an economist who sits on the Bank's rate-setting monetary policy committee, confirmed that several members – 'more than just me and fewer than a majority' – had not wanted an important report to endorse the rapid and sweeping fiscal retrenchment shortly after the election . . .
>
> Andrew Tyrie, chairman of the Treasury Select committee, grilled the governor about the worrying perception that the Bank's independence had been compromised. Speaking after the hearing, Mr Tyrie said: 'This is a very significant day in the history of the Bank of England's independence. A line may have been crossed, albeit with the best of intentions'.
>
> In a rare display of dissent over internal Bank matters, Mr Posen said there had been concern about a paragraph in the May Inflation Report that 'was talking about the particular speed with which to deal with fiscal policy. We were concerned that the statement could be seen as excessively political in the context of the election,' he said . . .
>
> Sushil Wadhwani, an economist and former member of the MPC, said the presence of a large budget deficit in Britain did not appear to be sufficient reason for Mr King to comment upon the fiscal plans of one political party since all parties agreed that to reduce the deficit was necessary. 'Rightly or wrongly, Mervyn has come to be seen as being much closer to the Conservative party than the Labour Party . . .' (Cohen et al. 2010)

In the UK there has been limited debate on the financial crisis, with no attempt through public hearings to analyse and explore the role of investment banks and the failing of the regulatory system. This has to be compared with the US experience where the Financial Crisis Inquiry Commission (FCIC) was established, which has been taking testimonies and having hearings since January 2010. The FCIC published their final report in January 2011, and its importance has been compared to the Pecora enquiry that was established in the aftermath of the Great Depression and which provided the regulatory framework for the Roosevelt administration in 1934. In the USA the Senate and House of Representatives have also had separate enquires on AIG, the Credit Rating Agencies and the derivatives market. The USA has also passed a major regulatory reform legislation under the Dodd-Frank Act of July 2010.

By contrast in the UK there has been no public enquiry on derivatives or credit default swaps, even though the UK dominates the global financial markets in these financial instruments. There was a Treasury Committee Report during 2009. The focus of the debate in the UK has shifted to a concern about public expenditure, which seems to be more abstract and removed from the human dimension. It is as if there is no need in the UK to have a public dialogue on the financial crisis but a concern to move the argument to public finances, which implicitly makes the reform of financial markets less of an issue. Talking about the need to reduce public expenditure does not directly relate to the human experience. Planned reductions in planned expenditure do not immediately concern the human experience, it is only when the reductions are implemented that a human dimension can be attached to the decision. Discussion on planned spending reductions is somehow an objective discussion rather than allowing for the subjectivity of human experience. The goal of reducing public expenditure to shrink the deficit becomes a discussion of the inevitability of economics as opposed to the politics of choices.

In the USA the Chairman for the Financial Crisis Inquiry Commission, Phil Angelides, in his opening statement on 13 January 2010, reflected on the major concern of his Commission. He outlined a series of paradoxes. On the one hand he said some commentators were talking of the Great Recession as being in the past tense while at the same time unemployment was still rising, with threatened foreclosures on some people's homes and others seeing their savings and pension plans disappear. On the other hand, banks and financial institutions were announcing record profits and major pay awards for top executives. The financial sector had received trillions of dollars from the Government. He said people were angry and argued that 'the concern of the commission would be a proxy for the American people to be their eyes and to therefore give voice to the voice-less'. He went on to say:

> Some already speak of the financial crisis in the past tense, as some kind of historical event. The truth is it is still here and still very real. Twenty-six million Americans are unemployed. Over 2 million families have lost their homes to foreclosure in the last three years . . . Retirement accounts and life savings have been swept away, vanished. People are angry. They have a right to be. The fact

that Wall Street is enjoying record profits and bonuses in the wake of receiving trillions of dollars in government assistance while so many families are struggling to stay afloat has only heightened the sense of confusion. I see this commission as a proxy for the American people, their eyes, their ears, and possibly also their voice. (Angelides 2010, p. 3)

THE POLITICS OF RECESSION

Economic data are like collection pieces in museums; they exist as external facts but need an explanation. Museum artefacts are symbols that in themselves do not explain history; each piece requires a narrative that can be located in histories and contexts. Likewise economic statistics do not speak for themselves: they need an interpretation, a narrator and a narrative. Furthermore, interpretation is influenced by the presence, and the co-existence, of multiple competing narratives. As Pierre Bezukhov found out in Tolstoy's *War and Peace*:

> The lodge split into parties, some accusing Pierre of Illuminism, other supporting him. At this meeting Pierre was for the first time struck by the endless variety of the human mind preventing any truth from ever presenting itself in the same way to any two persons. Even those brethren who seemed to be on his side interpreted him after their own fashion. (Tolstoy 1982, p. 512)

No one explanation can claim the status of being the one and only true story. All story tellers come from a specific story line. Market liberal thinkers have quickly responded to fill the vacuum of uncertainty by attempting to re-ascertain market liberal economics as the conventional wisdom. Galbraith (1958) in his book *The Affluent Society* coined the term 'conventional wisdom' referring to the assumptions that glued together market economic theory as a series of assumptions that could not be questioned.

> The conventional wisdom having been made more or less identical with sound scholarship, its position was virtually impregnable. The skeptic was therefore disqualified by his very tendency to go brashly from the old to the new. Were he a sound scholar he would remain with the conventional wisdom. (Galbraith 1958, p. 17)

The two most important words in the above quote are scholarship and impregnable. Market economists have created mathematical models on supply and demand equilibrium theories, always with the aim of making economics a science that marks a departure from other social sciences, including philosophy and sociology. The use of mathematics attempts to put the discipline of economics in the same category as physics and the hard sciences. Even when these models have been found wanting as the theory did not match the lived experience, the idea that markets are pervasive and market theory has proved to be impregnable. Therefore, this conventional wisdom, as defined and shaped by market liberals' assumptions and advocates, makes the case for government to exit the macro-economic policy framework. Market liberals argue that government easing of monetary policy now needs to be tightened because of the new dangers of inflation. However, the destruction of some 5 per cent of GDP seem to suggest that economies have a lot of under used capacity and that inflation poses no immediate threat.

Market liberals argue that the economy should return to normal in the sense of a return to a policy framework that existed prior to 2007. The finance industry's return to normal advocates a return to the deregulated policy framework, pointing out that regulation could harm growth. Some leaders in the financial sector do accept that a return to normal is not a viable policy and that some form of regulation is needed, and that governments need to produce regulation, but that intervention should be limited to some form of levy on bankers as a form of insurance against future bank failure. There is resistance to regulatory proposals on derivatives and the over-the-counter customized derivatives should be put on transparent clearing platforms. Regulation including the Volcker rule of splitting banks into narrow and investment banking is criticized as unnecessary regulation.

The priorities of economic policy are being implicitly redefined. In the new exit strategy debate the concern of unemployment is displaced by the worry about inflation. Even though unemployment continues to be a major problem reducing deficits becomes more important. Unemployment is dismissed as being voluntary. Workers are unemployed because they wait for jobs with higher rate of pay and because benefits act as a disincentive to work. Consumption expenditure and consumer confidence decline when unemployment is high. The 'exit now' advocates argue that government deficits are crowding out private investment and therefore hindering growth and employment growth.

The near shut down of the US government in April 2011 is evidence of a major ideological fault. Unemployment in the USA has started to decline, from a peak rate of 9.8 per cent in October 2010 to 8.8 per cent in April 2011. The November election has shifted the control of the House of Representatives to the Republican Party, with new lawmakers elected on pledges of less government and lower taxes. Republicans have threatened the shutdown of the US government unless there were major reductions in public expenditure. Democrats have resisted the process, arguing that reductions in public expenditure would hinder the recovery. By contrast

Republicans are arguing that the deficits and high public expenditure are crowding out the private sector.

The cure of unemployment is a labour market issue and not a macro-economy policy issue. Reducing taxes and insurance costs will provide the framework for business to hire more labour. Market economists and their mathematical models have tried to avoid being yet another interpretation by attempting to establish their scientific status – similar to that of physics, with the laws of gravity replaced by the laws of market supply and demand, equilibrium and rational individualism. Yet, economics, like sociology and politics, is contaminated by the human experience, and the attempt to create models that expunge the human dimension creates major discrepancies between abstract theory and the realities of lived experiences.

The narrative adopted in this book is the 'politics' of recession. The argument that there is a politics of recession suggests that recessions are man made. Recessions create winners and losers. Furthermore, recessions as paradoxes do not represent shared and common experiences. Some people will be moving to new jobs while others are faced with long-term unemployment. Recessions redefine geographical spaces of emerging and declining economic landscapes. Recessions redefine power relationships where unemployment has a threat effect to those in work resulting in declining wages and yet higher profits and higher productivity, the benefits of which are not shared throughout the economy.

Politics reflects deliberate policy. The concept of political choice suggests that policy outcome could have been different, when choice implies policy alternatives. Choice means a deliberate decision – the decision to do something and equally the non-decision which is the decision not to do something. The non-decision by bank regulators to ignore concerns in the deregulated derivatives markets was a decision not to do something. The focus on politics deconstructs languages associated with narratives that seek to explain recessions as an inevitable and inherent part of the market economy; the idea of the black swan event that allows market liberal economists wedded to rational expectations to keep their theory intact and explain the recession as a market outcome that cannot be foreseen.

Recessions are therefore not something which are inevitable or inescapable and therefore cannot be avoided, but rather that they are human constructs. Equally, the response to recession is political in that again the policy responses reflect policy choices and priorities. The politics of recession puts the focus on policy networks at both and the formal and informal levels, particularly between the finance industry and the policy makers. Since the financial sector is a central factor to economic policy the leaders who define the financial sector have comparative ease of access to the policy process:

One channel of influence was, of course, the flow of individuals between Wall Street and Washington. Robert Rubin, once the co-chairman of Goldman Sachs, served in Washington as Treasury secretary under Clinton, and later became chairman of Citigroup's executive committee. Henry Paulson, CEO of Goldman Sachs during the long boom, became Treasury secretary under George W. Bush. These personal connections were multiplied many times over at the lower levels of the past three presidential administrations, strengthening the ties between Washington and Wall Street. It has become something of a tradition for Goldman Sachs employees to go into public service after they leave the firm. The flow of Goldman alumni . . . not only placed people with Wall Street's worldview in the halls of power; it also helped create an image of Goldman (inside the Beltway, at least) as an institution that was itself almost a form of public service. (Johnson 2009, p. 5)

Finance has access to the central bank. In the midst of the banking crisis Hank Paulson, Ben Bernanke and Tim Geithner immediately made contact with the leaders of the five major banks as a means of finding a solution to the rescue of Bear Stearns. It was a similar event when decisions had to be made about the future of Lehman. Key members at the US Treasury the Federal Reserve met with Chief Executive Officers of the major investment banks to explore the possibility of finding a rescue package:

The *sine qua non* of the plan, as Secretary Geithner and others have pointed out, was a willing and capable merger partner . . . In the end, the rescue failed because we had no willing and capable merger partner to stabilize Lehman . . . As of that Friday [12 September 2008] there were two prospective Lehman acquirers: Bank of America and Barclays. On Saturday, September 13, Bank of America abandoned the potential acquisition of Lehman and reached an agreement to acquire Merrill Lynch. Barclays was the only remaining suitor. On Sunday, September 14, we learned for the first time that Barclays would not be able to deliver a key document to carry the merger to conclusion. (Baxter 2010, p. 11)

The shapers of economic policy were criticized for having too many close ties with leading bankers. However, averting the financial crisis required consensus between the leading bankers and the Federal Reserve. The story of the bail-out of Bear Stearns was played out between the US Treasury and Jamie Dimon of JP Morgan Chase with the Federal Reserve offering $29 billion in insurances that made possible the takeover of Bear Stearns by JP Morgan. The immediate focus of policy making was the survival of the financial sector. After the collapse of Lehman the decision of the US Federal Reserve to allow the bank to go into liquidation had been described as a major watershed. Major investors lost confidence and were involved in the fire sale of mortgage backed securities, hedge funds faced collapse and the market for paper dried up. There was no interbank lending. The US government could not allow AIG to go bankrupt. Governments had no choice but to provide the necessary funding in order to bring some stability to both the financial and the real sector sectors of the economy.

Between 1973 and 1985 the financial sector had contributed to 16 per cent of total corporate profits, in the 1990s this had increased to 21 per cent and in 2007 it had expanded to 41 per cent (Johnson and Kwak 2010). The importance of the financial sector to GDP and to tax revenues meant that governments had to listen more to an important and influential sector in the economy (Haldane 2010; Huffington 2010). It is estimated that there are now 26 finance lobbyists employed in Washington for every elected lawmaker, and that on average each member of Congress receives about $6.5 million a year in campaign contributions from special interests (Johnson and Kwak 2010). Between 1998 and 2008 the financial sector spent $1.7 billion on campaign contributions and $3.4 billion on lobbying agencies. These funds were targeted at highly influential lawmakers on the Banking Committee including Phil Gramm, Chris Dodd and Charles Schumer (Johnson and Kwak 2010) when it came to the repeal of Glass-Steagill in 1998 and the Commodity Futures Modernization Act that deregulated the over-the-counter derivatives markets. The growth of the financial sector, financial contributions to policy makers and the focus on lobbying of special interests leads to concerns of agency capture of regulators becoming interconnected with the interests of the financial sector and there is social capital capture of public institutions which means that government agencies are not always one step removed from the finance industry. The failure of the SEC to oversee broker dealers who have mis-sold securities to investors or to supervise investment advisers has been criticized as being an example of policy capture:

> During recent years, billions of dollars of ARS [Adjustable Rate Securities] were sold to investors by major brokerage houses as cash alternatives. In February 2008, the ARS market collapsed, with the result that investors were left holding illiquid securities. It is both evidence of the efficacy of state securities regulators and support for the proposition that a federal agency has been permanently captured that, before the ARS market collapsed in February 2008, several of the largest brokerage firms were selling many billions of dollars of securities to their customers throughout the country by means of misrepresentations as to the nature of these securities, while the SEC either was unaware of this or, if it was aware, took no action to stop them. (Crawford 2010, p. 9)

Governments are not empty shells to be filled by the ideas of others. Governments come to office with a series of worked-out policies and a 'selective perception' that is shaped by the proximity of political ideology and their policy priorities. They bring policy advisers – people who can be trusted in shaping policy with the civil service. The role of the adviser is to convey to the civil service the policy wishes of the minister. It is therefore more likely that governments will make use of the economic analysis provided by economists who produce a policy framework that is proximate to the government's way of thinking. It is therefore not true that governments come to office with an open mind, willing to look at all policy options and to select the policy that works best. Their selection of policy options always approximates to their selective perceptions. Governments take office with a set of preconceived ideas and therefore will listen to analysis that is close to those ideas.

The concept of politics both implicitly and explicitly represents a departure from arguments that portray markets as existing beyond human control, arguments that seek to equate markets with physics and imbue the laws of supply and demand with a status equal to the laws of gravity. In politics, markets become social constructs shaped and defined through a policy process. The study of politics aims to explore the influence of ideas and how the ideas of market liberal economists of rational expectations, efficient markets, individualism and choice were utilized to develop a series of policies of deregulation, repealing legislation that had been established as lessons from the Great Depression, but which after the mid-1980s were described as a hindrance to markets and economic prosperity.

Recessions create winners and losers. The present recession has, for example, resulted in steep increases in unemployment. The unemployment rate in the USA has now reached 15 million which is about 10 per cent of the US workforce. Unemployment has also risen in the UK, to 3.8 million. It is estimated that the recession has destroyed approximately 4 per cent of GDP and that the US economy will not recover the GDP losses until 2015. Recessions tend therefore to change economic geographies. Unemployment tends to be concentrated in industrial communities. Job losses in manufacturing are never replaced and workers who at the age of 50 plus have lost their jobs very often never return to the world of work.

Yet recessions also create winners. The winners of the present recession have been employers who have used the recession to reduce their workforce while at the same increasing the productivity of those in work. Profitability has increased in the new landscape. Those who have capital can now purchase homes at reduced prices. Near zero interest rates make borrowing cheaper for those households not saturated with debt.

Recessions also take different forms and shapes, which means that policy responses have to be located in different and changing contexts. The policy responses to the 2007 recessions have to be located in an economy that is more globalized, more interconnected, than it was in 1929. Furthermore, it is always that much easier to discuss recessions with the benefits of hindsight when the unfolding panic has stabilized and there is not that urgency that something needs to be done now at the present moment. Criticisms always have the benefits of a discussion that can take place when the climate is that much more stable. Despite the sophistications of economic forecasting models there has been an intellectual vacuum that seeks to explain the connections between the expansion of financial instruments, deregulation of financial sectors, the collapse of consumer confidence and the spill-over in the contraction of the real economy. All stock exchanges experienced losses of between 40 and 50 per cent of their values during the year 2008. The sharp declines in equities and in house prices have contributed to major declines in household net worth. It is estimated that in both the UK and the USA household net worth declined by 17 per cent. This has resulted in declines in consumer confidence as households have attempted to repair their financial losses through increased savings, which in turn have exacerbated major downturn and shrinkage in global and national GDP. In accordance with the rational expectations school where individuals are completely rational and have complete information, the fall in interest rates should have warned these rational expectations individuals that this would lead to a bubble in house prices, that house prices rises were an illusion, and therefore they should not have taken out equities against their homes. In 2008 the global economy contracted by 2 per cent – the first time such contraction has been experienced since 1945. The US GDP contracted by 4 per cent and UK GDP by 6.4 per cent. While there have been approximately 122 different recessions since 1945, recessions in one part of the world had always been countered with growth in other parts. What makes the present recession different is that all the major economies contracted. Japan, a major exporting country, has experienced a decline of 45 per cent in exports. Germany and China also experienced contraction in their export markets. The US consumer is no longer the engine of world economic growth

The present recession is often described as an exogenous event – a black swan that no economic forecasting group or sophisticated economic models were able to predict or forecast and that the near collapse of global financial markets put governments into a policy making straitjacket (Talib 2008; Taylor 2010). In these circumstance governments had no choice but to rescue the financial sector. The priority of economic policy making has had to be focused on the sustainability of the banking sector. The IMF forecast (IMF 2010) shows that the bank write down of debt was likely to reach $4.1 trillion and this has to be contrasted with a global GDP of $65 trillion.

According to market liberal theorists the cause of recession is always the government. Markets are efficient and allocate resources. Financial markets are the best way of allocating capital investment to the more successful companies. With a market liberal perspective therefore there are no bubbles and no recessions since prices always return to an equilibrium. It was the government that caused the housing bubble in creating policy that encouraged increased home ownership. Fannie Mae and Freddie Mac, both government-led institutions, were put under pressure to provide mortgages. Sub-prime mortgagees were directed at communities that should have not had access to mortgages since their incomes were never strong enough to pay off mortgage debt. Consumers were also blamed for borrowing too much, thinking their houses were an investment portfolio and assuming that house prices would continue to rise, so leveraging their houses to buy more expensive and larger houses.

However, this argument is based on a series of myths. First the idea that sub-prime loans to first-time buyers contributed to the financial meltdown is contradicted by research evidence published by the Centre for Responsible Lending (CRL 2007) which showed that the majority of loans made from 1998 through 2006 went to borrowers who already owned their own homes – 62 per cent of sub-prime loans were refinances, 30 per cent were for families who were moving from one house to another, and only 9 per cent were for first-time home purchase loans Sub-prime lending did not even increase homeownership. Home ownership has remained static at 64 per cent of the population, a similar figure to that in 1998. Furthermore, only ten per cent of all sub-prime loans went to first-time homebuyers. The FDIC Vice Chair Marty Gruenberg made this point in a speech in New York on 8 January 2008, when he said:

> it has been said that a lot of these homes were bought on a speculative basis and people who did that don't deserve help. That is true of some. But it is important to understand that the majority of subprime mortgages were refinancing of existing homes. In other words, these were homes in which the homeowner was living, with mortgages that the homeowner was paying and could afford. In many cases the homeowner was encouraged or induced to refinance into one of these subprime mortgages with exploding interest rates that the homeowner couldn't afford. (Dodd 2010, p. 12)

Soros (2010) has suggested that it is market participants that define and shape markets. Markets therefore do not exist in their own right:

> Rational expectations theory and the efficient market hypothesis are products of this approach. Unfortunately they proved to be unsound. To be useful, the axioms must resemble reality. Euclid's axioms met that condition; rational expectations theory doesn't. It postulates that there is a correct view of the

future to which the views of all the participants tend to converge . . . rational expectations theory was pretty conclusively falsified by the crash of 2008 which caught most participants and most regulators unawares. The crash of 2008 also falsified the Efficient Market Hypothesis because it was generated by internal developments within the financial markets, not by external shocks, as the hypothesis postulates. (Soros 2010, p. 1)

The emphasis on politics seeks always to show that markets do not exist as some exogenous event but they are socially constructed through human intervention. Government and interventions in the policy making process define and shape markets. The concept of inevitability suggests that recessions are events beyond the control of government. Recession is explained as the exogenous variable that could not be foreseen. The politics of recession reflects therefore a process of political judgements. The Glass Steagill Act of 1933 reflected lessons learned from the Great Depression. It set the framework of regulation of financial markets for the next 50 years. The Gramm-Leach-Bliley Act of 1999, which repealed Glass-Steagill, redefined the nature of financial markets by creating a less regulatory environment.

Context is important. The Reagan and Thatcher administrations sought to construct a climate at the ideological level of government non-intervention, and maintained that a climate of self-regulation in markets was better than government regulation. Self-regulation reflected the discipline of the market. Within a framework of self-interest, private enterprise would regulate itself as appropriate. This is important to understand because it explains the reluctance of regulators, including the Federal Reserve Board under the Home Ownership and Equity Protection Act (HOEPA), and other principal regulators including the Office of Thrift Supervision (OTS) and the Office of the Comptroller of the Currency (OCC), with the necessary statutory powers to stop predatory lending, to ensure better underwriting of mortgage lending. These regulators failed to put on the lid on the process. As early as the end of 2003 and the beginning of 2004, Federal Reserve staff began to observe deterioration of credit standards, yet the Federal Reserve Board failed to meet its responsibilities. Furthermore, when attempts were made at the State level to enact anti-predatory practices federal regulators pre-empted them. In 1996, the OTS pre-empted all State lending laws, while the OCC promulgated a rule in 2004 that, likewise, exempted all national banks from State lending laws, including the anti-predatory lending laws. These decisions created regulatory arbitrage in the hope of attracting additional charters, which in turn helped to bolster the budget of these regulators.

Underlying this whole chain of events leading to the financial crisis was the spectacular failure of the prudential regulators to protect average American homeowners from risky, unaffordable . . . exploding adjustable rate mortgages, interest only mortgages, and negative amortization mortgages. These regulators . . . routinely sacrificed consumer protection for short-term profitability of banks, undercapitalized mortgage firms and mortgage brokers, and Wall Street investment firms, despite the fact that so many people were raising the alarm about the problems these loans would cause. (Dodd, 2010, p. 14)

People's biographies and lived experiences differ from official statistics. While national economies as measured by GDP have experienced growth of around 3 per cent per annum during the past two decades, household incomes and take home pay for over 80 per cent of people has remained stagnant or actually declined (Hacker and Pierson 2010; Rajan 2010; Stiglitz 2010). The majority of people had not been enjoying the fruits of prosperity. Wages and household incomes have pointed to a definition of recession that existed before the official beginnings of recession as identified in 2007. Inflation-adjusted pay has actually declined since 2000, emphasizing the pressures of declining household income. Since 2000 inflation-adjusted wages grew only about 13 percent – the slowest pace since the 1960s. Recession for the majority therefore started well before 2007. The paradox is that while wages for 90 per cent of the population remained stagnant or were actually declining; the incomes for the top 10 per cent of households were increasing rapidly, especially for the top 1 per cent.

Summers (2010), speaking at Davos in January 2010, pointed out that while the data pointed to the USA coming out of recession in the last quarter of 2009, people in the USA were still experiencing a human recession. Between September 2007 and December 2009 some 8 million lost their jobs and the unemployment rate increased to 10 per cent of the US workforce.

What we are seeing in the United States, and perhaps in some other places, is a statistical recovery and a human recession. We're gratified by the most recent GDP figure. It suggests that the policies to contain economic collapse have been successful. What is disturbing is the level of unemployment. This is not just a cyclical but a structural phenomenon as well. Just to put it in a way it's not usually put, one in five men in the United States between the ages of 25 and 54 is not working right now. A reasonable extrapolation would be that following a reasonable recovery, it will still be one in seven, or one in eight, who are not working. That is in contrast to the mid-1960s, when 95% of men between 25 and 54 were working. (Summers 2010)

It is therefore important to locate the Great Recession in a longer timeframe and also to consider contexts that reach beyond explaining the Great Recession of 2007. The Gini coefficients as a measure of inequality at both the global and at the domestic levels have continued to confirm a trend of increased income inequalities. Income inequality has increased at the global level but also at the national levels. Studies of the Gini coefficient for most confirm growing income inequalities since the mid-1980s. Most of this inequality has been explained in terms of globalization and the wage disparities between those with high skills and manual workers. The argument is that manual workers in the UK and USA have now to compete with workers in China. Global labour markets have increased labour supply, thus contributing to wage disparities. Advanced economies have all experienced a decline in manufacturing employment. Steel making, ship building and ship repair, engineering and textiles are now global industries shaped by outsourcing, contracting out and changing economic geographies. The advanced economies have seen manufacturing employment shrink from 36 per cent of employment to 22 per cent during the past two decades.

During the past two decades increases in income inequalities have resulted in a concentration of wealth and income that has benefited the top 10 per cent of the population. In the USA the tax reductions of the Bush Government benefited the top 1 per cent of income earners. So while wages for the majority stagnated there were major income increases that benefited the top 1 per cent of earners. Declining take home pay in a way contributed to the present recession. Low interest rates and growing house prices allowed households to use their homes as collateral to increase household borrowing and expand their credit, and thus through leveraging, households experienced prosperity through debt that was not warranted by growth in wages or take home pay. The avenue of low interest rates, easy credit and increased house prices offered an avenue to household prosperity. Households were encouraged by experts that house prices would continue to rise. House prices reflected the economic fundamentals of high wages, low interest rates and pressures on land and housing. High house prices reflected real economics rather than a bubble. Households therefore used their homes as collateral to expand their borrowings and use the new money to purchase cars and other items of household consumption. Other households used the opportunity to move into new and larger homes.

Recessions therefore are not collective histories and experiences. While 10 per cent of the US population are unemployed, the other 90 per cent are in work. Those in work are not immediately threatened by unemployment. Those on high incomes are still buying high priced clothing and perfumes in high priced shopping malls.

All recessions lead to changes in landscapes and economic geographies. Britain emerged as the first industrial nation and dominated manufacturing into the 1880s, to be eventually overtaken by Germany and the USA (Mathias 1969). The decline of manufacturing in cotton, coal mining and steel production during the Great Depression of 1929 to 1931 resulted in the decline and eventual disappearance of the industrial communities that defined the geography of industrial Britain. In the mid-1950s approximately 50 per cent of the UK workforce were still involved in manufacturing. The world of manufacturing became an experience of decline. Between 1981 and 1987 the UK lost some 2.5 million jobs in manufacturing. Between 1970 and 2000 it is estimated that there has been a loss of approximately 35 million jobs in manufacturing in the OECD economies. Although other countries in Europe were also losing jobs, the UK still experienced the largest jobs losses – 2.5 million compared to 1.1. million in Germany and 1.4 million in France. The job losses were mainly described as a shake-out of the UK labour market. The experience of unemployment was of course painful for those who lost their jobs but it was a price worth paying, according to then Chancellor of the Exchequer Norman Lamont. Unemployment fluctuated between 2 and 3 million throughout the Thatcher years, compared to a figure of around 250,000 during the period from 1950 to 1974. However, Mrs Thatcher and her governments went on to win three consecutive elections. Unemployment had become a non issue. This was because the main job losses in coal, steel and engineering were mainly experienced in northern cities. Yorkshire had unemployment rates of 10 per cent in the 1980s, East Lancashire 10 per cent and South Yorkshire 10 per cent. Manufacturing during the period had shifted to new green field sites. By contrast parts of the south recorded unemployment rates of 4 per cent (Martin and Rowthorn 1986).

The decline of manufacturing did not lead to any major debate as to what would replace manufacturing. The assumption was that the creative destructions of markets would create the dynamics for economic growth. Attempts to answer the question of what replaces manufacturing employment was seen as illegitimate because that would lead to the centralized planning of government picking industrial winners. Just as the industrial revolution was the outcome of the invisible hand of the market that transformed the UK economy from agriculture to manufacturing, the invisible hand would guide manufacturing to new opportunities.

From the mid-1980s, therefore, the search was on for the New Economy. The digital revolution of computers, robotics and the information age was welcomed as representing the third industrial revolution, equal in magnitude to the coming of the railways and the telegraph. The information age would contribute to shrinking geographic spaces, and increasing trade, competition and productivity. The Fed Chairman Alan Greenspan argued the case of increased productivity that was, at the time, he argued, not being reflected in GDP estimates. Workers were being more productive and producing better quality goods, and that improved quality was not being reflected in GDP figures. If productivity was increasing, therefore, there was no problem of inflation.

Giddens (2001) referred to the New Economy as being the Knowledge Economy, arguing that power had shifted from hierarchical management styles to democratic work organizations that depended on the ideas and concepts created by the workforce. Employers now need the expertise of their labour force. Workers had knowledge power. Trade unions were an irrelevance in the new economy; workers could now bargain as individuals because of the knowledge they had acquired on which the success of the organization depended. Ideas and knowledge were the new sources of power. The manufacturing of a car could now be outsourced to countries that offered cheap labour as long as the advanced economies continued to provide the added value. Advertising, marketing and finance were the new sectors that provided the added value and the prosperity of the advanced economies.

The deregulation of the finance industry was perceived to be one of the major pillars of the New Economy. Dependence on the savings and deposits of individual savers could not provide the necessary finance to generate global economic prosperity. Banks had to find ways of making new loans. The solution lay in securitization. Instead of the banks holding on to individual mortgages and loans why not turn those loans into securities that could be sold to investors, providing new incomes streams for investors but also removing from the banks outstanding loans and therefore creating opportunities to provide new additional loans to new borrowers. Finance therefore was an important dynamic. The finance industry would create new high paying jobs that would provide new revenues to the government, but they needed an environment that allowed for financial innovation to make possible the promises of the New Economy.

Governments might make statements about the need to combat unemployment but that commitment might not necessarily be shared. The Obama stimuli of 2009 and 2010 were supported in some parts of America while others were highly critical. The mid-term elections of November 2010 confirmed the fragmentation of US opinion on responding to the recession. The Tea Party movement, a coalition of groups favouring lower taxes and less government, had pledged to reverse the Obama administration's health reforms and also the reforms of the financial sector. Their priority is reducing government deficits, reducing taxes, abandoning health reform proposals and even shifting away from any regulatory proposals on the financial sector. The present financial meltdown has created the politics of contentment and political arithmetic of creating a series of public policies that create coalitions of majorities. In the USA, therefore, Republicans resist health reforms as creating too much government, but at the same time support Medicare because Medicare is popular with senior citizens. In the UK the government seeks to reduce public expenditure by focusing on pension contributions, retirement and tuition fees for university students, while a number of universal benefits for senior citizens have been protected.

CONCLUSIONS

Recessions are paradoxes. There are winners and losers and issues of power and influence are redefined. The Great Depression of 1929 was not a shared experience. Some workers in the staple industries who lived in old industrial communities experienced long-term unemployment and poverty but others found jobs in the new growth sector of aircraft building, automobiles and chemicals. Recessions redefine economic landscapes. As to the present recession, it is the advanced economies that have experienced economic slowdown: China, Brazil, India and other emerging economies have experienced growth. There are major regional differences and different sectors of the economy are impacted. Governments in the advanced economies have had no alternative but to provide the necessary funding to stabilize the financial sector, while the spill-over to the real economy has resulted in major increases in unemployment. In contrast to the willingness to find the necessary financial resources to stabilize finance, governments have been less willing to provide relief for the long-term unemployed. The finances need to bail out the financial sector have resulted in policies of austerity towards public provision. The risk taking by the finance industry in over-extending loans to property markets has resulted in a major write down of banking assets, which in turn has resulted in declining house prices, sharp declines in equity markets and losses for pension and retirement funds.

The recession in the financial sector has meant a slowdown in consumer demand as consumers have tried to repair declining savings. The spill-over to other sectors of the economy has meant that employers have sought to increase productivity by making a number of their employees redundant. In the retail sector the labour shake-outs have resulted in major increases in the output of the existing workforce. Private sector companies are running large financial surpluses. Consumers have shifted from zero savings to 5.6 per cent of GDP. Government is the only viable consumer in the economy and yet its response is austerity and a reduction in government consumption.

The concept of a politics of recession points to the idea of policy choices, to the role of ideology and the presence of specific interests. The present recession was not inevitable but represents the outcome of policy decisions. Recessions create winners and losers. They alter the landscapes of power relations. After 20 years of virtually stagnant wage rises and rises in inequality it would seem that the present recession has created further increases in inequality and further concentrations of power.

REFERENCES

Angelides, P. (2010) Opening Remarks of Phil Angelides, Chairman of the Financial Crisis Inquiry Commission at the Hearing on 'The Role of Derivatives in the Financial Crisis', 13 January, Washington, DC.

Baxter, T.C. (2010) Statement By Thomas C. Baxter, Jr. Executive Vice President and General Counsel Federal Reserve Bank of New York, Financial Crisis Inquiry Commission, 1 September.

Bernanke, B. (2010) 'Lessons from the Failure of Lehman Brothers', Statement by Ben S Bernanke, Chairman Board of Governors of the Federal Reserve System before the Committee on Financial Services, U.S. House of Representatives, Washington, DC, 20 April.

Bosworth, M. and A. Smart (2009) 'The Wealth of Old Americans: The Subprime Debacle', Brookings Institute, November.

Brunnermeier, M. (2010) 'Deciphering the Liquidity and Credit Crunch 2007–2008', Financial Crisis Inquiry Commission, Washington, DC, 27 February.

Cohen, N., D. Pimlott, C. Giles and G. Parker (2010) 'Bank of England Divisions are Laid Bare', *The Financial Times*, 25 November. Available at: http://www.ft.com/cms/s/0/25ad090e-f887-11df-8b7b-00144feab49a.html#axzz1QaMcLEKb

Crawford, D. (2010) Testimony of Denise Voigt Crawford Commissioner, Texas Securities Board and President North American Securities Administrators Association, Inc. Before the United States Financial Crisis Inquiry Commission, 14 January.

CRL (2007) 'Sub Prime Lending a Net Drain on Home Ownership', CRL Issue Paper No 14, 27 March.

Dodd, C. (2010) The Restoring American Financial Stability Act 2010. Senate Report 111-176. Available at: http://www.gpo.gov/fdsys/pkg/CRPT-111srpt176/html/CRPT-111srpt176.htm

Financial Crisis Inquiry (FCIC) (2011) *Final Report of the National Commission on the Causes of the Financial and Economic Crisis in the United States*. New York: Public Affairs.

Galbraith, J.K. (1958) *The Affluent Society.* Harmondsworth: Penguin Books.

Geanakoplos, P. (2010) 'Solving the Present Crisis and Managing the Leverage Cycle', Financial Crisis Inquiry Commission, Washington, DC, 27 February.

Giddens, A. (2001) *The Global Third Way Debate.* Cambridge: Polity Press.

Gourinchas, P. (2010) 'U.S. Monetary Policy, "Imbalances" and the Financial Crisis: Remarks Prepared for the Financial Crisis Inquiry Commission Forum', Washington, DC, 26–27 February.

Hacker, J. and P. Pierson (2010) *Winner-Takes-All Politics: How Washington Made the Rich Richer – and Turned Its Back on the Middle Class*. London: Simon and Schuster.

Haldane, A.G. (2010) 'The Debt Overhang', speech given at a Professional Liverpool Dinner, 27 January, by Andrew G Haldane, Executive Director Financial Stability Bank of England. Available at: http://www.bis.org/review/r100202d.pdf

Huffington, A. (2010) *Third World America: How Politicians are Abandoning the Middle Class and Reneging on the American Dream*. New York: Crown Press.

IMF (2010) *Global Financial Stability Report*. Washington, DC: IMF.

Johnson, S. (2009) 'The Quiet Coup', *The Atlantic Monthly*, May. Available at: http://www.theatlantic.com/magazine/archive/2009/05/the-quiet-coup/7364/

Johnson, S. and J. Kwak (2010) *13 Bankers: Wall Street Takeover and the Next Financial Meltdown*. New York: Pantheon Books.

Martin, R. and B. Rowthorn (1986) *The Geography of De-industrialization*. London: Macmillan.

Mathias, P. (1969) *The First Industrial Nation: The Economic History of Britain 1700–1914*. London: Methuen.

McDonald, L. (2009) *A Colossal Failure of Common Sense: The Incredible Inside Story of the Collapse of Lehman Brothers*. London: Edbury Press.

Rajan, B.G. (2010) *Fault Lines: How Hidden Fractures Still Threaten The World Economy*. Princeton, NJ and Oxford: Princeton University Press.

Sorkin, A. (2009) *Too Big to Fail: Inside the Battle to Save Wall Street*. London: Allen Lane.

Soros, G. (2009) 'The Game Changer', *The Financial Times*, 29 January, p.10.

Soros, G. (2010) 'Anatomy of Crisis – The Living History of the Last 30 Years: Economic Theory, Politics and Policy', presentation by George Soros, Chairman of Soros Fund Management, LLC and Founder of the Open Society Institute at the INET Conference, King's College, 8–11 April.

Stiglitz, J. (2010) *Free Fall, America, Free Markets and the Sinking of the World Economy*. London: W.W. Norton and Company.

Summers, L. (2010) 'The US Economic Outlook' paper presented at the 2010 Annual Meeting of the World Economic Forum in Davos, Switzerland, 29 January.

Talib, N.N. (2008) *The Black Swan: The Impact of the Highly Improbable*. London: Penguin Books.

Taylor, J. (2010) 'The Financial Crisis and the Policy Responses: An Empirical Analysis of What Went Wrong', paper presented at the Financial Crisis Inquiry Commission, 2 September, Washington, DC.

Tolstoy, L. (1982) *War and Peace*. London: Penguin Books.

Towns, E. (2010) Opening Statement of Chairman Edolphus Towns, Committee on Oversight and Government Reform, 27 January.

Wessel, D. (2010) *In Fed We Trust: Ben Bernanke's War on the Great Panic*. New York: Three Rivers Press.

3. Explanations of the financial meltdown and the present recession

The present economic crisis started in June 2007 and is still unfolding, with high rates of unemployment, an ongoing banking crisis in the euro zone, large public sector deficits in many of the advanced economies and unresolved problems of global trade imbalances. Explanations of the crisis are contestable, reflecting competing discourses and narratives. The languages that define each of these narratives are incommensurate in the sense that they offer competing views of the world and allow little room for agreement as to causes and what needs to be done.

> To say that a particular network of concepts is contestable is to say that the standard and criteria of judgement it expresses are open to contestation. To say that such a network is essentially contestable is to contend that the universal criteria of reason, as we can understand them, do not suffice to settle these contests. (Connolly 1983, p. 225)

In a debate launched in the pages of *The Financial Times* during July 2010, Wolf (2010) pointed to the fierce debate on the themes of austerity and stimulus between market liberal 'cutters' and Keynesian 'postponers'. Ferguson (2010) and Taylor (2010) favoured immediate reductions in public expenditure.

> The evidence is very clear from surveys on both sides of the Atlantic. People are nervous of world war-sized deficits when there isn't a war to justify them. The remedy for such fears must be the kind of policy regime-change . . . which the Thatcher and Reagan governments successfully implemented. Then, as today, the choice was not between stimulus and austerity. It was between policies that boost private-sector confidence and those that kill it. (Ferguson 2010)

Ferguson's plea was a return to the Reagan/Thatcher Revolutions, despite the fact that under Reagan deficits had exploded to finance defence spending and the Thatcher government had actually failed to reduce public expenditure as a ratio of GDP. Even after all the privatizations, public expenditure was higher in 1992 then when the Thatcher Government took office in 1979 (Mullard 1993).

On the other side of the debate the stimulus sympathizers (postponers), including De Long (2010), Skidelsky and Kennedy (2010) and Summers (2010), pointed out that while the deficit was a problem, in the context of recession there was a problem of demand which had been caused by major declines in household net worth. Households had responded to the financial meltdown by increasing their savings and paying off debt. In the context of falling aggregate demand the government was the consumer of last resort:

> where an economy's level of output is constrained by demand and the central bank has at best a limited ability to relax that constraint because it cannot reduce interest rates to below zero, fiscal policy can have a significant impact on output and employment. Through either direct spending or tax cuts that promote private spending, hiring or investment, governments possess a range of tools to raise demand directly. As increased demand boosts incomes, these measures raise output further. The result will be economic growth and reduced joblessness. To the extent that expansionary fiscal policies affect growth, their impact on future indebtedness is attenuated as tax collections rise, transfer payments fall, and the ability of the economy to support debt increases. (Summers 2010)

Wolf (2010) pointed out that no one was really sure as to which narrative was right and that people needed to make up their own minds. However, the debate was important because policy makers have proceeded to construct public policies that approximated to the specific discourse they favoured and therefore the outcomes of their policy choices would soon unfold as the economy assimilated the policy changes. The question for the policy makers was whether their course of favoured treatment would have adverse effects and what contingency policies did they have to deal with such adverse effects:

> To tighten or not to tighten that is the question . . . That is the issue addressed in the Financial Times this week, echoing the fierce debates of the 1930s . . . Readers must make up their own minds on the merits of the arguments this week . . . My own strong sympathies are with the postponers. But on one thing everybody agrees, this debate matters. We cannot be sure who is right. But we can be sure if policymakers get it wrong the results may well be dire. Physicians must prepare to respond swiftly to adverse reactions to their favoured course of treatment. (Wolf 2010)

The UK coalition government has planned to reduce deficits by £80 billion during this Parliament. Public sector deficits are perceived as crowding out the private sector through high interest and employing resources that could be used more productively in the private sector. This argument is central to the government's case, despite countervailing evidence that shows interest rates as close to zero and UK Treasury bills with yields of below 3 per cent and no evidence that the financial markets have lost confidence in Britain. Equally the most recent OBR (Office for Budget Responsibility) forecast shows unemployment and low growth persisting to 2015.

In the following sections it will be suggested that there are three major areas of contestability. These include the role of government and disagreements about whether government policies have succeeded in stabilizing financial markets or whether the government, through intervention, undermined the workings of markets which in turn resulted in increased uncertainty. The second area of contestability is the question of whether the recession was inevitable, which suggests that this was an exogenous event which was difficult to forecast, or whether it was unavoidable since it represented the outcome of a series of policy decisions which eventually resulted in bubbles in housing and financial markets. The third area relates to problems of ideas and ideals and to what extent the paradigm of markets influenced a policy of deregulation, as well as the role ideas played in the financial crisis. It shall also be argued that the process of contestability creates the possibility of locating explanations of the financial crisis under five categories, namely:

1. The pragmatists
2. Market liberal fundamentalists
3. The Institutionalists
4. The Keynesian collectivists
5. The structuralists.

CONTESTABLE TERRAIN 1: THE ROLE OF GOVERNMENT

The responses of governments to the crisis included the partial nationalization of banks, exchanging equity for asset backed securities, providing guarantees on loans and the purchase of assets. The IMF calculates that the global costs of the bail-outs was around $16 trillion. The US Government under TARP provided $700 billion to deal with the problems of capital and liquidity requirement in the banking sector. Starting with the collapse in house prices in June 2007, the bail-out of Bear Stearns in March 2008, the bankruptcy of Lehman in September 2008, followed by the rescue of AIG a few days later, economies seemed to be falling off a cliff. With the real threat of contagion spilling over to other investment banks, there was an increased possibility that the fragile financial markets would also affect the collapse of major industries because of the freezing of asset backed commercial paper. Also at risk were the pensions and savings of millions of households. The primary goal of government was therefore the need to stabilize financial markets to provide the necessary guarantees and to stop major runs on the banking sector.

In the UK the Labour Government of Gordon Brown took partial ownership of Northern Rock, Lloyds and Royal Bank of Scotland, while in the US, Secretary Paulson and Fed Chairman Bernanke put together a $700 billion programme to stabilize US financial markets. Hank Paulson (2010b) in his recent memoirs argued that his rescue package ran up against the prevailing ideology of the Republican Party and that he had to negotiate the rescue through the leadership of the Democrats. There is major disagreement about the role of government. The area of concern is whether government intervention did stabilize the financial markets and avoided a Depression similar to the Great Depression of 1929 or whether the bail-outs actually reinforced a climate of moral hazard which then allowed financial institutions to sustain their high levels of leverage without seeking to improve their liquidity or capital margins?

The Pragmatists' Interpretation

The pragmatists' interpretation (Wessel 2010) is a time-related series of accounts that reflected the immediacy of the crisis. The pragmatists' major concern was trying to make sense of the crisis while it was still unfolding. These policy makers directly involved in the process of seeking to stabilize the financial markets did not have the benefit of hindsight, but at the time were trying to create order from disorder. The responses of Secretary to the US Treasury Paulson (Paulson 2010a), Chairman Bernanke of the Federal Reserve, and the New York Federal Reserve Chairman Geithner were piecemeal, but in the end the measures seemed to work as the financial system did return to some form of stability. Wessel has called these pragmatists the four musketeers, whom, he argued, within a period of two weeks had between them changed the landscape of the US financial sector through forced mergers of investment banks, making Morgan Stanley and Goldman Sachs bank holding companies.

In a recent article in the *New York Times* Warren Buffet (2010) praised the role of the Government in stabilizing the economy:

> Just over two years ago, in September 2008, our country faced an economic meltdown . . . One of Wall Street's giant investment banks had gone bankrupt . . . A.I.G., the world's most famous insurer, was at death's door. Indeed, all of corporate America's dominoes were lined up, ready to topple at lightning speed: 300 million Americans were in the domino line as well. Well, Uncle Sam, you delivered . . . I would like to commend a few of your troops. In the darkest

of days, Ben Bernanke, Hank Paulson, Tim Geithner and Sheila Bair grasped
the gravity of the situation and acted with courage and dispatch. (Warren
Buffet 2010)

In the immediate aftermath of 2007 a window of opportunity seemed to
open, at least for a short while, for an emerging consensus of a readiness to
accept that the deregulatory environment in financial markets and the lack
of oversight by regulators had contributed to the crisis. The shift from an
originate and hold model of banking to an originate and distribute model
had resulted in a moral deficit (Stiglitz 2010), with markets participants,
including bankers, lawyers, brokers and households, pursuing short-term
gains in fees and enjoying high levels of compensation, which, in the long
term, proved to be unsustainable.

In 2007 those policy makers who favoured improved regulation of the
securitization process to put these instruments on clearing platforms and
make these derivatives more transparent seemed to be in the ascendant.
Within this framework the expansion of a derivatives market which was
unregulated, especially in the emergence of credit default swaps, was
accepted as being a major contributor to the financial crisis (Dinallo 2010;
Gensler 2010; Masters 2010):

> As the notional value of CDS went from slightly less than $10 trillion in 2004 to
> roughly $60 trillion at the end of 2007, mortgage-backed securities (MBS) went
> from roughly $1.5 trillion in 2004 to its peak of $3.5 trillion in 2007 before both
> started a decline. The simultaneous rise and fall of the CDS market and the
> MBS market reflects the interplay between weak rating agency practices with
> respect to CDOs, reliance on CDS protection of CDOs by AIG and other insur-
> ers, such as Ambac and MBIA, declining mortgage underwriting practices and
> the failure of banks to do proper due diligence when packaging the mortgages.
> Ultimately each of these factors helped feed into the housing bubble. Once the
> housing bubble burst in 2007, mortgage securitization collapsed, the demand
> for CDS protection proportionately decreased and the writers of CDS, like
> AIG, started suffering significant losses. (Gensler 2010, p. 9)

There seemed to be agreement that the regulatory system was broken
and that markets could be improved through better regulation. Policies on
bank regulation, control of leverage and increased capital requirements
did not create much controversy about the future shape of policy reform.
The CEOs of Goldman Sachs and JP Morgan, in giving evidence to the
FCIC enquiry in January 2010, both supported the proposal to regulate
the previously unregulated derivatives markets, with the CEO of Goldman
Sachs making the case for central clearing:

> With respect to OTC derivatives, Goldman Sachs supports the broad move
> to central clearinghouses and exchange trading of standardized derivatives. A

central clearinghouse with strong operational and financial integrity will reduce bi-lateral credit risk, increase liquidity and enhance the level of transparency through enforced margin requirements and verified and recorded trades. This will do more to enhance price discovery and reduce systemic risk than perhaps any specific rule or regulation. (Blankfien 2010, p. 11)

Dimon (2010) in his testimony pointed to the process of securitization and how the shift to an originate and distribute model in banking had resulted in poor underwriting standard for mortgage borrowing. Dimon also pointed to problems of predatory lending and the dishonesty of mortgage brokers,

As the housing bubble grew, new and poorly underwritten mortgage products helped fuel asset appreciation, excessive speculation and far higher credit losses. Mortgage securitization had two major flaws that added risk: nobody along the chain had ultimate responsibility for the results of the underwriting for many securitizations, and the poorly constructed tranches converted a large portion of poorly underwritten loans into Triple A-rated securities. In hindsight, it's apparent that excess speculation and dishonesty on the part of both brokers and consumers further contributed to the problem. (Dimon 2010, p. 9)

The pragmatists' central argument was that the incoming Obama administration had to focus on a series of regulatory reforms to prevent future financial meltdowns. Advocates for regulatory reform urged the new administration to create a Consumer Protection Agency to deal with future predatory lending and to ensure that households were sold mortgages that they could understand and that were transparent. Regulators including Gary Gensler (2010) at the CFTC and Eric Dinallo (2010), former Superintendent of the New York State Insurance Department, all argued that the unregulated derivatives markets had to be standardized and put on exchange and trading platforms that had transparent prices similar to clearing and trading on the stock exchange which shows daily price movements. James Dimon, giving evidence to the FCIC, confirmed that 80 per cent of the so-called over-the-counter customized derivatives could be standardized and put on clearing platforms.

When the crisis hit and huge swaths of the American financial system got caught in the run on the parallel banking system, many came running to the Federal Reserve for liquidity and for protection. The emergency financial response to the run that started in the parallel financial system was necessary to protect our economy from an even greater calamity. But if our regulatory and supervisory systems had had the tools and authorities to prevent risks from accumulating in unregulated sectors of the financials system in the first place, such a large emergency response would not have been necessary. That is a key reason why financial reform is so essential. (Geithner 2010, p. 4)

The Market Fundamentalists

Within this temporal framework, as the banks stabilized and the panic seemed to recede, there was an emerging literature that sought to criticize the measures taken during the immediacy of the crisis. The second series of explanations came from those who can be categorized as market fundamentalists, whose starting points were existing theoretical frameworks and who sought in turn to fit the events of 2007 within these existing models. Within this category are Wallison (2008) and the writers for the CATO Institute such as Schwartz (2010), Taylor (2010), Kyle (2010) and Kohlhagen (2010) whose common theme was that government intervention was the major contributor to the crisis, including the misguided policies of bailing out the banks, the Troubled Asset Relief Programme (TARP), and attempting to regenerate the economy through stimulus measures and high public sector deficits. This approach has a number of layers that includes government housing policy, the policy of low interest rates, the subsidies to government sponsored agencies (GSEs), including Fannie Mae and Freddie Mac, moral hazard and the bail-out of Bear Stearns.

Taylor (2010) blames the meltdown on the government undermining his 'Taylor rule', namely of fixing the interest rate in relation to an inflation rate. The focus is the Federal Reserve and interest rate policy followed by Alan Greenspan. The argument is that Greenspan kept interest rates too low for too long which in turn contributed to the housing bubble. Furthermore, the Federal Reserve misdiagnosed the crisis by arguing that the problem of the banks was one of liquidity, leading to the government decision to purchase mortgage backed securities through the Troubled Asset Relief Programme (TARP):

> I have provided empirical evidence that government actions and interventions caused, prolonged, and worsened the financial crisis. They caused it by deviating from historical precedents and principles for setting interest rates, which had worked well for 20 years. They prolonged it by misdiagnosing the problems in the bank credit markets and thereby responding inappropriately by focusing on liquidity rather than risk. (Taylor 2010, p. 9)

Other market fundamentalists have pointed to the Clinton/Bush administrations' housing policies, aimed at encouraging wider home ownership, including tax deductions on mortgages, and Freddie Mac and Fannie Mae for their monopoly position in the housing market (Kohlhagen 2010; Kyle 2010). Providing targets for Fannie Mae and Freddie Mac created increased risk in mortgage backed securities. The policy of low interest rates created by Greenspan in 2003 meant that low interest fed into the housing bubble because of expectations that interest rates would remain low, which in turn encouraged people to take on more debt:

> In the case of the housing price boom, the government played a role in stimulating demand for houses by proselytizing the benefits of home ownership for the well-being of individuals and families. Congress was also more than a bit player in this campaign. Beginning in 1992 Congress pushed Fannie Mae and Freddie Mac to increase their purchases of mortgages going to low- and moderate-income borrowers. In 1996, HUD, the department of Housing and Urban Development, gave Fannie and Freddie an explicit target: 42 percent of their mortgage financing had to go to borrowers with incomes below the median income in their area. The target increased to 50 percent in 2000 and 52 percent in 2005 (Schwartz 2010, p. 7)

According to market fundamentalists, therefore, there was no problem with derivatives or credit default swaps. Derivatives confirm that markets are working; swap deals reduce the costs for business, while credit default swaps provide accurate pricing mechanisms, and therefore rational expectations and efficient markets models of the economy do not need to revised or questioned.

> Credit default swaps (CDSs) have been identified in media accounts and by various commentators as sources of risk for the institutions that use them, as potential contributors to systemic risk, and as the underlying reason for the bailouts of Bear Stearns and AIG. These assessments are seriously wide of the mark. They seem to reflect a misunderstanding of how CDSs work and how they contribute to risk management by banks and other intermediaries. In addition, the vigorous market that currently exists for CDSs is a significant source of market-based judgments on the credit conditions of large numbers of companies. Although the CDS market can be improved, excessive restrictions on it would create considerably more risk than it would eliminate. (Wallison 2008, p. 1)

Government intervention, including the bail-out of banks, created a chemistry of moral hazard, with financial institutions coming to the conclusion that they were too big to fail. In an open letter to Chairman Ben Bernanke of the Federal Reserve, a series of commentators criticized the Federal Reserve for continuing to intervene in the economy through quantitative easing:

> We believe the Federal Reserve's large-scale asset purchase plan (so-called 'quantitative easing') should be reconsidered and discontinued. We do not believe such a plan is necessary or advisable under current circumstances. The planned asset purchases risk currency debasement and inflation, and we do not think they will achieve the Fed's objective of promoting employment. (e21 Team 2010)

The important issues in this quote were the twin references to inflation and employment. Despite the counter evidence that the US economy had contracted by around 5 per cent of GDP as well as evidence of access capacity, the concern of these commentators was that the Federal Reserve through monetary easing was likely to cause inflation. The implicit argument rested on the market theory that government was crowding out the private sector. Secondly, their argument was that employment should not be the concern of the Federal Reserve. For them, unemployment would be resolved within the dynamics of labour markets, which again implied that unemployment was voluntary and at present the unemployed had a preference for leisure as they waited for better days and higher wages.

CONTESTABLE TERRAIN 2: PROBLEMS OF INTERPRETATION – INEVITABILITY AS AGAINST POLICY CHOICE

The second layer has been the disagreement of interpretation as to whether the financial crisis was either an event that was difficult to predict or whether the financial crisis was the product of the policy process. Was the financial crisis an exogenous event with governments having to respond to the external challenge, or was it endogenous, caused by a series of policy choices? The sudden declines in house prices were accompanied by the Credit Rating Agencies downgrading asset back securities from triple-A to below investment grade, which led to increased uncertainty in financial markets with investment banks finding themselves under pressure to provide additional collateral in the REPO markets and the eventual freezing of interbank lending.

The Institutionalists

Some CEOs at the major investment banks, including Fuld (2010), who was the CEO of Lehman, and Cayne (2010) the CEO of Bear Stearns, made the case that no one could have anticipated the magnitude of the financial crisis. Since bubbles are difficult to predict or regulate markets need to be left alone so that economies could very quickly recover from such disruptions. The common response was to adopt the Minsky moment (Whalen 2008) view of crisis as being the result of a series of inevitable stages leading from caution to stability, and then stability in itself would lead to euphoria, irrational exuberance and eventual bubbles. Alan Greenspan, the previous chairman of the Federal Reserve, in his testimony to the FCIC on 9 March 2010 pointed out that attempts to crush bubbles through higher interest rates would cause more damage to the economy than allowing bubbles to burst and governments should confine themselves to providing a safety net for those who lost their jobs in the immediate period of such a disruption:

> At some rate, monetary policy can crush any bubble. If not 6½%, try 20%, or 50% for that matter. Any bubble can be crushed, but the state of prosperity will be an inevitable victim. Unless there is a societal choice to abandon dynamic markets and leverage for some form of central planning, I fear that preventing bubbles will in the end turn out to be infeasible. Assuaging their aftermath seems the best we can hope for. Policies, both private and public, should focus on ameliorating the extent of deprivation and hardship caused by deflationary crises. (Greenspan 2010b, p. 9)

The counter-argument was to see the financial crisis as human made. The financial crisis was therefore not a exogenous factor, but rather the outcome of a series of policy choices. Johnson's (2009) central argument was that the financial sector has had a major influence on the policy process in America. The finance industry in the USA has gained prominence because of what Johnson calls cultural capital as a belief system. The financial sector over the past two decades had grown from 4 per cent of GDP to 9 per cent of GDP and its contribution to corporate profits has increased from 16 per cent to 40 per cent:

> these various policies – lightweight regulation, cheap money, the unwritten Chinese-American economic alliance, the promotion of homeownership – had something in common. They all benefited the financial sector. Policy changes that might have forestalled the crisis but would have limited the financial sector's profits – such as Brooksley Born's now-famous attempts to regulate credit-default swaps at the Commodity Futures Trading Commission, in 1998 – were ignored or swept aside. (Johnson 2009, p. 7)

Reinhart and Rogoff in their historical studies of financial crises have pointed out that most crises start in the banking or housing sector where bubbles are formed because of high leverage and increased risk exposure. Reinhart and Rogoff associate the financial with the policy of liberalization and deregulation in financial markets that started with the years of President Reagan in the USA and Prime Minister Thatcher in Britain, where both governments committed themselves to deregulation and a retreat of the state. The repeal of Glass-Steagill in 1999 and the Commodities Modernization were a series of a policies that created the climate of deregulation:

> While each financial crisis no doubt is distinct, they also share striking similarities in the run-up of asset prices, in debt accumulation, in growth patterns, and

in current account deficits. The majority of historical crises are preceded by financial liberalization. While in the case of the United States, there has been no striking de jure liberalization, there certainly has been a de facto liberalization. New unregulated, or lightly regulated, financial entities have come to play a much larger role in the financial system, undoubtedly enhancing stability against some kinds of shocks, but possibly increasing vulnerabilities against others. (Reinhart and Rogoff 2008, p. 4)

The CFMA legitimized a process where new financial instruments such as over-the-counter derivatives did not have to be traded in exchanges with transparent price movements; instead the new derivatives became customized where each transaction was unique. Unregulated markets for mortgage backed securities (MBS), collateralized debt obligations (CDOs) and credit default swaps (CDS), contributed to the financial crisis because of their lack of transparency, the uncertainty of counter-party exposure and the absence of posting of collateral. AIG is seen as the major example of having sold a series of credit default swaps which at one level generated streams of income for AIG in the short term and which could be defined as profits for the company, without AIG having to post collateral. When these insured bonds were downgraded in July 2007 and AIG was asked to post collateral by Goldman Sachs, AIG very quickly lost liquidity and also its triple-A ratings. The US government eventually had to step in and meet the CDS contract of AIG at a total cost of $180 billion. AIG sold approximately $400 billion worth of insurance without having to post collateral.

The unregulated marketplace in credit derivatives was a central cause of a near systemic collapse of our financial system. Credit default swaps played a major role in the financial problems at AIG, Bear Stearns, Lehman and the bond insurance companies. A major cause of our current financial crisis is not the effectiveness of current regulation, but what we chose not to regulate. This lack of regulation has been devastating for thousands of New Yorkers and every taxpayer in the United States. We must see that this does not happen again. Credit default swaps must be regulated and sellers must be required to hold sufficient capital. That will make them more expensive, but it will mean the guarantee has real value. (Dinallo 2010, p. 10)

The institutionalists' arguments (Gorton 2009; Haldane 2010; Johnson and Kwak 2010) seek to put the emphasis on the limits of the shadow banking system and their reliance on short-term unsecured funding in the REPO markets, which in turn turned into bank runs similar to those of the 1880s and early 1900s. The government regulators failed to oversee the growth of bank holding companies and showed no interest in dealing with the growth of leverage and the levels of capital requirements. Gorton (2009) points out that the financial crisis of 2007 was a bank run similar to 1907 when depositors demanded their money back; this time the panic started in the shadow banking sector, with the depositors in the REPO markets not rolling over the debt of investment banks, while also demanding larger haircuts on the banks' collateral.

> The key question for understanding the panic is: Why were non-subprime-related asset classes affected? Subprime mortgage originations in 2005 and 2006 totalled about $1.2 trillion . . . a large number to be sure, but not large enough to cause a systemic crisis. How was the shock turned into a panic? . . .
>
> Uncertain about the solvency of counterparties, repo depositors became concerned that the collateral bonds might not be liquid; if all firms wanted to hold cash – a flight to quality – then collateral would have to decline in price to find buyers. The run on repo is, again, akin to previous panics. 'Withdrawal' corresponds to an increase in haircuts. (Gorton 2009, p. 38)

The regulatory system had allowed for regulator arbitrage as financial institutions sought to be regulated by a principal regulator that did not have the capacity or expertise to oversee highly complex institutions. Bank risk management in the finance industry, the brokers who sold sub-prime mortgages and the rating agencies and their models in the rating of triple-A asset backed securities in exchange for higher fees, have all been described as broken systems that needed to be reformed.

> Compounding the problems at these financial institutions was a financial regulatory system that was archaic and outmoded. Our regulatory framework was built at a different time for a different system, and it has not kept pace with the rapid changes in the financial industry. I noted during my time at Treasury the enormous gaps in authority, duplication of responsibility, and unhealthy jurisdictional competition. No single regulator had responsibility for oversee-ing the stability of the system. The result was that regulators were often unable to supervise the firms they oversaw adequately, they did not see the impending systemic problems that progressed towards a crisis, and they did not have the tools to contain all the harms that unfolded as institutions began to collapse. (Paulson, 2010a, p. 7)

Bernanke (2010) attempted to separate out the differences between what he called triggers and structural explanations of the recession. Bernanke's major theme was that the decline in house prices and sub-prime loans were in the category of trigger explanations, in the sense that their impact on financial losses totalled between $500 billion and $1 trillion and that a global economy of $65 trillion should have been able to absorb these losses without creating the major global financial crisis of 2007. The IMF has forecasted that total government bail-outs have amounted to approximately $16 trillion. In the USA, household net worth had declined by $12 trillion while home owners have seen something like $6 trillion wiped from their home ownership equity.

with more than $1 trillion in subprime mortgages outstanding, the potential for losses on these loans was large in absolute terms; however, judged in relation to the size of global financial markets, prospective subprime losses were clearly not large enough on their own to account for the magnitude of the crisis. (Indeed, daily movements in global equity markets not infrequently impose aggregate gains or losses equal to or greater than all the subprime mortgage losses incurred thus far.) Rather, the system's vulnerabilities, together with gaps in the government's crisis-response toolkit, were the principal explanations of why the crisis was so severe and had such devastating effects on the broader economy. (Bernanke 2010, p. 3)

Bernanke argues that the structural weaknesses were related to changes in the financial markets. These changes included the increased reliance of the investment banks Bear Stearns, Lehman, Merrill Lynch and Goldman Sachs on short-term unsecured financing through the REPO markets and mutual funds that supplied funding to the banks on very short-term loans. Once the mutual funds lost confidence in collateral deposited they asked for increased margins, which in turn put pressure on investment banks to sell assets in a market with no demand for these asset backed securities. This made it difficult for the banks to price these securities, which meant that they had to rely on computerized models. Bernanke agrees with the Gorton thesis that there was a run in the shadow banking sector:

the reliance of shadow banks on short-term uninsured funds made them subject to runs, much as commercial banks and thrift institutions had been exposed to runs prior to the creation of deposit insurance. A run on an individual entity may start with rumours about its solvency, but even when investors know the rumours are unfounded, it may be in their individual interests to join the run, as few entities can remain solvent if their assets must be sold at fire-sale prices. (Bernanke 2010, p. 17)

In a presentation in 2008 Blinder pointed to what he called the 10 possible culprits that could be associated with the financial meltdown of 2007 and the ongoing economic crisis. The list of culprits comprised:

1. *The 'Masters of the Universe'*, including the bond markets where in the midst of low interest and low yield on safe assets in 2003 they went in search of higher yield securities and were willing to increase their leverage as a means of increasing performance but also increasing risk.
2. *American citizens and the assumptions they made that house prices would continue to rise*. The irrational exuberance of increases in house prices resulted in more households taking out equity on their homes to meet personal consumption. The sub-prime mortgages, including

adjustable mortgages, put these households at risk. Householders lost approximately $6 trillion of equity in their homes.

3. *The mortgages lenders, including brokers, who sold mortgages to consumers, sub-prime mortgages and yield high interest but also higher fees.* Non-document loans, so-called liar loans and NINJA (No Income, No Job, and No Assets) loans were generated by brokers who knew that these high-risk mortgages would be sent down the pipeline to investment banks to be securitized. Underwriting standards were undermined in a world of high fees and high compensation for the brokers.

4. *The bank regulators that failed in supervising investment banks within their areas of supervision.* Regulators were aware of an ascending ideology of deregulation and leaving the market to itself. Regulatory arbitrage meant that banks went in search of principal regulators that pledged a lighter touch. Some of these principal regulators did not have the capacity nor the necessary expertise to supervise complex bank holding companies

5. *The private labelled mortgages*: the expansion of derivatives, the securitization of mortgages into mortgage backed securities (MBS) and also the creation of collateralized debt obligations (CDOs) and the CDS (credit default swaps) market where none of these new instruments were regulated. It is estimated that the notional value for over-the-counter derivatives (OTC) increased to $650 trillion in a global economy of $65 trillion while the market for credit default swaps increased (CDS) to $60 trillion – about four times the size of the US economy. As the financial meltdown became clearer it was the investment banks that were left holding the majority of these securities. As asset prices declined and banks had to price these securities to market value they were forced to write down a large amount of their assets which in turn shrunk their capital ratios.

6. *The Credit Rating Agencies that rated mortgage backed securities and other asset backed securities as triple-A*, and yet within a few months these securities were downgraded below investment grade. The issuer pays model created a conflict of interest problem, with CRAs reluctant to refuse to rate a bond since the issuers would always go to another competing rating agency to get a rating. The business model created by the CRAs undermined their commitment to objectivity and impartiality in the ratings process.

7. *The securitization process.* The unregulated over-the-counter derivatives market made it difficult to discover the connections between counter-parties. AIG selling CDS to banks without laying out collateral meant that the cost of insurance was underpriced, and the lack

of transparency created problems of price discovery. The problems faced by Bear Stearns and Lehman confirmed their precarious position in depending on short-term lending in the REPO markets. These arguments were countered by those who point out that the derivatives and CDS market actually contributed to economic prosperity. Derivatives reduced the cost of companies that aimed to hedge the future increases in energy costs, fuel and agriculture products, which in turn allowed these companies to reduce their risks:

> OTC interest rate derivatives did not cause, amplify, or materially spread the financial crisis. OTC interest rate derivatives, which provide valuable interest rate hedging opportunities to global corporations, investors, and individuals, and enhance global resource allocation efficiency had absolutely no material effect whatsoever on the financial crisis. (Kohlhagen 2010, p. 1)

8. *The Securities and Exchange Commission (SEC) and the failure to supervise the bank holding banks.* The SEC was reluctant to supervise the over-the-counter derivatives market. Free market thinking meant that regulators were relying on financial markets to regulate themselves.

9. *The failure of leadership.* The argument is that President George Bush was disengaged from communicating the nature of the crisis, relying on Treasury Secretary Paulson and Bernanke at the Federal Reserve to deal with the crisis, but there is also an awareness that the bail-outs run against the ideology of the administration and the commitment to markets. The initial reaction by the Treasury was passive, allowing the Federal Reserve to take the lead in dealing with the crisis. No one explained to the people the role of the TARP and the decision to spend $700 billion in rescuing the financial market.

10. *The question of who allowed Lehman to fail?* In spite of the attempt at rescuing Bear Stearns, with the government providing guarantees to ensure the take-over of Bear Stearns by JP Morgan, the government made the decision to allow Lehman to fail, which raises the question as to whether this exposed a problem of ideology with the government bail-out of Bear Stearns so that there was now a mark in sand for no further bail-outs. These decisions created a context of uncertainty. The immediate fall-out was the crisis at AIG, and then when the Reserve Fund Mutual Fund 'broke the buck' as investors found that their deposits were no longer guaranteed, which in turn resulted in the drying up of the commercial paper market which put the wider US economy in danger.

CONTESTABLE TERRAIN 3: IDEAS AND IDEALS

Bootle (2009) in his study of the financial crisis pointed out that the major explanatory factor was at the level of ideas and ideology and the influence of those who gave support to the theory of efficient markets in the formulation of policy:

> it was the efficient markets theory that really led people up the garden path . . . This theory holds that whatever information is available about the prospects for an asset that this is embodied in the current market price . . . The textbook version of capitalism free and uncontrolled has all along been a fairy tale. But finance capitalism has enacted the fairy tale in real life with witches, hobgoblins and wicked stepfathers along with the fairy godmother. (Bootle 2009, p. 23)

Bootle (2009) went on to argue that the theory of efficient markets become a form of a religious fundamentalism that was not open to question, even when the reality of economic conditions was undermining the assumptions of efficient markets:

> It is striking how difficult it is to keep a bad idea down. Not only are there still adherents to the 'crowding out' view, even in depression conditions, another version of the idea has sprung up. It is as though what the Keynesians are fighting is one of those creatures of Greek mythology that, as soon as you cut off its head, sprouts another one. (Bootle 2009, p. 197)

Likewise Kaletsky (2010) has also tended to put the focus on ideology and the role of efficient markets and rational expectations arguments, and the influence these ideas had on policy makers.

> The quixotic demands to choose between fully predetermined individual micro foundations and uniform rational expectations should have been laughed out of court . . . Not only did these methodologies seem to turn economics into a mathematically-based science, but they had the further flattering feature of allowing the model-building economists to decree the universal laws of motion [to] be obeyed by all humanity. Rational expectations did not just raise economics to the same status as physics they elevated economists to the role that Newton had reserved for God. (Kaletsky 2010, p. 169)

Rational expectations and the theory of efficient markets became the dominant ideas that influenced the context and landscapes of policy making after 1980, heralded by the Presidency of Reagan and his commitment to markets. The climate of continuing financial stability that had been brought about by Roosevelt's regulatory framework provided the opportunity and the context to break free from these regulatory frameworks, as memories of the Great Depression were also fading into the mists of time. Fox (2009) sees the ascendance of the rational expectations and efficient markets theorists as a paradox in the sense that the theories flourished in a climate of stability, a stability that had been brought about by a regulatory framework developed in the aftermath of the Great Depression of 1929:

> The efficient market hypothesis, the capital asset pricing model, the Black-Scholes option-pricing model, and all the other major elements of modern rationalist finance arose toward the end of a long era of market stability characterized by tight government regulation and the long memories of those who had survived the Depression. These theories' heavy reliance on calmly rational markets was to some extent the artefact of a regulated, relatively conservative financial era – and it paved the way for deregulation and wild exuberance. (Fox 2009, p. 320)

Leaders in financial markets gave support to the arguments of free deregulated markets for allowing the industry to produce its own rules of behaviour. Arguments for a Ricardian Equivalence, financial and resource crowding, meant that the role of government was limited. Rational markets advocates point to the random walks in financial markets, that financial markets reflected the balance of investment and savings, that markets therefore allocated investment decisions efficiently and that financial markets therefore confirmed intrinsic value.

The contribution of these ideas to the financial meltdown is that they provided the conventional wisdom and the science for deregulation. Those who, therefore, argue that derivatives and credit default swaps were central to financial meltdown are also arguing that it was the argument for deregulated regulators that therefore contributed to the climate of deregulation

The Keynesian Collectivists

By contrast, those who come from a Keynesian tradition (Krugman 2009; Skidelsky and Kennedy 2010; Stiglitz 2010) tend to argue that the problem is of demand deficiency and falling consumption resulting from the loss of household wealth, which leaves the government as the most viable consumer. In the context of recession, therefore, the government should utilize the excess of savings to invest in infrastructure projects.

> The government, Keynes argued, is the only agency that can prevent total spending in the economy from falling below a full or acceptable employment level. If private spending is depressed, it can restore total spending to a reasonable level by adding to its own spending or reducing taxes. In doing so it will be adding to a deficit that is already the result of falling tax revenues and rising

benefits due to the recession. The deficit, though, has the function of sustaining the level of total spending and output in the economy. Any attempt to reduce it before a strong momentum to private sector recovery is established will make matters worse. Once the economy has started to grow, the deficit incurred during the recession will automatically shrink to a pre-recession level. Deliberate steps to eliminate the 'structural' (ie non-recession induced) deficit should be postponed until the recovery is firmly entrenched. With the budget balanced, or even in surplus, at high employment, continued growth will steadily reduce the national debt as a percentage of gross domestic product. This is what happened after the second world war. (Skidelsky and Kennedy 2010)

This category of explanations also includes those who argued that unfettered markets and deregulation resulted in market failure. Markets failed because of the externality problems of there being a divergence between individual interests and public interests. Individual interests included the interests of brokers, lawyers and investment bank managers who collected fees in the securitization process. The shift from an originate and hold model of banking to an originate and distribute model created a climate of disavowal of responsibility, with individual self-interest eventually harming the wider public interest.

Within this category are also those explanations that connect the financial meltdown to the thesis of the savings glut in the emerging economies and China. Savings outstripped investment demand, which in turn meant a surfeit of savings searching for higher yields. The process of securitization, mortgage backed securities, CDOs and synthetic CDOs, emerged because of an existing demand for these products. Also included in this category are arguments that revisit the Minsky moment, whose authors argue against rational individualism and point to evidence of herding the idea of uncertainty rather than the measuring of risk.

The Structuralists

Finally, there are explanations which seek to locate the crisis in issues related to the wider structure of society, including the growth of income inequality and how governments sought to resolve the problem of inequality through low interest rates, increased leverage and debt, which contributed to increases in house prices, allowing households to take out equity on their homes as a means of improving their well-being. In this way governments did not have to confront the more difficult issue of designing policies that aimed to improve take-home pay or to redistribute income through taxation and improved social provision (Geisst 2009; Rajan 2010; Reich 2010). In addition to income inequality concerns, the concentration of wealth and power as income is concentrated in the top 0.01 per cent of earners, which provides a landscape for the influence of narrow interest groups to shape the policy process (Hacker and Pierson 2010; Stiglitz 2010).

The study of wages and income equality can be located into two distinct periods: the years 1950 to 1974, which Krugman (2007) calls the Great Compression, and the years 1980 to the present which he categorizes as the Great Divergence. The period of the Great Compression is associated with continuing increases in wages and full employment. During the period 1945 to 1973 productivity and family incomes both doubled. The median income in 1947 in the US amounted to some $21,700, which by 1973 had increased to $44,380, an increase of 2.8 per cent per annum, so while productivity had increased 103.7 per cent incomes had also increased by 103.9 per cent. In contrast, during the Great Divergence, which started in 1980, output increased 3.5 times as much as family incomes. During the next 27 years median income increased by 25 per cent, which was about 1 per cent per annum except for a brief interlude between 1995 and 2000 when median incomes were increasing at 2.2 per cent. However, after 2000 median income actually declined by 0.7 per cent annum. From 1973 to 2000 wages increased from $44,380 in 1973 to $54,000, an increase of 0.7 per cent per annum, so while productivity increased by 102 per cent, incomes increased by 20 per cent. So for the period, for 90 per cent of the population, incomes increased by 12.5 per cent, while the top 10 per cent of earners experienced a 40 per cent increase and the top 1 per cent, 75 per cent. However the study of the top 1 per cent needs to be broken down even further, with the top 0.1 per cent experiencing an increase of 117 per cent, and the top 0.01 per cent, 156 per cent.

In addition, income tax policy changes also contributed to income inequality. Before Ronald Reagan's election in 1980, the top income tax bracket stood at or above 70 per cent, where it had been since the Great Depression. Reagan dropped the top bracket from 70 per cent to 50 per cent, and eventually pushed it all the way down to 28 per cent. Since then, it has hovered between 30 and 40 per cent. If President Obama lets George W Bush's 2001 tax cut expire for families earning more than $250,000, the top bracket would increase from 35 per cent to just under 40 per cent, still well below the tax levels of the 1950s and the 1970s. The tax composition reveals some more shifts. At the Federal level progressive taxes made up 60.8 per cent of the total tax in 2000. By 2005 this had declined to 56.4 per cent. Meanwhile, regressive taxes increased from 38.9 to 43.1 per cent. Corporation taxes under Roosevelt amounted to 5.6 per cent of GDP. During the Truman and Eisenhower administrations this had declined to 4.5 per cent, while under Nixon and Ford the tax had declined further, to 2.7 per cent, then under Clinton to 2.4 per cent and in 2007 to 1.3 per cent, which became the lowest level of corporate tax since 1940.

Rajan (2010) has outlined a series of arguments that go beyond economic explanations and instead put the focus on social issues, which he
describes as fault lines. Included in his list of fault lines are the increase
in the concentration of wealth and the growth in income inequality, and
the decline in the number of students attaining degree qualifications in the
USA, which together have contributed to America becoming less globally
competitive and has also contributed to economic slowdown. Rajan has
pointed to the problem of stagnant wages for the majority of Americans,
the weak safety net to deal with long-term unemployment and political
paralysis.

These factors, he argues, explain why the government used housing
policy and easy credit as a form of panacea, since this was a policy of least
resistance compared with alternative strategies of increasing taxes and redistributing income through public expenditure on health, education and
social security:

> Politicians have looked for other ways to improve the lives of their voters. Since
> the early 1980s the most seductive answer has been easier credit. In some ways
> it is the path of least resistance. Government-supported credit does not arouse
> as many concerns from the Right at the outset as outright income redistribu-
> tion would . . . Politicians love to have banks expand housing credit, for credit
> achieves many goals at the same time. It pushes up house prices, making house-
> holds feel wealthier and allows them to finance more consumption. (Rajan
> 2010, p. 31)

Geisst (2009) has also taken up the connection between stagnant wages
and rising house prices. Credit card debt and taking out equity on homes
as housing prices were rising provided the avenue to higher consumption,
even if this was not warranted when wages and household income are
taken into consideration: 'The increase in house prices and the heightened
use of credit cards were accompanied by low growth in real wages as had
been the case for two decades. To achieve the American Dream average
American families were going into more debt given the low growth in
incomes' (Geisst 2009, p. 166).

Easy credit, the expansion of credit cards, and easier mortgages created
the possibility for higher levels of consumption that benefited both households and the economy. It was a strategy that, at least in the short term,
only seemed to create winners. However, the equity and housing bubble
confirmed that the strategy of consuming wealth while increasing household debt was in the long run not sustainable. The drawing out of equity
was directed to consumption without increasing investment.

The question of whether politicians used easy credit and housing policy
as a palliative to deal with the problem of rising income inequalities

without having to deal directly with issues of taxation and redistribution of income, is difficult to ascertain since political actors can always deny such intent. After all, politicians can point out that in a democracy they reflect the wishes of their voters and affordable housing seemed to resonate with the wishes of their electors.

Wages for 90 per cent of workers in the USA have been rising at a slow pace since the middle of the 1970s. While productivity and the economy have continued to grow, the distribution of the proceeds of the economy has been directed towards the top 10 per cent of earners, and becomes even more highly skewed when the incomes of the top 1 per cent are looked at (Piketty and Saez 2003).

In their study, *Winner-Take-All Politics*, Hacker and Pierson (2010) point out:

> From 1979 until the eve of the Great Recession, the top 1 per cent received 36 per cent of all gains in household incomes. Economic growth was even more skewed between 2001 and 2006, during which the share of income gains going to the top 1 per cent was over 53 per cent. That's right: More than 50 cents of every dollar in additional income pocketed by Americans over this half decade accrued to the richest 1 in 100 households. (Hacker and Pierson 2010, p. 3)

CONCLUSIONS

The concern of this chapter has been to provide some framework for reviewing the continually expanding literature that seeks to explain the nature of the financial crisis. The reading of the literature confirms that these commentaries are contestable, reflecting serious and fierce debates, as there were in the 1930s, as to causes of and remedies for the recession. The stakes are also high since these narratives also seek to shape, define and influence the policy process.

In the immediate aftermath of the financial crisis, and even as events were still unfolding between June 2007 and September 2008, there was, for a short while, an emerging consensus that the commitment to deregulated markets that started in the early 1980s had come to an end. The financial meltdown confirmed that markets needed to be regulated. Pragmatists and institutionalists agreed that there was need for reform that included the regulation of OTC and CDS markets to put these into central clearing and trading platforms and to make these deregulated markets open to price discovery to reduce counter-party risk and make these derivatives more transparent. There was also consensus on the need for reform in the banking sector, especially on leverage, capital requirements and liquidity. The Dodd-Frank Bill of July 2010 reflects that emerging consensus.

Market fundamentalists have sought to challenge that reformist agenda, arguing instead that it was intervention by government that had prolonged the recession. Market fundamentalists criticized the bank bail-outs, as creating a major problem of moral hazard. Furthermore, they argued that the securitization process had contributed to economic prosperity because of the process of spreading risk, which in turn had reduced the cost of borrowing. The US mid-term elections in November 2010 seemed to confirm a major shift in sentiment, since the newly elected Republican law makers have strongly argued the case for less government, and their primary aim is to reform the Frank Dodd regulatory reforms.

The Keynesian collectivists' and the structuralists' arguments are attempts to connect the recession with household income inequality and the concentration of wealth. The slow growth in incomes during the past 20 years confirms a shift from the 20 years after World War Two when both median incomes and productivity were rising. While GDP has continued to increase since the 1980s, most of the fruits of the new income have been concentrated towards the top 1 per cent of earners. The policy of low interest rates and easy credit provided the avenue for median income households to increase their consumption and living standards, which came at the cost of higher household debt. The UK government commitment to reduce public expenditure by £80 billion during the next five years and the recent Commission (FCIC 2011) recommendations in the US to increase the pensionable age to 70, reduce Medicare and other social provision polices, would result in increased inequality in both countries. However, other countries, including Greece and Ireland, have had to reform welfare provision to deal with mounting public sector deficits as they try to stabilize their financial markets.

REFERENCES

Bernanke, B. (2010) Statement by Ben S. Bernanke Chairman Board of Governors of the Federal Reserve System before the Financial Crisis Inquiry Commission Washington, DC, 2 September.
Blankfien, L. (2010) Testimony to the Financial Crisis Inquiry Commission Hearing on the Role of Derivatives in the Financial Crisis, 13 January. Available at http://fcic-static.law.stanford.edu/cdn_media/fcic-testimony/2010-0113-Blankfein.pdf
Blinder, A. (2008) 'Origins of the Financial Crisis', lecture delivered at Princeton University, the Wood Wilson School of Public and International Affairs, 11 November.

Bootle, R. (2009) *The Trouble with Markets: Saving Capitalism from Itself.* London: Nicholas Brealey Publishing.

Buffet, W. (2010) 'Pretty Good for Government Work', *New York Times*, 11 November. Available at: http://www.nytimes.com/2010/11/17/opinion/17 buffett.html

Cayne, J. (2010) Testimony of James E. Cayne Before the Financial Crisis Inquiry Commission, 5 May.

Connolly, W.E. (1983) *The Terms of Political Discourse.* Oxford: Martin Robertson.

De Long, B. (2010) 'It is Far Too Soon to End Expansion: The Austerity Debate', *The Financial Times*, 20 July.

Dimon, J. (2010) Testimony to the Financial Crisis Inquiry Commission Hearing on the Role of Derivatives in the Financial Crisis, 13 January. Available at: http://fcic-static.law.stanford.edu/cdn_media/fcic-testimony/2010-0113-Dimon. pdf

Dinallo, E. (2010) Testimony to the Financial Crisis Inquiry Commission Hearing on the Role of Derivatives in the Financial Crisis, 1 July.

e21 Team (2010) 'An Open Letter to Ben Bernanke', *Economic Policies for the 21st Century*, 15 November. Available at: http://economics21.org/commentary/ e21s-open-letter-ben-bernanke

Ferguson, N. (2010) 'Today's Modern Keynesians have Learnt Nothing Since the 1930s: The Austerity Debate', *The Financial Times*, 20 July.

Financial Crisis Inquiry (FCIC) (2011) *Final Report of the National Commission on the Causes of the Financial and Economic Crisis in the United States.* New York: Public Affairs.

Fox, J. (2009) *The Myth of the Rational Market: A History of Risk, Reward, and Delusion on Wall Street.* New York: HarperCollins.

Fuld, R.S. (2010) Written Statement of Richard S. Fuld, Jr. Before the Financial Crisis Inquiry Commission, 1 September.

Geisst, C. (2009) *Collateral Damage: The Marketing of Consumer Debt to America.* New York: Bloomberg Press.

Geithner, T. (2010) Testimony Before the Financial Crisis Inquiry Commission on the Causes of the Financial Crisis and the Case for Reform, 6 May. Available at: http://fcic-static.law.stanford.edu/cdn_media/fcic-testimony/2010-0506- Geithner.pdf

Gensler, G. (2010) Statement of Gary Gensler, Chairman, Commodity Futures Trading Commission before the Financial Crisis Inquiry Commission, 1 July. Available at: http://www.cftc.gov/pressroom/speechestestimony/opagensler-48. html

Gorton, G. (2009) 'Slapped in the Face by the Invisible Hand: Banking and the Panic of 2007', paper prepared for the Federal Reserve Bank of Atlanta's 2009 Financial Markets Conference: Financial Innovation and Crisis, 11–13 May.

Greenspan, A. (2010a) Testimony of Alan Greenspan, Financial Crisis Inquiry Commission, 7 April.

Greenspan, A. (2010b) *The Crisis*, second draft, 9 March.

Hacker, J. and P. Pierson (2010) *Winner-Takes-All Politics: How Washington Made the Rich Richer – and Turned Its Back on the Middle Class.* London: Simon and Schuster.

Haldane, A.G. (2010) 'The Debt Overhang', speech given at a Professional Liverpool Dinner, 27 January.

Johnson, S. (2009) 'The Quiet Coup', *The Atlantic Monthly*, May.

Johnson, S. and J. Kwak (2010) *13 Bankers: Wall Street Takeover and the Next Financial Meltdown*. New York: Pantheon Books.

Kaletsky, A. (2010) *Capitalism 4.0: The Birth of a New Economy*. London: Bloomsbury.

Kohlhagen, S.W. (2010) Testimony of Steven W. Kohlhagen, Former Professor of International Finance, University of California, Berkeley, and Former Wall Street Derivatives Executive to the Financial Crisis Inquiry Commission Hearing, 30 June.

Krugman, P. (2007) *The Conscience of a Liberal*. New York: W.W. Norton and Company Ltd.

Krugman, P. (2009) 'How Did Economists Get it so Wrong?', *The New York Times*, 6 September.

Kyle, P. (2010) 'Reforming the OTC Derivatives Markets', Testimony to the Financial Crisis Inquiry Commission Hearing on the Role of Derivatives in the Financial Crisis, Testimony and Evidence Testimony to the Financial Crisis Inquiry Commission Hearing on the Role of Derivatives in the Financial Crisis, 1 July.

Masters, J. (2010) Testimony to the Financial Crisis Inquiry Commission Hearing on the Role of Derivatives in the Financial Crisis, 1 July.

Mullard, M. (1993) *The Politics of Public Expenditure*. London: Routledge.

Paulson, H.M. (2010a) Testimony by Henry M. Paulson, Jr. Before the Financial Crisis Inquiry Commission, 6 May.

Paulson, H.M. (2010b) *On the Brink: Inside the Race to Stop the Collapse of the Global Financial System*. New York: Business Plus.

Piketty, T. and E. Saez (2003) 'Income Inequality in the United States, 1913–1998', *The Quarterly Journal of Economics*, CXVIII(1).

Rajan, R. (2010) *Fault Lines: How Hidden Fractures Still Threaten the World Economy*. Oxford and Princeton, NJ: Princeton University Press.

Reich, R. (2010) *After Shock: The Next Economy and America's Future*. New York: Alfred A Knopf.

Reinhart, C. and K. Rogoff (2008) 'Is the 2007 US Sub-Prime Financial Crisis So Different? An International Historical Comparison', *American Economic Review*, **98**(2): 339–344. Available at: http://www.aeaweb.org/articles.php?doi= 10.1257/aer.98.2.339

Schwartz, A. (2010) Statement of Alan D. Schwartz before the Financial Crisis Inquiry Commission, 5 May.

Skidelsky, R. and M. Kennedy (2010) 'Future Generations Will Curse Us for Cutting in a Slump', *The Financial Times* 27 July. Available at: http://www.ft.com/cms/s/0/307056f8-99ae-11df-a852-00144feab49a.html#axzz1Qxb7q4bY

Stiglitz, J. (2010) *Free Fall, America, Free Markets and the Sinking of the World Economy*. London: W.W. Norton and Company.

Summers, L. (2010) 'America's Sensible Stance on Recovery', *The Financial Times*, 18 July.

Taylor, J. (2010) 'The Financial Crisis and the Policy Responses: An Empirical Analysis of What Went Wrong', paper presented to the Financial Crisis Inquiry Commission, Washington, DC, 2 September.

Wallison, P. (2008) 'Everything You Wanted to Know about Credit Default Swaps – But Were Never Told', American Enterprise Institute for Public Research, Washington, DC.

Wessel, D. (2010) *In Fed We Trust: Ben Bernanke's War on the Great Panic*. New York: Three Rivers Press.

Whalen, C. (2008) 'Understanding the Credit Crunch as a Minsky Moment', *Challenge*, **51**(1): 91–109.

Wolf, M. (2010) 'Why the Battle is Joined Over Tightening', *The Financial Times*, 19 July. Available at: http://www.ft.com/cms/s/0/f3eb2596-9296-11df-9142-00144feab49a.html

4. Derivatives and securities: the finance industry

INTRODUCTION: DERIVATIVES AS CONTESTABLE TERRAIN

The political polarization generated in the analysis of the derivatives markets was confirmed in the most recent FCIC Report (FCIC 2011) where in the final report there was a division between Democrat commissioners signing the majority report and Republican commissioners submitting two dissenting statements. The majority commissioners report made the case that unregulated markets in over-the-counter derivatives were one of the major causes of the financial crisis. The majority FCIC report stated:

> without any oversight, OTC derivatives rapidly spiraled out of control and out of sight, growing to $673 trillion in notional amount. This report explains the uncontrolled leverage; lack of transparency, capital, and collateral requirements; speculation; interconnections among firms; and concentrations of risk in this market . . .
>
> Companies sold protection – to the tune of $79 billion, in AIG's case – to investors in these newfangled mortgage securities, helping to launch and expand the market and, in turn, to further fuel the housing bubble . . .
>
> Goldman Sachs alone packaged and sold $73 billion in synthetic CDOs from July 1, 2004, to May 31, 2007. Synthetic CDOs created by Goldman referenced more than 3,400 mortgage securities, and 610 of them were referenced at least twice. This is apart from how many times these securities may have been referenced in synthetic CDOs created by other firms. (FCIC 2011, p. 27)

Commissioner Wallison (2011) in his statement of dissent made the case that it was the government housing policy of extending home ownership and using the Community Reinvestment Act (CRA) to persuade banks to lend to high-risk borrowers that eventually created a context were 27 million out of a possible 55 million home owners were likely to default:

> Using this standard, I believe that the *sine qua non* of the financial crisis was U.S. government housing policy, which led to the creation of 27 million subprime and other risky loans – half of all mortgages in the United States – which

were ready to default as soon as the massive 1997–2007 housing bubble began to deflate. If the U.S. government had not chosen this policy path – fostering the growth of a bubble of unprecedented size and an equally unprecedented number of weak and high risk residential mortgages – the great financial crisis of 2008 would never have occurred. (Wallison 2011, p. 2)

The issue of whether the OTC derivatives did contribute to the financial crisis was always likely to be controversial. Derivatives were not just benign financial instruments; the ideology, the politics, the way these instruments were structured, the modelling, the rating process and the legislative framework reflected different levels of contestability. Policy makers and advisers who, over the previous two decades, had advocated, shaped and defined the policy framework of deregulation and commitments to non-intervention resisted arguments that pointed to the possibility that the experimentation with free markets had contributed to the financial crisis The processes of securitization and the growth of an unregulated over-the-counter (OTC) derivatives markets, alongside the shadow banking system, had contributed to the financial crisis. Black (2008) has pointed to the resistance and strong ideological commitment of policy makers, leaders of financial markets, regulators and rating agencies to the concept of free markets:

> Ideologically driven (non) regulators have strong personal and ideological incentives to cover up the scale of the problem and to blame it on anything other than their policies. The history of science shows the immense reluctance to admit that existing paradigms have been falsified. This problem is particularly acute for neo-classical finance and economics scholars because the theories that have been falsified by the ongoing crises are the foundations of modern finance. Neo-classical economists' methodology, which they asserted made them the only social scientists worthy of the name, has also been falsified. The pricing models that were their most sophisticated development have failed. (Black 2008, p. 4)

The derivatives process reflected conflicting ideologies, issues of power and conflicts of interests, Tett (2009) in her study of the financial meltdown, explained the process of derivatives as follows:

> In most societies, elites try to maintain their power not simply by garnering wealth, but by dominating the mainstream ideologies, both in terms of what is said, and also what is *not* discussed. Social 'silence' serves to maintain power structures . . .
> Credit was considered too 'boring' or 'technical' to be of interest to amateurs. It was a classic area of social 'silence'. Insofar as any bankers ever reflected on that silence (which very few ever did) most assumed that it suited their purpose well. Free from external scrutiny, financiers could do almost anything they wished. (Tett 2009, pp. 252 and 253, original emphasis)

Secondly, the contestability of the OTC market reflected the debate on processes of regulation and deregulation. The Reagan/Thatcher decade initiated the process of deregulation, the retreat of the state and liberalization of financial markets. Between 1980 and 2007 the light touch of regulation was in ascendance. Even those with the power to regulate recognized that the climate favoured a deregulation regulator. President Reagan signalled his intentions to drive a liberalization agenda when he appointed Alan Greenspan to the Chairman of Federal Reserve to replace Paul Volcker. That decision confirmed the recognition that Greenspan would push for deregulation of financial markets. Greenspan as a Republican was perceived to be a true believer in deregulated markets while Volcker was a Democrat who was judged as being more pragmatic, less ideological and less committed to the idea that markets could regulate themselves.

> Regulation of the over-the-counter derivatives market was virtually eliminated in 2000 with the enactment of the Commodity Futures Modernization Act. And since that time, no federal regulator has regulatory authority over that market, or oversight of that market. Moreover, states have been prohibited from enforcing their anti-gaming and anti-bucket shop laws with respect to derivatives. By June 2008, less than eight years after deregulation, this market grew to more than $680 trillion in notional amount and played, I think, a major role in derailing our financial system and harming the economy. (Born 2010, p. 53)

Finally, there were the vested interests that have actually benefited financially from a deregulated environment and therefore aimed to resist attempts at re-regulation that would jeopardize their fees, their earnings and the business model of their organizations. The OTC market was a $640 trillion business that created major earnings for the financial sector. Equally, non-financial corporations as end users of derivatives also lobbied and campaigned in resisting policy reforms. Airline companies extolled the value of derivatives for offering lower costs, hedging on the future of fuel costs, and export companies on future trading on currencies. Mr David Dines, President of Cargill Risk Management, in his testimony to the Senate Agriculture Committee on 4 June 2009 defended the benefits of derivatives for his industry as follows:

> It is important to note that while we have witnessed the greatest economic crisis in 80 years, and perhaps the most volatile commodity market Cargill has ever seen, OTC contracts in the agriculture, energy, and foreign exchange markets performed well, did not create systemic risks, and in fact helped many end-users manage and hedge their risks during this very difficult time The imposition of mandatory clearing and mandatory margining of tailored hedges will have a significant drain on working capital at a time when capital is highly constrained and credit is in short supply. There will be a liquidity drain on those companies. (Dines 2009, p. 7)

In his testimony on 18 November 2009 to the Senate Committee on Agriculture, Nutrition and Forestry, Neil Schloss, Vice President and Treasurer of the Ford Motor Company, outlined the benefits of OTC as follows:

> Today, a substantial proportion of our derivatives are at Ford Credit, with about 60% of our interest rate derivatives being utilized to hedge asset-backed securitization transactions. As of September 30, 2009, Ford Credit's securitization funding totalled about $57 billion, or about 60% of our $94 billion in managed receivables. The securitization and other funding Ford Credit uses enables it to provide financing to the vast majority of Ford's 3,000-plus dealers and over 3 million active consumer accounts in the U.S. alone. (Schloss 2009, p. 3)

For end users derivatives have been described as being one of the major pillars for the success of their businesses, even though the process of the deregulated derivatives market did not take off until 2000 with the introduction of the Commodity Futures Modernization Act (CFMA). Prior to the CFMA all traded options in foreign exchange interest rates were traded in transparent regulated exchanges. The CFMA produced a process where swaps were moved from regulator regimes. A swap was therefore not a security nor an insurance. The CFMA amended the Securities and Exchange Acts of 1933 and 1934 so that the definition of 'security' did not include credit default swaps. The Commodity Futures Trading Commission (CFTC) and the Securities and Exchange Commission (SEC) were prohibited from regulating those swap agreements, except for their anti-fraud enforcement authority. Therefore, by ruling that credit default swaps were not gaming and not a security, the way was cleared for the growth of the market. But there was one other issue. If some swaps – covered swaps – were considered insurance, then they would be regulated by state insurance departments. The capital and underwriting limits in insurance regulation could have threatened the rapid growth in the market for these derivatives. So, at the same time, in 2000, the New York Insurance Department was asked a question that related to naked credit default swaps (CDS): they were asked whether naked CDS was an insurance where, in a naked CD, the buyers and sellers do not have a direct interest. The New York Insurance Department replied that such a circumstance was not an insurance since the buyer of the premium was not suffering a loss. Insurance is defined as making whole the experience of suffering a loss and replacing that loss.

> Clearly, the question was framed to ask only about naked credit default swaps with no proof of loss. Under the facts we were given, the swap was not 'a contract of insurance', because the buyer had no material interest and the filing of a claim does not require a loss. But the entities involved were careful not

> to ask about covered credit default swaps. Nonetheless, the market took the Department's opinion on a subset of credit default swaps as a ruling on all swaps and, to be fair, the Department did nothing to the contrary. In sum, in 2000 as a society we chose not to regulate credit default swaps, whether as insurance, as a security or gaming. (Dinallo 2010, p.7)

The OTC derivatives market – an unregulated market – became a substitute for official currencies and commodities futures trading markets which take place on trading exchanges with continuous highly transparent price discovery. The OTC market by contrast is highly customized and since each transaction is seen as being unique it is difficult to agree on price discovery. However, in his testimony and evidence to the FCIC, the CEO of JP Morgan Chase Mr Jamie Dimon pointed out that up to 70 per cent of the OTC market can be arranged within standard trading platforms. The argument that OTC markets are therefore highly customized reflects more the interests of broker dealers who can generate more fees from customized derivatives and therefore a monopoly of knowledge when it comes to the marking of price, and also end users who use customized derivatives; with having to put up minimal collateral to hedge their exposure, this in turn reduces their borrowing costs, but at the same increases the exposure of lenders if these corporations default.

Adair Turner (2010) Chairman of the Financial Services Authority (FSA) in a speech at the CASS Business School, reflecting on the controversy he had created in his Prospect Article (Turner 2009), when he had argued that financial transactions could be deemed as socially useless and not contributing to the social good, suggested that it would have been better had he used the twin terms 'economically useless' or of 'no economic value added'.

> Last August, some remarks of mine caused controversy. I suggested that some of the activities which went on in the trading rooms of some banks in the run up to the financial crisis were 'socially useless'. People have asked me whether I regret those comments. The answer is no, except in one very small respect. Which is that I think it would have been better to use the phrase 'economically useless' or 'of no economic value added'. For my purpose was to provoke a debate about the functions which banks and near banks play in the economy, and about whether and under what circumstances we can be confident that the impact of their activities will be beneficial for the real economy and thus for human welfare. (Turner 2010, p. 1)

Turner (2010) aimed to explore the influence of economic ideas on policy makers. Within financial markets and regulators the predominant ideas since the 1990s had been that liquidity was always beneficial for the economy, that financial innovation was to be welcomed because it increased investors' choice, and, finally, that regulatory policies were to be limited only to cases where such intervention was beneficial to the market. Turner argued that these key elements were an inherent part of the regulators' DNA. Furthermore, this conventional wisdom had also been encouraged by the International Monetary Fund, which stressed the advantages of the free flows of capital.

The risk management mathematical models that sought to minimize risk had become the cause of increased risk. The models had relied on data that was expunged from economic context. The post-World War Two world, for example, showed continuing growth but the model builders did not take into consideration the context of the policy process that had contributed to the continuing prosperity and financial stability from 1950 to 1974, including legislation such as the Glass-Steagill Act of 1933, Keynesian economics, increased government and full employment with rising wages. The models could not and did not capture the differences between periods of pre-regulation and post-regulation. The mathematical models were based on abstract assumptions far removed from the realities of the policy process. The data was decontextualized:

> of course, all models are wrong. The only model that is not wrong is reality and reality is not, by definition, a model. But risk management models have during this crisis proved themselves wrong in a more fundamental sense. They failed the Keynes' test – that it is better to be roughly right than precisely wrong. (Haldane 2009, p. 2)

The social silence that Tett (2009) referred to reflected the absence of resistance and how policy makers embraced the concept of deregulation. There was no attempt to educate the public as to the implications of an unregulated OTC derivatives market. The social silence was of major benefit to the financial sector because there was no attempt to legislate on scrutiny, on transparency or accountability.

Blythe Masters who had pioneered the first CDS, speaking at the Securities Industry and Financial Markets Association (SIFMA) in October 2008 acknowledged the role of complexity and the lack of accountability that had characterized the expansion of the OTC markets:

> Our industry needs to rebuild its reputation and the first step is to acknowledge accountability and to own the responsibility of rebuilding a more systematically sustainable business model. Financial engineering was taken to a level of complexity which was unsustainable . . . But it is important to distinguish tools and their users. (Blythe Masters, quoted in Tett 2009, p. 294)

Proponents of derivatives have been equally quick to point to the contribution derivatives made to economic growth. Cohn (2010) giving testimony and evidence to FCIC answered the question on social value as follows:

> I would love to answer that. Multiple factors of social value. Number one, pricing transparency. Number two, we brought new capital into the market. Number three, we were able to build more diversified portfolios. Number four, it provided ability to short. Number five, it provided different ways of risk transference through the system which allowed the underlying mortgage market to grow. (Cohn 2010, p. 73)

Market liberal advocates have persisted with the theme that derivatives and the securitization process vindicated the efficient markets theory. The deregulated OTC derivatives and securitizations allocated resources efficiently and effectively. The consensus within the financial community was that derivatives provided the necessary framework for global prosperity after the 1990s.

The International Swaps and Derivatives Association (ISDA) has always taken the position of advocating for a deregulated derivatives market and spent the past two decades lobbying and seeking to persuade policy makers that market participants involved in the derivatives process could regulate themselves, and that they and their customers could look after their own self-interest through an unregulated market. During the mid-1980s, in the aftermath of the derivatives debacle, with concerns raised by Proctor and Gamble and the bankruptcy of Orange County, a prevailing view was then emerging that the growing derivatives business needed to be regulated. Yet by the mid-1990s these regulatory proposals were in retreat. President Clinton signalled his preference to the ISDA and the Group of 30 report that derivatives should be allowed to flourish in an unregulated market.

In the midst of the financial meltdown the defenders of unregulated OTC markets were still making the case that the derivatives markets had in no way contributed to the financial crisis. One such example was Mark Bricknell who had led the lobbying against regulation during the 1990s on behalf of the International Swaps and Derivatives Association (ISDA), and, speaking at the Annual Meeting of ISDA in Vienna in 2008, he declared that he could still defend the derivatives market, even in the midst of financial crisis:

> Twenty years ago we set out to design a business guided by market discipline because we believed that it should be an even better guide to good behaviour than regulatory proscription. The credit crunch gives good evidence that market discipline has guided the derivatives business better then regulation has steered housing finance. Hayek believed that markets would create a rhythm

of their own that are self healing. That is something we should remember and honour today. (Mark Bricknell, quoted in Tett 2009, p. 294)

However, at that same conference, another ISDA member, Paul Calello, in a keynote speech recognized the tide was turning and that voluntary regulation had proved to be inadequate: 'We cannot expect as usual. There will be new regulation and there should be. Voluntary efforts are not enough.' In line with other market liberal fundamentalists Bricknell argued the case that the recession of 2007 was not due to derivatives but due to policy failures of government intervention in the housing markets, encouraging banks to extend home ownership, and the Federal Reserve's lax monetary policy which created the context for higher risks and higher rates of borrowing.

CHANGING ECONOMIC LANDSCAPES

During the past two decades the processes of derivatives and securitization had become highly associated with global economic prosperity. The Anglo American market liberal financial model was perceived to be the model of success to be exported to the emerging economies. Deregulation, liberalization and privatization of finance were seen as essential for economic development. During a 15-year period that started in 1990, the British economy experienced uninterrupted growth. Unemployment levels fell to under 1 million, compared to the recent experiences of the 1980s when unemployment had peaked at 3 million. Inflation rates below 2.5 per cent reinforced the argument that the independence of the central bank and a macroeconomic policy focused on inflationary targets had reduced inflationary expectations. The Labour Government was able to claim that previous eras of boom and bust had become history. Public finances were in good shape. Government annual borrowing at 3 per cent of GDP and a national debt to GDP ratio of 40 per cent of GDP were well within the euro zone macro-economic constraints. The Labour Government could also claim that the Annual Comprehensive Reviews and Public Sector Agreements had allowed the government to reduce the deficits while at the same providing additional resources for health, education and social security without increases in the tax burden and with no increases in the overall levels of public expenditure. Equally in the USA the period was hailed as the Age of Moderation, of low inflation, continuing growth and low unemployment.

Between 1990 and 2007 the financial sector had become a major contributor to economic growth in both the US and UK economies. While in the early 1990s the financial sector had contributed to approximately

3 per cent of GDP, by 2007 this had grown to 9 per cent of GDP in the UK and 5 per cent of GDP in the USA. In terms of corporate profits the financial sector had grown from 15 per cent of corporate profits in 1990 to 40 per cent in 2007. The period between October 1998 and June 2007 could be described as being the Golden Decade for the finance industry. Banks' share prices increased almost 60 per cent. The derivatives markets of structured collateralized debt obligations (CDOs) contributed to fees and bank profits. Brokers and traders were being paid average incomes of $380,000 and bonuses which were at least 10 times their incomes. The financial sector was therefore becoming an important part of the macro-economy, contributing to GDP, higher incomes and higher government revenues. In 2007 London accounted for 42.5 per cent of world issues of foreign exchange and interest rate derivatives, and New York 24 per cent (Haldane 2010). In terms of the CDO markets, the US market share was 40 per cent and London 37 per cent (Haldane 2010). The Bank of International Settlements (BIS) estimated the derivatives market to be worth around $640 trillion in 2007 while the CDS market was worth $65 trillion. These figures have to be put in the context of a global GDP of $65 trillion, which meant that derivatives were worth 10 times global GDP and the CDS market was equivalent to world GDP. According to Fitch (FitchRatings 2009), 90 per cent of $640 trillion of these derivatives were held by ten banks that included Goldman Sachs, JP Morgan Chase, Morgan Stanley, Bank of America and Barclays, while the five largest banks were responsible for 88 per cent of the $60 trillion CDS market. The FCIC estimated that at the end of 2009 Goldman Sachs held $1.2 trillion in OTC derivatives to the notional amount of $45.6 trillion, more than four times the GDP of the USA.

> This leverage was the result of requiring little or no margin collateral to be posted to ensure other dealers' bets. Together, these three factors formed the preconditions for a contagion between institutions as well as between markets. The large volume of trading between swaps' dealers spawned an interlocking web of very large exposures among the 20 or so largest dealers. (Masters 2010, p. 24)

The years 2007 and 2008 changed all that. The defaults in the sub-prime that over-spilled in the CDO and CDS markets confirmed how fragile the financial system had become. Asset prices fell by an average of 40 per cent between 2008 and the middle of 2009 while house prices declined by over 30 per cent. Household net worth declined by 15 per cent while prices of banks' shares lost 60 per cent of their value so that in 2009 they were worth less than at the beginning of the decade. The IMF estimates that global bank losses will amount to over $14 trillion:

Our financial sector has grown disproportionately in relation to the rest of our economy. Whereas the financial sector claimed less than 15 percent of total U.S. corporate profits in the 1950s and 1960s, its share grew to 25 percent in the 1990s and to 34 percent by 2008. Financial services are essential to our modern economy, but the excesses of the past decade were a costly diversion of resources from other sectors of the economy. We must avoid policies that encourage such economic distortions. (Bair 2010, p. 5)

During a period of 20 years the economies of the developed countries had come to depend on selling and buying houses and using the financial markets to make the selling of housing possible. The Case-Shiller index of house prices showing major increases in the USA was equally applicable in the UK, Spain, Ireland, Canada, and a number of economies with different housing policies, yet where house price increases had become the major contributor to economic prosperity. The question that needed to be answered urgently was whether the increase in house prices reflected economic fundamentals of growth in incomes and people's willingness to pay more for their homes, or were the increases in house prices purely reflecting house price inflation as a result of cheap mortgages and low interests rates?

It is interesting that since the financial crisis there has been an emerging consensus that the model of dependence on consumer demand and financial markets needs to be rebalanced and countries with trade deficits have to deal with the question where does future growth come from. The declines in households' net worth have already resulted in major shifts in consumption and household savings. While house prices and equity prices were rising, households were saving less and consuming more, relying on the idea that the increases in their assets portfolios would pay for their retirements. The major declines in these assets' prices after 2000 meant that consumers had to repair their losses through increased saving, so that in the US whereas savings were less than 1 per cent of GDP in 2004, savings in 2010 had increased to 6 per cent of GDP.

The continuing decline of manufacturing exports as a share of GDP over two decades that started around 1980 and the outsourcing of production to emerging economies resulted in increased reliance on financial markets, the retail services and the housing market to provide the new engines of economic growth, employment and prosperity. Whereas during the period 1950 to 1970 manufacturing in the advanced economies accounted for 24 per cent of GDP by the 1990s this had declined to 22 per cent of GDP. The UK experienced the highest rates of labour shake-outs in manufacturing during the 1980 and early 1990s when approximately 3.2 million jobs were lost. By contrast, the declines in manufacturing were less severe in Germany and Japan. While in 2007 UK manufacturing represented 18 per cent of GDP, in Japan and Germany manufacturing still accounted for 22 per cent of GDP. This is important to understand in the sense that as both the USA and the UK after 2007 experienced major reductions in GDP and large trade deficits, Japan and Germany could still continue to rely on the strength of their manufacturing exports. Furthermore, the debate on global imbalances of large trade surpluses held by exporters and large trade deficits by countries that had relied on consumption in part reflected policy choices on manufacturing. While the major exporters, including Germany, Japan and China, had provided subsidies and government assistance to manufacturing, the UK and the USA embraced a more rigorous free market commitment that said that the economy is changing and the decline in manufacturing represented the supply and demand laws of markets.

The concepts of the New Economy, the Information Age Revolution and the Knowledge Economy were all utilized to explain the transition from manufacturing to service economies. This transition was explained as being part of the evolution in the advanced economies – a sort of maturation from basic manufacturing to the focus on added value. Information technology was contributing to great increases in productivity and therefore the growth in economies after the mid-1990s was seen as being founded on economic fundamentals. The increases in house prices reflected economic prosperity. In the UK the debate on the knowledge economy pointed to a Britain that was now focused on producing added value through financial markets, insurance and advertising. The decline of manufacturing was a non-issue since new sectors were replacing coal mining, steeling making and textiles.

The growth of the service sector and the financial sector in particular were seen as the new pillars for economic transition. The expansion of the financial sector was encouraged under the auspices of President of Ronald Reagan and Prime Minister Margaret Thatcher, as each political leader sought to liberalize financial markets through reducing regulation and aimed to make London and New York the major hubs of global finance.

The market for OTC derivatives became highly complex, opaque and interconnected. The processes of securitization created contexts that made the financial markets vulnerable and fragile because market participants did not have sufficient knowledge on counter-party risks. Investors who hedged their mortgage backed securities by buying CDS were not sure that their credit counter-party would be able to meet margin calls as mortgage defaults increased (Masters 2010; Patterson 2010). The CDS market amplified the financial crisis. The OTC market was a future options market yet these derivatives were excluded from futures traded markets. The notional estimate for this OTC market was approximately $640 trillion which was about 10 times global GDP. The notional value of the CDS market was $60 trillion. Once the financial crisis broke CDS insurance stopped working. The near collapse of Bear Stearns, the Lehman bankruptcy and the near collapse of AIG added to the fragility of the financial sector:

> But in the financial tsunami of late 2008, the swaps (CDS) were dysfunctional. The deleveraging had grown so powerful that most banks and hedge funds weren't willing to buy insurance from anyone; that meant swaps that were supposed to protect investors weren't working as promised. Many were afraid the seller of the insurance might not be around much longer to pay up if the underlying bond defaulted. (Patterson 2010, p. 270)

The majority of non-financial corporations utilized the new OTC market because the transactions were highly customized to the needs of that specific corporation. Transaction costs were low because there was no collateral to be posted. The CDS form of insurance was cheaper than conventional statutory insurance. The OTC derivatives market was opaque and without clear price setting. Asset backed securities became highly specialized and customized with little market trading or price discovery. Prices were set through the modelling of risks. In the unregulated market there was no need to post daily collateral to reflect price changes. Furthermore, this opaqueness generated problems of contagion due to the uncertainty of risk. Defaults in sub-prime mortgages resulted in spillovers for all other forms of mortgage backed securities, even those bonds that were made up of traditional 30-year mortgages and were performing, showing defaults of less than 1 per cent. The sharp declines in house prices meant that these securities now had to be marked to the market, and banks had to review prices for their assets, which often meant accepting write downs and selling assets in markets that were not performing. The construction of new financial instruments for asset backed securities meant that mortgage backed securities (MBS) entries were repeated for different CDOs. The diversification of risk became highly correlated since all assets were moving in the same direction.

FINANCIAL MARKETS

In the following sections it shall be argued that the relationships between OTC derivatives and the financial meltdown needs to be analysed at four levels. First, there is the issue of contexts and the question why this market expanded within a framework of deregulation. The derivatives market was limited to institutional investors. These investors were defined as being sophisticated investors and therefore both the investment banks and the investing institutions knew what was best for their clients. Over-the-counter derivatives confirmed the ultimate ascendancy in market liberal thinking. Over-the-counter derivatives did not have to be regulated because it was assumed that participants would regulate themselves and that it was always better for these sophisticated investors to regulate themselves than for government to intervene:

> In my view, with the benefit of hindsight the Commodity Futures Modernization Act was an unmitigated disaster. It is one of the worst pieces of legislation that I've ever seen with regard to the economy. And, you know, today we are still trying to fix a big problem, but it's a long battle. (Masters 2010, p. 37)

Secondly, there is the question of who benefited from the expansion of the deregulated over-the-counter derivatives markets? Was it mainly the financial sector that benefited which in turn meant higher fees and higher levels of compensation for broker dealers and the chief executives of the major banks? The Royal Bank of Scotland had gross capital assets of over $2 trillion before the collapse of the bank in 2007. This was greater than the UK GDP. In the USA the major investment banks grew their assets tenfold during the period 1990 to 2007 so that the five major investment banks' assets amounted to 60 per cent of US GDP.

The third issue is whether the growth of derivatives could be attributed to government housing policies that encouraged wider home ownership and so fostered the expansion of sub-prime and Alt-A high-risk mortgages. The increased demand for housing contributed to higher house prices, so the question is to what extent did the growth in derivatives reflect government housing policies. A recent OECD report (OECD 2010) has made such a connection, as have free market advocates (Kohlhagen 2010; Kyle 2010; Wallison 2011).

> Over-the-counter on credit derivatives, in general, and credit default swaps in particular, had absolutely no role whatsoever in causing the financial crisis . . . the cause of the financial crisis was quite simply the commitment by the United States Government to bring home ownership to the next group of people who previously had not been able to own their own homes. (Kohlhagen 2010, p. 14)

Kohlhagen (2010) and Wallison (2011) have both argued that housing policy was the major contributory factor that contributed to the financial crisis. Their argument points to housing policy under both the Clinton and Bush Governments where the major concern was the expansion of home ownership. Home ownership between 1990 and 2006 increased from 64 per cent to 69 per cent: that additional 5 per cent increase represented new home owners who were highly at risk of defaulting. Government policy aimed at increasing incentives to banks to lend to high-risk groups meant that loan originators aware of the new risk created derivatives to spread the risk of loans. According to Kohlhagen, derivatives markets represented a series of 'enablers' to the crisis rather than being the cause of the financial crisis.

The major error with the Wallison/Kyle/Kohlhagen argument is that sub-prime mortgages totalled between 500 billion and $1 trillion and although this was a large amount relative to a US economy of $14 trillion and a global economy of $65 trillion, the sub-prime mortgage crisis could have been contained and not turned into a major global financial crisis. Secondly, there is no evidence that CRA encouraged lower quality underwriting of mortgages. Thirdly, the issue of house price inflation was a global phenomenon; house prices were increasing worldwide. There was a major investment boom in housing in the UK, Ireland and Spain, all countries with different housing policies to those of the USA, so the increase in house price was not just a US problem. Equally, the sharp declines in house prices were also on a global scale. Speculators in the sunnier climes of Spain and Portugal build houses as future second homes for British home owners looking for a place in the sun. The sharp declines in house prices in 2006 and 2007 meant there were now fewer buyers for second homes in Spain, which in turn left contractors and builders with unsold houses and falling prices. Banks and finance houses exposed to the housing booms were left with falling assets prices. In Ireland the optimism associated with the growth of the Celtic miracle also resulted in a major housing boom.

A further criticism that can be levelled against Wallison is the issue of households who had surrendered years of equity in their homes as they were encouraged to remortgage their properties, and in the process of remortgaging for the sake of buying a new home or using the additional finance to purchase consumer goods, these households, that originally had traditional 30-year mortgage, were put in jeopardy of losing their homes. These households lost equity. They were not the new additional owner-occupiers encouraged by the Clinton/Bush housing policies. The growth of securitization and derivatives created a large pool of cheap credit. This was therefore not a story of first-time buyers. The majority who traded the equity in their homes were existing home owners who had previously always met their mortgage repayments.

So the question that Wallison should have been asking is, why were households risking the equity in their homes by refinancing their mortgages? Rajan (2010) has pointed out that this process reflected a climate of stagnant wages where housing therefore became the means through the which the government could make people feel their standards of living were rising while their take home pay remained unchanged. The increase in house prices improved households' net worth. In the climate of rising asset prices these households were encouraged to use the equity in their homes to purchase consumer goods, which also helped to generate economic growth through increased consumption.

The Wallison thesis rests on a theory of inevitability. Government policy seeks to create a climate of expanding home ownership and in that process new owners enter the housing market – these new owners are high risk. Inevitably, banks and the financial sector created a process of securitization and derivatives to deal with this high risk. Mortgage backed securities and synthetic CDOs were the finance industry's response. Wallison points out that 26 million home owners, equivalent to 50 per cent of those with mortgages, had sub-prime mortgages and were therefore prone to default. However, the estimates for default for sub-prime mortgages were between $550 million and $1 trillion in a housing asset class worth $22 trillion.

Finally, there is the issue of moral hazard. Merrill Lynch, Bear Stearns, Lehman, Wachovia and Washington Mutual, all major market participants in the US and global financial markets, were all highly exposed to mortgage backed securities and credit default swaps. All of these institutions held too many asset backed securities to expand their balance sheets. Kyle (2010) in his testimony to the FCIC argued the case that these institutions were involved in risk shifting, ensuring that they retained profits when the market was on the upside, and therefore taking risks of exposure and leverage in the knowledge that on the downside the government would intervene and would not allow these institutions to fail.

The Kyle argument represents purely an assertion, since, according to their evidence, leaders of the major financial institutions made no assumptions that they would be bailed out by the government. There might have been mistakes of risk management and over leverage but this had more to do with assumptions about the housing market, and furthermore, in the context of increasing profits, no one was able to bring the growing bubble to a halt.

In the analysis of the derivatives debate, market liberal advocates have tended to argue the case that the unregulated derivatives markets provided the liquidity that contributed to the growth of the global economy since the mid-1990s. Derivatives provided lower cost access for corporations to new borrowing and investment; the process of securitization facilitated higher levels of consumer demand. The problem therefore was not the derivatives markets but the role of government. Government housing policy provided the means for the financial sector to create instruments that aimed to hedge the borrowings of high-risk new home owners.

Secondly, there was the context that government would always intervene and not allow banks to fail.

Thornburg Mortgage, a publicly traded mortgage lender that specialized in Alt-A mortgages greater than $400,000 directed at wealthy borrowers, still had 99.6 per cent of its mortgages performing when the company went bankrupt. However, the decision by UBS in August 2007 to declare losses of $11.3 billion on its mortgage backed securities and write off $13.7 billion of investment in US mortgages meant that all participants in Alt-A mortgages had to mark down their assets. Between December 2007 and March 2008 Thornburg received redemption calls totalling $1.78 billion and only had liquid assets worth $1.67 billion: these calls of $600 million exceeded the available liquidity and Thornburg was declared insolvent. The study of Thornburg is important because it shows that the financial crisis could not be attributed purely to sub-prime mortgages.

Within the OTC derivatives markets there was an absence of price transparency that would have been available on exchanges where price changes were reflected daily. The disagreements between Goldman Sachs and AIG on Goldman's collateral calls were related to a problem of price transparency, a lack of market pricing, and the ability of Goldman Sachs to create marks in the markets. The OTC market created complex interconnected swaps between the major broker dealers that were difficult to disentangle once the crisis started. The levels of risk could no longer be judged accurately because of the lack of price transparency and levels of exposures between counter-parties. The credit derivatives market, which mainly involved credit default swaps (CDS), was a pseudo form of insurance since the so-called insurance seller did not have to post daily collateral to reflect exposure, and, furthermore, CDS insurance was qualitatively different from statutory insurance. In the CDS market the asset backed securities were marked to the market while statutory insurance was based on actuarial principles.

> I would like to reiterate that during this crisis one single factor stood out in its potential to destroy the financial system as a whole: The massive interlocking web of over-the-counter derivatives' exposures among the biggest Wall Street swaps dealers. Many financial institutions might have gone bankrupt or suffered severe losses from the crisis, but the system as a whole would not have been imperiled were it not for the propagation of unregulated derivatives markets. (Masters 2010, p. 28)

The unregulated OTC derivatives market provided the context for contagion between the major derivatives dealers for three reasons. First, there was a lack of transparency of who was holding which exposure that made it difficult for counter-parties to see when individual firms were taking excessive risks. Counter-parties buying insurance from monoline insurers like MBIA and AIG did not really know how much CDS AIG had been selling and whether it would be able to honour these commitments. Investors purchasing mortgage backed securities did not really know the content of their bond and to what extent they were exposed to sub-prime defaulting loans, so that even MBIA, that had traditional loans, could not separate these from loans that contained high levels of new mortgages. There was also a lack of price transparency since most of the swap deals were not being traded in conventional futures or equity markets. The opaqueness of price discovery might have helped the dealers in generating fees and higher compensation but in the longer term the lack of price discovery resulted in the near collapse of this market. Secondly, there was the problem of interconnectedness between the major swap dealers. A company requiring a fixed interest rate for an adjustable interest rate needed a dealer to purchase that adjustable rate, and equally the dealer needed to find another dealer wanting the exposure. So in a market that had grown to $600 trillion it was becoming very complex for dealers to net out their exposures. This web of connections therefore created the potential for a domino effect, so that if one dealer defaulted other dealers would also default. Thirdly, losses did not have to be very high because all the dealers were highly leveraged.

> Estimates of the market were as high as $62 trillion, though lately the market has been reduced to an estimated $55 trillion. By comparison, as of the second half of this year, there was only about $6 trillion in corporate debt outstanding, $7.5 trillion in mortgage-backed debt and $2.5 trillion in asset-backed debt, according to data from the Securities Industry and Financial Markets Association. That's a total of about $16 trillion in private sector debt. So it appears that swaps on that debt could total at least three times as much as the actual debt outstanding. (Dinallo 2008, p. 13)

DERIVATIVES

The derivatives market has been described as being an institutional marketplace, that is as confined to institutional investors who are therefore described as being sophisticated traders and consequently not treated as clients by investment banks but as counter-parties in the construction of securities. This perspective was included in the US President's Working Group report in 1999, while European regulators also held a similar view that sophisticated traders needed less regulation than the broader investing public. For example, the UK's regulatory approach was different for investment services offered to 'sophisticated' investment professionals than the approach for investment services offered to other investors. During the period between 2005 and 2007, it is estimated that investment banks issued about $1.1 trillion of CDOs. As these products were downgraded from triple-A ratings to below investment grade, investment banks, including Goldman Sachs, Merrill Lynch and JP Morgan defined the buyers of CDOs as being 'sophisticated investors' – a legal term dating back to the US Securities Act of 1933 and extended to OTC derivatives in 2000. Banks were free to treat the buyers as counter-parties, rather than customers to whom they owed a duty of care.

The investors in the OTC markets were therefore wholesale funds including mutual money funds and pension funds. The ratings of triple-A by the ratings agencies of all mortgage backed securities, CDS and CDO was essential if these market participants were going to purchase the new bonds.

The generic term derivative comes from the word derive, and derivatives are instruments whose values are derived from values that can be exchanged for a price in markets; for example, creating a future derivative on aviation fuel or fuel for a farmer derived from oil prices. Insuring the future price of wheat is decided in commodity markets. Bonds have maturity dates and annual payments. Bonds and Treasury Bonds are used as derivatives since these are described as being liquid and are recognized as collateral. Exchange rate currencies and interest rates are derivatives. The growth in derivatives has been associated with the breakdown of the Bretton Woods settlement in 1974 and the new uncertainties that followed in macro-economic policy. Since the dollar was no longer the anchor for currency, convertible currency countries had to cope with flexible exchange rates and interest rates that were now decided in global financial markets. Currencies now reflected the sentiment of markets. Derivatives and securities in the 1970s were seen as a response to the uncertainty of exchange rates and interest rates. Derivative and securities were therefore deemed as being highly beneficial because they permitted the development of risk management in the volatile flexible currency and interest rates markets. The Foreign Exchange SPOT FX is sighted as a working example in the derivatives market. Approximately $3.2 trillion are traded daily on the FX. The foreign exchange market is highly transparent, with exchange rates being posted on platforms throughout the day to reflect changes in sentiments and trades in different currencies. Seventy per cent of foreign exchange trading happens over the counter.

OTC derivatives have become a vital part of our economy. According to the most recent data, 92% of the largest American companies and over 50% of mid-sized companies use OTC products to hedge risk. Recently, many of our

clients have expressed great concern on the affects of the proposed legislative
and regulatory changes on their businesses. Clients such as BP, Chesapeake,
Constellation and Cargill are very worried about the unintended consequences
of these policy proposals, particularly at a time when our economy remains
fragile. (Lenczowski 2009, p. 3)

The repeal of Glass-Steagill in 1999 and the removal of securities
from the Securities Act of 1933 created a framework for a derivatives
market that was outside the ambit of specific regulators or agencies to
supervise the derivatives industry. Alan Greenspan, the then Chairman
of the Federal Reserve, had championed the new non-regulatory framework, arguing that markets were better at dealing with issues of efficient
resource allocation than governments, and that it was better for financial
institutions to regulate themselves.

Derivatives were mainly traded over the counter which meant that most
transactions were completed by two counter-parties in a swap contract
usually underwritten by an investment bank that acted as market maker.
There was no central clearing platform for these swap deals and therefore
no transparency in the making of markets and prices. Derivatives markets
were not open to competition posted on stock exchanges. The quality of
opaqueness was important because the narrowness of knowledge created
forms of knowledge estates and therefore higher fees. Derivatives could
be defended as providing an essential service by helping institutions to
balance their short-term risks and also to cut the cost of capital, which in
turn generated additional investment.

There was a policy network of dealers and traders who often traded
between themselves. According to a BIS survey, OTC trades were shaped
and made by the 12 largest banks while 48 per cent of all transactions were
dominated by five major banks.

THE OTC DERIVATIVES MARKET

In his opening address on the hearings on derivatives in September 2010,
Chairman Angelides of the FCIC made the following remarks:

> The sheer size of the derivatives market is as stunning as its growth. The
> notional value of over-the-counter derivatives grew from $88 trillion in 1999 to
> $684 trillion in 2008. That is more than 10 times the size of the gross domestic
> product of all nations. Credit derivatives grew from less than a trillion dollars at
> the beginning of this decade to a peak of $58 trillion by 2007. As I have explored
> this world, I feel a little like I've walked into a bank, opened a door, and seen a
> casino as big as New York, New York. As the financial crisis came to a head in
> the fall of 2008, no one knew what kind of derivative-related liabilities the other

guys had. Our free markets work when participants have good information. When clarity mattered most, Wall Street and Washington were flying blind. (Angelides 2010, p. 2)

Derivatives in themselves are not harmful. These are instruments – it was the way they are used and the climate and context that allowed and encouraged how they are used and defined that made the difference. Therefore, the concern was how derivatives were being traded in an unregulated market. This meant that within this unregulated market there was no need to treat these swaps as options that could be traded in transparent open markets. Credit default swaps that were perceived to be insurance were traded outside the statutory insurance framework. The case studies of Bear Stearns (Cohan 2009), Merrill Lynch (Farrell 2010) and Lehman (McDonald 2009) confirmed the exposure by these institutions to mortgage backed securities and CDOs so that when house prices started to decline they had to mark to market these assets and confirm losses, which in turn resulted in investors seeking redemptions. Lack of oversight in the Fixed Income Commodities and Currency (FICC) desk at Merrill allowed for an exposure at Merrill to a CDO market that led to losses of $30 billion on their mortgage backed securities. Bear Stearns became highly reliant on the REPO markets. AIG increased their exposure to CDS from $30 billion to $78 billion.

Market advocates have argued that these institutions were implicitly relying on a taxpayers' bail-out, shifting risk to taxpayers in the knowledge that they were too big to fail and that the government had no alternative but to find the necessary financing. The US government bailed out AIG at a cost of $180 billion buying 78 per cent of AIG shares, while guaranteeing the debt of Bear Stearns to $29 billion to ensure the merger with JP Morgan. By contrast Lehman was allowed to go into bankruptcy, and JP Morgan Chase and Goldman Sachs were turned into bank holding companies. Merrill Lynch was bought by Bank of America.

> Bear Stearns's failure in March had highlighted many of the flows in the regulatory structure of the US financial system . . . financial companies active in our markets had all gotten into one another's businesses. The products they designed and sold had become infinitely more complex . . .
>
> The regulatory structure, organized around traditional business lines had not begun to keep up with the evolution of the markets. As a result the country had a patchwork system of state and federal supervisors dating back 75 years. (Paulson 2010, p. 125)

Paulson did not ask why the regulatory system was so fragmented and unable to keep up with these innovations. Why were regulators at the SEC and Federal Reserve unable to deal with AIG or the investment banks?

President Reagan had encouraged a climate of deregulation. During the following years there was no attempt to review the capacities of regulators or to empower regulators to oversee the new process. When the Chairperson of the Commodity Futures Trading Commission (CFTC), Brooksley Born, pointed out that she was worried about the lack of supervision in the OTC markets she was admonished by the Chairman of the Federal Reserve Alan Greenspan, Robert Rubin and Larry Summers that she would undermine the confidence of the markets and would damage economic prosperity. The Participants in derivatives wanted to operate in free markets. The patchwork of federal and state regulators benefited the finance sector since they could choose between systems of regulation. Regulatory arbitrage with regulators competing for bank charters and offering a light touch of regulation, became the new conventional wisdom. It was these processes that generated the inadequate patchwork of regulation. Congress even passed legislation to omit securities from the Securities Act of 1933 and also ensured that the CFTC had no supervisory role in the derivatives market.

SECURITIZATION

The process of securitization could be likened to a revolution in finance. Banks that held long-term corporate loans and were exposed to defaults found new ways of buying insurance against the possibility of default. By paying a premium to a willing counter-party the banks could now shift the obligation of default. Furthermore, the bank could now hold capital against the exposure. Banks that had previously held mortgages for the lifetime of that mortgage could now package a number of mortgages held on their books and sell these as mortgage backed securities (MBS) to financial investors. The outstanding mortgages were now no longer on the banks' balance sheets. The investors received streams of income generated by the MBS. In the meantime in structuring these mortgages into CDOs the banks also received fees. The banks could now become involved in new loans and therefore extend mortgages to a larger number of people. Banks were no longer limited in making loans that related to bank deposits and customer savings. They were no longer constrained by the economic context of their locality. They could attract investors beyond national boundaries. Investors were promised a potential income from these mortgages for an extended period. Housing was defined as a sound investment since people always needed homes. Housing data was showing that house prices were rising and therefore in cases of default investors could seek foreclosures on collateral that was rising in price.

The most basic derivative was the mortgage backed security (MBS) also called the residential mortgage backed security (RMBS). The MBS's contents were a series of pooled mortgages. Originators, brokers and lenders offered mortgages to individual households. These mortgages were not held by the originator but sold to an investment bank who pooled the mortgages and sold these to a Special Investment Vehicle (SIV). Starting in 2004 and 2005, with the sharp increases in sub-prime originations, the asset backed securities (ABS) CDO market took off. ABS CDO volume roughly doubled each year starting in 2003. Total issuance jumped from $22 billion in 2003 to $58 billion in 2004, $106 billion in 2005, and $217 billion in 2006. Issuance then dropped in 2007 to $162 billion and virtually disappeared in 2008.

According to McDonald (2009) the MBS procedure at Lehman included a form of factory process where a mortgage backed security would involve one thousand mortgages each worth about $300,000 making a CDS worth $300 million. Adjustable rate mortgages at an initial rate of 1 to 2 per cent which would be adjusted upwards after two years would create $500 repayment on each mortgage and $500,000 for a thousand mortgages per month giving a potential yield of $6 million a year. The next stage of the MBS was therefore to break the $300 million into 300 $1 million bonds that would offer a coupon of 7 to 8 per cent.

> The Head Office did not care one way or another whether the loans were sound or not, because the mortgage broker would sell them on to Lehman or Merrill Lynch within a month. Lehman did not care much either because once the bonds were sold the problem was no longer theirs. (McDonald 2009, p. 108)

CREDIT DEFAULT SWAPS

Within the derivatives market the credit derivative has been the major contestable instrument. Generally credit derivatives represented the transfer of credit risk. The process of the single named corporate bond credit was where the bank that had lent money to a major corporation wanted to defray the risk of that entity corporation or bond going to default. During this process the investment bank sought an insurance company that would sell insurance against the default (CDS). In this way the bank continued to receive interest payments from the corporation but also maintained a traditional relationship with their client.

Credit default swaps (CDS) were a financial instrument introduced into the market after the repeal of Glass-Steagill with the intention of providing insurance to cover losses to banks and bondholders when a particular bond or security went to default, or when the stream of revenue behind the loan became insufficient to meet the payments that were promised. The major insurers that became involved in CDS included bond insurers like MBNA, Ambac and AIG. As the market for the credit default swaps expanded from around $900 billion in 2000 to around $58 trillion in 2007 this was seen as a great opportunity for these companies to provide insurance in a market which was seen as having a small risk of defaulting. Furthermore, the new derivatives had all been graded as triple-A by Moody's, S & P and Fitch.

CDS have been described as being similar to car or health insurance, with the buyer buying protection and paying monthly premiums and the seller of insurance accepting liability and therefore being able to meet the insurance claim. At first sight a CDS deal does resemble a form of insurance, in that the buyer pays premiums with the assurance of a pay-out on the occurrence of an event, and therefore some buyers of CDS do have 'insurable interests'. However, the Commodity Futures Modernization Act (CFMA) passed in the USA in 2000 liberalized the CDS market so that it was no longer necessary for CDS buyers to have insurable interests. A hedge fund could now buy a CDS on a particular company, even though it had no shares or other financial interest in that company. The term 'naked CDS' is applied to such situations, in contrast to covered CDS. According to McDonald, talking about trading a CDS:

> This is nothing more than a bet, for instance, that a mortgage company will go broke and its bond value will sink to 4 cents on the dollar. We are talking about a bet that would allow a bond holder to go to an investment bank and say 'I hold 1 billion dollars worth of bonds in Country Wide. The coupon is 5 per cent which is one per cent more than a similar Treasury bond. I give you 90 per cent of that 1 per cent if you insure me for the present value of the bond all the way to zero. In that transaction the bank will collect 9 million dollars a year in insurance unless the corporation goes down. More often the Bank will sell the CDS to a Hedge Fund. (McDonald 2009, p. 60)

Credit default swaps are not insurance since they are marked to market which means the value of the swap has to reflect the current market value. As values changed, CDS sellers were required to post more collateral. That capital strain could produce sudden liquidity problems for the sellers. The seller may own enough assets to provide collateral, but the assets may not be liquid and thus not immediately accessible. When many sellers are forced to sell assets, the price of those assets falls and sellers are faced with taking large losses just to meet collateral requirements. As the prices of the assets are driven down by forced sales, mark-to-market losses increase and the collateral posting cycle continues. Meanwhile, the underlying assets may continue to perform – paying interest and the principal in full.

The estimates for the growth of the credit derivatives market vary widely because these credit derivatives took place privately and were bilateral as OTC derivatives. The estimate by the British Banking Association show CDS growing from $900 million to over $20 trillion in 2007. The Bank of International Settlements (BIS) estimates CDS as worth $45 trillion in 2007 and ISDA estimates show derivatives markets growing to $35 trillion in 2007. The British Bankers Association (BBA) survey shows that the notional amount of credit derivatives was $180 billion in 1997 and had grown to over $20 trillion in 2006. ISDA started doing annual surveys in 2001 and reported notional amounts of $632 billion that year – slightly less than the BBA reported in 2001 – but over $34 trillion in 2006, which was materially more than the BBA reported in that year. According to ISDA, the market peaked at $45 trillion in 2007. The Bank for International Settlements (BIS) began collecting statistics in 2004 and sized the market at $43 trillion in notional amount in June 2007 and $58 trillion in December 2007. Unlike the other data sources, the BBA survey broke the market down by product type: for example, in 2006 it reported that 33 per cent of credit derivatives were single-name CDS, 30 per cent were full index CDS (in contrast to index tranches, as discussed below), and 17 per cent were synthetic CDOs.

The decline in house prices that started in 2006 soon had spill-over effects on the mortgage backed securities (MBS) that many swaps were supporting, and which began to lose value in 2007. Increases in the number of households defaulting on their mortgages meant that the payment streams of MBS were falling and investors began to fear that the swaps, originally meant as a hedge against risk, could suddenly become huge liabilities. Bond insurers like MBNA and Ambac that had underwritten large amounts of the swaps saw their shares plunge in late 2007. Goldman Sachs and Société Générale both asked AIG to increase their collateral to cover their CDS exposure. By September 2008 AIG realized that they could not meet the redemptions and were fearing bankruptcy. The Federal Reserve attempted to provide about $80 billion of funding for AIG but this soon proved to be insufficient. The holders of CDS were now asking AIG for their default swaps to be repaid. Eventually the Federal Reserve and the US Treasury bought up the outstanding AIG contracts for $29 billion and put these in Maiden Lane III.

The swap market was bilateral, private and opaque, and therefore the value of the CDS market would always be at best an estimate. Greenberger (2010) estimated that the CDS market was worth between $35 trillion and $65 trillion in notional value. However, the opaqueness of this unregulated market did create major problems of uncertainty because counter-parties did not know their levels of exposure. Greenberger argued that in 1999 the government had to make the decision whether to treat these swaps as futures, meaning that, by virtue of the Commodity Exchange Act of 1933 these swaps would be cleared which meant that each swap deal was backed by adequate capital through the collection of margins. The situation of Goldman Sachs getting into a dispute with AIG on CDS payments would not have occurred since price discovery would have been constant.

> you wouldn't have situations like September 15th, 16th, where AIG wakes up finding out all of a sudden it owes $80 billion on its credit default swap book. That's the clearing aspect. And if it were regulated, it would be exchange traded. That is to say, transparent. The market would know. The regulators would know what is out there, and there would be a market-driven price mechanism associated to these products. We had a fork. We could have either done that, or we could do what Congress did in 2000, which was to decide for their reasons that this market would be completely unregulated. That is to say, no clearing. No exchange trading. (Greenberger 2010, p. 7)

SYNTHETIC COLLATERALIZED DEBT OBLIGATIONS

A CDS covers a single entity. The CDS premium provides an income stream to the CDS seller. A synthetic CDO is comprised of a number of CDS. The CDO now provides an income stream from a series of companies buying insurance and from the sellers. The pooled CDO is bought by a Special Investment Vehicle (SIV). The SIV now owns the pooled CDO, which it sells as a series of tranches according to the exposure their clients are willing to take, so that senior tranches represent the lowest risk and mezzanine higher risks.

Synthetic CDOs were a series of securities that were mainly composed of swaps premiums that paid in relation to future default. The person who bought into synthetic CDOs could choose the most vulnerable companies and for a small layout purchase a synthetic CDO. Two case studies highlight the problem of derivatives and the relationship between investment banks as the arranger of CDO and their investors. The question that arises is related to the issue of conflict of interest. Does an investment bank sell a security to a client because it knows it is good for the client or does the investment bank see the client as a counter-party who is aware of the risk and the exposure and therefore the bank does not play a fiduciary or advisory role to that investor.

The much cited case of Goldman arranging the CDO Abacus 2 raised a number of issues. Abacus 2 was structured by Goldman Sachs for the

Paulson Hedge Fund. Paulson chose a number of CDS to go into the list and paid Goldman a fee of $15 million a year as premium for insuring the listed synthetic CDO. Goldman then searched other counter-parties to take the long side of the swap, including IKB, a German Bank. Goldman did not make clear to the counter-party that John Paulson was taking the short side or that Paulson was involved in selecting the entries. Goldman told the FCIC Inquiry that they had acted as the market makers bringing counter-parties together. Abacus 2 failed within six months. Paulson made $1 billion profit for his hedge fund while the counter-parties had to seek government aid to help with their losses.

In the case of Vertical 2007-1, UBS of Switzerland structured the $1.5 billion product. In internal memos, UBS staff referred to the content of the CDO as vomit and crap entries which were obviously highly toxic and which the Bank of America wanted off its books. Barely two months later, Vertical 2007 collapsed. One of the buyers, Pursuit Partners, a hedge fund, has since sued UBS, alleging that the bank knew before it sold the deal that it would fall apart, that UBS had already been alerted by S & P that the CDO would be downgraded.

Haldane (2009) argued that all insurance against default was mispriced by around 60 per cent. Prosperity and continuing increased asset and house prices led to the assumption that these assets would continue to rise in price and therefore assumed low insurance premiums. In the new climate of prosperity, and as banks' profits increased, the risk takers were now in the ascendance while the risk management teams became the laggards. Describing the climate at Lehman Brothers, McDonald (2009) explained their ascendance as follows: 'Their words were not so much heard as acclaimed. Their budgets were enormous, their bonuses magnificent, their freedoms enviable. And the risks they took were nothing short of awesome' (McDonald 2009, p. 111).

Warren Buffett, CEO and Chairman of Berkshire Hathaway, had no problem in pointing out that the deregulated OTC derivatives were the new weapons of mass destruction that had the potential of undermining the US economy. In his 2002 Annual Report to Berkshire Hathaway he described the new instruments as a call for money to change hands at some future date with the amount to be determined by one or more reference items such as interest rate, stock prices or currency values. As far as Buffett (2002) was concerned the new financial instruments created after the mid-1980s had become too complex, too sophisticated, created by mathematicians and engineers whose models on risk management were too far removed from the realities of economies. The collateralized market was like hell: one that was easy to enter but almost impossible to exit:

Charlie [Munger] and I are of one mind in how we feel about derivatives and the trading activities that go with them; We view them as time bombs both for the parties that deal in them and the economic system. In our view derivatives are financial weapons of mass destruction, carrying dangers that while now latent, are potentially lethal. (Buffet 2002, p. 16)

The process of securitization allowed and encouraged speculation. AIG sold CDS to Goldman Sachs, insuring around 17 billion for around 1.5 million when other insurers were charging higher rates. The decision to sell CDS by AIG was perceived as creating easy revenues since it was assumed that as the CDS were rated as triple-A therefore they did not need to be hedged. Goldman Sachs felt they needed to insure their CDO and found AIG willing to sell that insurance. AIG mispriced their CDS exposure.

The Gramm-Leach-Bliley Act of 1999 that repealed Glass-Steagill and the Commodity Futures Modernization Act of 2000, created an unregulated market for 'swaps'. These swaps were exempt from the Securities Act of 1933, were not covered by insurance legislations and were also exempted from gaming laws. Credit default swaps acted as a form of insurance in the sense that those who had exposure to a bond could hedge against the risk of default by going to a CDS seller who for a premium sold CDS insurance to the buyer on an entity defaulting. However, CDS insurance was qualitatively different from conventional insurance. In the latter case insurance companies relied on statutory accounting which therefore took the long-term view of their exposures and used actuarial models of mortality rates and life expectancy to decide the actuary principle of insurance. Within CDS the accounting was marked to market and therefore the so-called insurance company had to post collateral or capital if a bond fell below a certain level. This process allowed an insurance company like AIG to operate as a hedge fund that had insufficient reserves to back up its promises. AIGFP was permitted to do this because of the triple-A ratings that were allocated to its subsidiary insurance companies. However, AIGFP did not have the statutory rights to borrow from the insurance subsidiaries. If AIGFP had been a stand-alone company no other companies would have done business with the holding company. However, AIGFP sold $2.7 trillion of CDS but had posted no collateral nor shown it had the reserves to meet these requirements.

This changed, in my view, 100 years of known capital requirements and led to our Century's version of shadow banking. My essential thesis is that these changes permitted AIG and FP and other institutions to sell wildly under-capitalized pseudo-insurance and other core 'financial products' that previously had well-known capital requirements, reserving, and net capital requirements. (Dinallo 2010, p. 17)

SHADOW BANKING

The period from 1934, when deposit insurance was enacted, until the crisis of 2007 could be defined as the 'Quiet Period' in banking history, compared to the frequency of runs on banks in the 1880s, 1907 and then during the Great Depression of 1929. Paradoxically, the Quiet Period led to the view that banking panics were a thing of the past. Furthermore, during the thrift and banking crisis of the 1980s, a series of reforms were enacted specifically designed to improve the financial regulatory system and to prevent future similar crises. These rules significantly strengthened bank regulation and provided banks with strong incentives to operate at higher capital levels with less risk. But at the same time, they created unintended incentives for financial services to grow outside of the regulated sector in the so-called shadow banking system. In the 20 years following these reforms, the shadow banking system grew much more quickly than traditional banking. It is estimated that by 2007 the so-called shadow banking system was worth the equivalent of $8 trillion, which was the same value as the regulated banking sector. At the onset of the crisis, it is estimated that half of all financial services were conducted by institutions not subject to potential regulation and supervision. Products and practices originated by the shadow banking system have proven particularly troublesome in this crisis. Many of these non-banks grew to be too large, too complex and too interconnected. The events that unravelled starting in August 2007 represented a classic banking panic similar to those of the 1880s and 1907 when people queued outside banks to retrieve their savings. The bank panic of 2007 was also about people asking for their money back, but this time it was not individuals queuing outside banks, but mutual funds pensions funds that had allowed lending to the investment banks through the short-term REPO markets, and when these banks became vulnerable the REPO market dried up and investment banks had no access to overnight lending.

A banking panic is a systemic event because the banking *system* cannot honour its obligations and is *insolvent*. Unlike the historical banking panics of the 19th and early 20th centuries, the current banking panic is a wholesale panic, not a retail panic. In the earlier episodes, depositors ran to their banks and demanded cash in exchange for their checking accounts. Unable to meet those demands, the banking system became insolvent. The current panic involved financial firms 'running' on other financial firms by not renewing sale and repurchase agreements (repo) or increasing the repo margin ('haircut'), forcing massive deleveraging, and resulting in the banking system being insolvent. (Gorton 2009, p. 1)

Here the question is how to define the daily transactions on financial markets. Do these reflect and confirm the efficient markets hypothesis of resources always being directed to more efficient corporations reflecting continuing changes in information, or do these transactions represent a series of bets of what is likely to happen to a certain stock at some future date. In the first case market participants are unable to predict the market because it reflects a myriad of transactions. By contrast if the later case is true then the issue is not so much a random walk down Wall Street, but a series of participants who through their actions define and shape the market. The explosion in MBS reflected the optimism of investors that house prices would continue to rise. The expansion of the CDS market after 2006 reflected the sentiments of those who argued that the housing market had peaked and that there were likely to be large numbers of defaults.

Professor Robert Shiller asked why there were major discrepancies between economic fundamentals and what happens in financial markets (Fox 2009). Within the real economy companies take a long term to absorb new investment and new technology and adjust productivity, and yet financial markets turnovers occur on a daily basis. The real sector seemed to be so much slower than the financial sector. Does the financial sector have superior knowledge of what is likely to happen to the economy in the future, is a question that Schiller asked when he studied the performance of stock prices and actual dividends paid by companies

THE LIMITS OF DERIVATIVES

Bernanke (2010), in his testimony to the FCIC, argued that explanations of the financial crisis need to separate out triggers from structures. Trigger explanations including sub-prime mortgages could not explain the global financial crisis. The problem was the structure and the fragility of the financial system. First, commercial banks became involved in the securitization process, bundling up their loans into securities, passed into off-balance-sheet special vehicles, thus evading Basel capital requirements. Investment banks devised structured products such as collateralized debt obligations (CDOs) with tranches of different risks/rewards, using mixes of securitized loans 'alchemised' into higher ratings, and then sold on. Investment banks applied CDSs to CDOs to produce 'synthetic' CDOS, where only the credit risks, not the loan packages, needed to be sold on.

At the first sign of trouble – defaults in the relatively small sector of sub-prime loans – this unregulated system folded like a pack of cards. The rush to the exit by leveraged hedge funds sent CDOs' prices in a downward spiral. With CDOs impossible to price, even senior tranches became toxic. With most institutions holding unknown amounts of toxic assets of unknown value, trust evaporated and markets froze.

REFERENCES

Angelides, P. (2010) Opening Remarks of Phil Angelides, Chairman of the Financial Crisis Inquiry Commission at the Hearing on the Role of Derivatives in the Financial Crisis, 30 June, Washington, DC.

Bair, S. (2010) Sheila Bair, Chairman Federal Deposit Insurance Corporation, Evidence to the Financial Crisis Commission, 14 January.

Bernanke, B. (2010) Ben S. Bernanke, Chairman Board of Governors of the Federal Reserve System before the Committee on Financial Services U.S. House of Representatives, 20 April, Washington, DC.

Black, W. (2008) Prepared Testimony of William K. Black Associate Professor of Economics and Law University of Missouri – Kansas City, Before the Committee on Agriculture, Nutrition & Forestry of the United States Senate, 12 October, Washington, DC.

Born, B. (2010) Financial Crisis Inquiry Commission Official Transcript Hearing on The Role of Derivatives in the Financial Crisis, 30 June, Washington, DC.

Buffet, W. (2002) *Berkshire Hathaway Inc 2002 Annual Report*.

Cohan, W.D. (2009) *House of Cards: How Wall Street's Gamblers Broke Capitalism*. London: Allen Lane.

Cohn, G. (2010) Testimony from Gary D. Cohn, President & Chief Operating Officer, The Goldman Sachs Group, Inc. before the Financial Crisis Inquiry Commission, 30 June, Financial Crisis Inquiry Commission Official Transcript Hearing on The Role of Derivatives in the Financial Crisis, 30 June, Washington, DC.

Dinallo, E. (2008) Testimony to the United States Senate Committee on Agriculture, Nutrition, and Forestry Hearing on the Role of Financial Derivatives in the Current Financial Crisis, by Superintendent Eric Dinallo, New York State Insurance Department, 12 October.

Dinallo, E. (2010) Testimony To the Financial Crisis Inquiry Commission Hearing on the Role of Derivatives in the Financial Crisis by Former Superintendent Eric Dinallo, New York State Insurance Department, 1 July, Washington, DC.

Dines, D. (2009) Evidence and Testimony on Over the Counter Derivatives to the Senate Committee on Agriculture and Forestry, 18 November, Washington, DC.

Farrell G (2010) *Crash of the Titans: Greed, Hubris and the Fall of Merrill Lynch and the Near Collapse of Bank of America*. New York: Crown Business.

FCIC (2011) *Final Report of the National Commission on the Causes of the Financial and Economic Crisis in the United States*. New York: Public Affairs.

FitchRatings (2009) 'Global Credit Derivatives Survey: Surprises, Challenges and the Future', 20 August.

Fox, J. (2009) *The Myth of the Rational Market: A History of Risk, Reward and Delusion on Wall Street*. New York: Harper Collins.

Gorton, G. (2009) 'Slapped in the Face by the Invisible Hand: Banking and the Panic of 2007', paper prepared for the Federal Reserve Bank of Atlanta's 2009 Financial Markets Conference: Financial Innovation and Crisis, 11–13 May.

Greenberger, M. (2010) Testimony of Michael Greenberger, Law School Professor, University of Maryland School of Law, to the Role of Derivatives in the Financial Crisis Financial Crisis Inquiry Commission, Hearing Dirksen Senate Office Building, 30 June, Washington, DC.

Haldane, A.G. (2009) 'Rethinking The Financial Network', speech delivered at the Financial Student Association, April, Amsterdam.

Haldane, A.G. (2010) 'The Debt Overhang', speech given at a Professional Liverpool Dinner, 27 January.

Kohlhagen, S. (2010) Testimony to the Financial Crisis Inquiry Commission Hearing on the Role of Derivatives in the Financial Crisis, 1 July.

Kyle, P. (2010) Reforming the OTC Derivatives Markets: Testimony to the Financial Crisis Inquiry Commission Hearing on the Role of Derivatives in the Financial Crisis, 1 July.

Lenczowski, M. (2009) Testimony of Mark Lenczowski, JP Morgan Chase & Co. (JPMC), Senate Agriculture Committee, 4 June.

Lewis, M. (2009) *The Big Short: Inside the Doomsday Machine*, New York: W.W. Norton.

Masters, B. (2008) 'Through the Turmoil', Opening Address, SIFMA Annual Meeting, New York, 28 October. Available at: http://events.sifma.org/2008/292/event.aspx?id=8566

Masters, M. (2010) Testimony of Michael W. Masters, Managing Member/Portfolio Manager, Masters Capital Management, LLC, before the Financial Crisis Inquiry Commission, Financial Crisis Inquiry Commission, Official Transcript Hearing on the Role of Derivatives in the Financial Crisis, 30 June, Washington, DC.

McDonald, L. (2009) *A Colossal Failure of Common Sense: The Incredible Inside Story of the Collapse of Lehman Brothers*. London: Ebury Press.

Patterson, S. (2010) *The Quants: How a New Breed of Math Whizzes Conquered Wall Street and Nearly Destroyed It*. New York: Crown Business.

Paulson, H. (2010) *On the Brink*. New York: Business Plus.

Rajan, R. (2010) *Fault Lines: How Hidden Fractures Still Threaten the World Economy*. Oxford and Princeton, NJ: Princeton University Press.

Schloss, N. (2009) Evidence and Testimony on Over the Counter Derivatives to the Senate Committee on Agriculture and Forestry, 18 November, Washington, DC.

Tett, G. (2009) *Fool's Gold: How the Bold Dream of a Small Tribe at J.P. Morgan Was Corrupted by Wall Street Greed and Unleashed a Catastrophe*. New York: Free Press.

Turner, A. (2009) 'What Do Banks Do, What Should They Do and What Public Policies Are Needed to Ensure Best Results for the Real Economy?', CASS Business School, 17 March.

Turner, A. (2010) 'What Do Banks Do, What Should They Do and What Public Policies are Needed to Ensure Best Results for the Real Economy?', speech delivered at CASS Business School, 17 March.

Wallison, P. (2011) 'Dissenting View by Peter Wallison', in *Final Report of the National Commission on the Causes of the Financial and Economic Crisis in the United States*. New York: Public Affairs.

5. Credit Rating Agencies and their contribution to the financial meltdown

INTRODUCTION: CONNECTING THE RATING AGENCIES TO THE FINANCIAL CRISIS

The central concern of this chapter is to explore the question of whether the Credit Rating Agencies (CRAs) contributed to the financial crisis of 2007. In debating this issue there are two perspectives: one presented by the senior managers of the CRAs who pointed out that all major market participants, including the CRAs, did not predict the depth of the financial crisis and that the crisis was an exogenous event. The alternative view tends to put the emphasis on institutional failures, including deficiencies in the mathematical models used by the CRAs, the conflict of interests inherent in the user pays model and the quasi monopoly positions of the CRAs. Evidence produced in testimonies by analysts and Moody's and Standard & Poor's (S&P) tended to put the focus on market share that undermined the ethics of independent impartial analysis.

In the following sections it shall be argued that the study of the ratings process confirms the view that the priority of the management teams at the CRAs to maintain market share and to issue a rating for a bond, even when their analysts expressed concern about the soundness of the securities was a contributory factor in the financial meltdown.

There have been a number of factors outlined at different enquiries to try and explain how the CRAs failed to forecast major downgrades in such a short space time of time when it was the taken for granted assumption that triple-A ratings had a minimum life expectancy of seven years (Raiter 2010). These explanations included:

1. The CRA business issuer pays model which altered the priorities of the CRAs as they became more focused on generating fees and higher profits.
2. The issue of conflict of interest between the commitment of the impartial agency and issuer fees that undermined the ethics of the research

based analysis and the ascendance of the new managerialism of the CRAs.

3. The failure of the mathematical models mainly because the data did not reflect the new mortgages and relied on classic 30-year traditional mortgages. The new adjustable rate mortgages, teaser mortgages and non-documented mortgages were qualitatively different from traditional mortgages. Furthermore there was a reluctance by the CRAs to deploy revised mathematical models.

4. Evidence given by analysts at a number of enquiries that showed the reluctance of some analysts to rate some issues, only to be ignored, marginalized and in some cases made redundant by their management teams.

5. Despite the heavy workloads the CRAs were understaffed and new staff being recruited did not have sufficient expertise to deal with the need for due diligence in dealing with issuers of asset backed bonds.

6. The legal framework did not provide a context for CRAs to be taken to courts for lack of diligence and for error in the ratings of bonds. CRAs were therefore exempt from legal accountability for their performance.

The Securities and Exchange Commission Report of September 2008 *Report of Issues Identified in the Commission Staff's Examinations of Select Credit Rating Agencies* (SEC 2008b) starts with the following remark:

> Beginning in 2007, delinquency and foreclosure rates for subprime mortgage loans in the United States dramatically increased, creating turmoil in the markets for residential mortgage-backed securities backed by such loans . . . The rating agencies performance in rating these structured finance products raised questions about the accuracy of their credit ratings generally as well as the integrity of the ratings process as a whole. (SEC 2008, p. 3)

The SEC Report concluded that while the workloads of the CRAs on the new asset backed securities increased, especially on the collateralization of CDOs, the rating agencies were not employing sufficient expert staff to deal with the new demands. Secondly, despite the anxiety of some analysts in the rating process, the asset backed securities were still rated as triple-A. Finally the SEC Report pointed to the lack of transparency in the ratings decisions, the use of risk models and adjustment to these models which were not always transparent.

> the rating agencies examined did not always fully document certain significant steps in their subprime RMBS and CDO ratings process. This made it difficult or impossible for Commission examiners to assess compliance with their established policies and procedures, and to identify the factors that were considered in developing a particular rating. (SEC 2008b, p. 23)

Warren Buffett (2010), CEO of Berkshire Hathaway, and Raymond McDaniel, CEO at Moody's (2010), in their evidence to the FCIC hearings on 2 June 2010, both pointed out that no one could have forecasted the sharp decline in house prices during 2007. The sharp reductions reflected a major exogenous event that was not predicted. Warren Buffett described the continuing increases in house prices after 2000 as being a form of narcotic for the majority of people in America. Low interest payments and continuing increases in house prices encouraged families either to trade and move into larger homes, taking larger mortgages or using their homes as collateral to borrow monies from banks and improved household consumption. Senior managers of the CRAs, in their submission of testimonies and giving evidence at various Senate, House of Representatives and financial crisis enquiry hearings, have tended to argue the case that their decision to downgrade to below investment grade of $4 trillion of asset backed securities that they had previously rated as triple-A did not represent a failure of the ratings agencies, but rather reflected the wider context of market forces. No market participant was able to predict the depth of the crisis. The ratings agencies were modelling their ratings on the history of the assets that formed a mortgage backed security. Raymond McDaniel (2010), CEO of Moody's, explained the deterioration of the asset backed securities as follows:

> With respect to CRAs, some market observers have expressed concerns that credit ratings did not better predict the deteriorating conditions in the U.S. subprime mortgage market and the impact on the credit quality of residential mortgage-backed securities ('RMBS') . . . Moody's is certainly not satisfied with the performance of our ratings during the unprecedented market downturn of the past two years. We, like many others, did not anticipate the unprecedented confluence of forces that drove the unusually poor performance of subprime mortgages in the past several years. (McDaniel 2010, p. 7)

As far as McDaniel was concerned, therefore, the failure to predict the fragility of the housing market was not just confined to the CRAs but other market participants had equally not been able to predict the financial crisis. Market forces prevailed and implicitly, therefore, the CRAs could not be blamed.

The Credit Rating Agencies' connection to the financial crisis was related to their failure in acting as gatekeepers when it came to the ratings of the asset backed securities for mortgages, car loans and card credit loans. The highly coveted triple-A ratings undersigned by the two major Credit Rating Agencies (CRAs) – Moody's and Standard & Poor's – were undermined when, within a period of 18 months, bonds that had been rated as triple-A were downgraded by the same CRAs to below investment grade.

After 2005 the CRAs were described as being in factory mode when it came to the ratings of asset backed securities including residential mortgage backed securities (RMBS) and collateralized debt obligations (CDOs).

The FCIC (2010) estimated that Moody's and S&P rated some 10,000 securities as triple-A between 2005 and 2007 and that Moody's had rated $4.7 trillion in RMBS and over $400 billion in CDOs. During the same period, the incomes for the CRAs grew from $3 billion to $6 billion, with the CEOs earnings incomes similar to the CEOs on Wall Street. Ninety per cent of these triple-A securities were downgraded after July 2007 to below investment grade. These major downgrades contributed directly to the financial meltdown since banks and regulated investors were now holding securities below investment grade, which meant that they had to write down losses on these assets. The ratings process and the downgrading of these securities were therefore defined as being a major failure of the ratings agencies.

> Most subprime and Alt-A mortgages were held in residential mortgage-backed securities (RMBS), most of which were rated investment grade by one or more CRA. Furthermore, collateralized debt obligations (CDOs), many of which held RMBS, were also rated by the CRAs. Between 2000 and 2007, Moody's rated $4.7 trillion in RMBS and $736 billion in CDOs. The sharp rise in mortgage defaults that began in 2006 ultimately led to the mass downgrading of RMBS and CDOs, many of which suffered principal impairments. Losses to investors and writedowns on these securities played a key role in the resulting financial crisis. (FCIC 2010, p. 1)

Chairman Levin of the Senate Sub-Committee for Investigations (Levin 2010), in his opening address on the Hearings on the CRAs identified the issue of conflict of interest as being the factor that connected the CRAs to the financial crisis:

> Those toxic mortgages were scooped up by Wall Street firms that bottled them in complex financial instruments, and turned to the credit rating agencies to get a label declaring them to be safe, low-risk, investment grade securities. For a hundred years, Main Street investors trusted U.S. credit rating agencies to guide them toward safe investments . . . But now, that trust has been broken . . . At the same time, the credit rating agencies were operating with an inherent conflict of interest, because the revenues they pocketed came from the companies whose securities they rated. (Levin 2010, p. 2)

Senator Coburn (2010), Vice Chairman to the same Senate Sub-Committee for Investigation, in his opening remarks to the same hearings on 23 April 2010 made the case that because the three ratings agencies had, by their designation as NRSRO (Nationally Recognized Securities Ratings Organizations), obtained a monopoly position in the ratings process, they had abused their monopoly position. Moody's and S&P were responsible for 94 per cent of ratings. Furthermore, investors perceived the ratings given by the CRAs as having the seal of government approval. Investors therefore relied on the ratings agencies despite the CRAs' disclaimers on due diligence and the ratings. The Vice Chairman then went on to suggest that the CRAs ought to lose their NRSRO status and the area of ratings be opened to competition:

> The NRSRO designation had become for many investors a 'government seal of approval.' The ratings they assign have received the tacit blessing of the government . . . By requiring investors to purchase only AAA assets, it created an incentive for ratings to be *high*, though not necessarily *accurate*. If we are ever going to fix these problems we are going to need to start by ending the regulatory use of ratings. Second, we need to tear down the NRSRO designation and open up ratings to competition where reputation is more important than being in a government-approved club. (Coburn 2010, p. 1)

Partnoy's (2006) major concern was the issue of conflict of interest associated with the issuer pays business model that the CRAs created after 1974. The CRAs had become the 'gate opener' for the issuer of the securitized bonds rather than the gatekeeper. The CRAs' major focus became the ratings of structured products since these generated new revenues to the CRA:

> credit rating agencies continue to face conflicts of interest that are potentially more serious than those of other gatekeepers: they continue to be paid directly by issuers, they give unsolicited ratings that at least potentially pressure issuers to pay them fees, and they market ancillary consulting services related to ratings. Credit rating agencies increasingly focus on structured finance and new complex debt products, particularly credit derivatives, which now generate a substantial share of credit rating agencies' revenues and profits. With respect to these new instruments, the agencies have become more like 'gate openers' than gatekeepers; in particular, their rating methodologies for collateralized debt obligations (CDOs) have created and sustained that multi-trillion dollar market. (Partnoy 2006, p. 60)

Mr Eric Kolchinsky, who was employed as a CDO analyst and was later dismissed by Moody's, in giving evidence to the FCIC hearing on 23 April 2010 pointed to the unequal relationship between the issuers of the asset backed securities who were mainly the investment banks and the CRA. Kolchinsky argued that the issuer could mislead the CRA about the contents of a pooled asset and that there were no penalties for issuers who lied to the CRA. Furthermore because of pressure of market share, which had become the prevailing mood with the CRA, it made it difficult for the analyst to walk away from a deal:

For practical purposes, we would not walk away from a deal. We couldn't say no, so that would be the most obvious penalty, that you do in any normal business, So once that avenue is closed off because you want to increase market share, there's no penalty. We were in the position of being a quasi regulator, which means we had no power to compel people to give us information. We had no power to check the veracity of their statements. So that, without the – without the ability to say no to a deal, without the ability to compel, you just were left in this sort of limbo where you tried very hard, and many people tried very hard to force the information out. But at the end of the day, with push comes to shove, people could lie to you without a penalty. (Kolchinsky 2010b, p. 43)

THE CREDIT RATING AGENCIES AND THE CHANGING ECONOMIC CONTEXT

In the mid-1970s the CRAs had started to charge fees and moved from subscriber fees to an issuer pay model. In making this change the CRAs argued the case that the issuer pay model did not represent a conflict of interest since individual issuers tended to be small, generating about 1 per cent of CRA revenues, so that losing an issuer to a competitor was a non-issue (SEC 2003). However Macey (2003) was able to point out that this argument was only relevant as long as the CRAs were rating corporate bonds. However, that context changed after 2000 when the CRAs' main business became the ratings of MBS and CDOs and where the market was now dominated by 12 underwriters that accounted for 80 per cent of the deals and when losing a deal became a major concern. Moody's could not afford to lose a rating to another competitor like S&P or Fitch. Each rating agency was determined to maintain market share. The loss of market share signified failure and loss of confidence on the part of the issuers. This created a climate where the concern was market share and where analysts had to explain their reluctance to agree on a rating; and if analysts proved to be difficult they were removed:

> The failure of the rating agencies can be seen as an example of regulatory capture, a term used by economists to describe a scenario where a regulator acts in the benefit of the regulated instead of the public interest.
> In this case, the quasi regulators were the rating agencies, the regulated included banks and broker/dealers, and the public interest lay in the guarantee which taxpayers provide for the financial system. (Kolchinsky 2010b, p. 19)

This concentration of issuers had shifted the balance of power to the issuers who could now argue they could always go to a competing rating agency to get a rating if the rating agency was proving to be difficult. In this new climate rating agencies found it difficult to walk away from a deal:

I'll start with an analogy to describe the market players. Picture the organizations in the financial markets as animals roaming an open plain. The hedge funds were wolves, hunting in packs, eating what they killed. The investment banks were a now extinct species of predatory cats, saber-toothed tigers, larger and more powerful than the hedge funds. The money center banks were the elephants, big, indestructible, almost a feature of the landscape. And the rating agencies? They were definitely the goats – specifically, the scapegoats. The analogy is almost perfect. From the perspective of the other market players, rating agencies fought over scraps to perform a necessary but lowly task . . .

The last reason that large rating agencies like Moody's are too popular as scapegoats is the glaring conflict of interest at the heart of their business model. They are paid by the issuers they rate. (Witt 2010, p. 7)

There were three possible mechanisms by which the CRAs influenced the financial crisis of 2007. First, the rating agencies were facilitators of the process because of their triple-A ratings of asset backed securities, including residential mortgage backed securities (RMBS) the collating of collateralized debt obligations made up of different RMBS and synthetic CDS. These triple-A ratings increased the demand for these asset backed securities by institutional investors including pension funds. Secondly, the original lenders of mortgages could now offload their holdings of mortgages to investment banks that turned these mortgages into pools of mortgage backed securities with the original lender now having new funds to generate new mortgages. This process of securitization contributed to a climate of disavowal of responsibility. Mortgage originators no longer had the responsibility for holding to a mortgage until the mortgage had been paid off. The investment banks that securitized these mortgages had no major concern for due diligence, since their aim was to get a rating for the securities and being able to offload these to the investor. Equally, the ratings agencies made clear on their websites that they had no responsibility for due diligence and that therefore it was up to the investor to carry out due diligence in making the decisions to purchase an asset backed security. Originators of mortgages, including mortgage brokers, now had the incentive to sell high cost mortgages to consumers since these higher cost mortgages provided them with higher income fees. Third, the triple-A rating reduced capital requirements to be held by banks, which in turn created a climate for higher leverage by banks and increased exposure to mortgage pools. Triple-A ratings meant reduced risks on assets which in turn required less capital requirements. Institutional investors, including pension funds, diverted their portfolios to mortgage backed securities so that when the crunch came these institutional investors were faced with heavy loss, which in turn affected pension payments and municipalities that had invested in RMBS securities. Finally, the decision to revise downwards the ratings of large numbers of MBS and CDOs during July 2007 also contributed to undermining an already brittle market confidence. CDO sales dried up in 2008 and banks were left with large numbers of unsold mortgage pools.

One of the many paradoxes during the financial meltdown of 2007 was what seemed to be a rush by the major investment banks in the securitization of a number of mortgage-based CDOs when the signals were already clear that the housing market had peaked and house prices were starting to fall. The Zandi Report (Zandi et al. 2006) had already in October 2006 predicted a crash in house prices. Furthermore, there were other reports during 2007. However, in October 2006, immediately after the release of the Zandi Report, the CDO rating jumped from $20 billion to $40 billion. In January 2007, after the issue of a second report by Moody's, the rating again jumped from $10 billion to $55 billion. In the space of 90 days the ratings of CDOs jumped by 60 and 70 per cent. When the logic would have been to slow down the number of ratings, securitizations actually assumed a more rapid pace. Moody's increased the rate of CDO ratings after October 2006 from $10 billion a month to $40 billion in April 2007. In October 2006, with the housing market showing the first signs of decline in house prices – by 2 per cent – and an increase in the number of defaults, Moody's report, authored by Chief Economist Mark Zandi (Zandi et al. 2006), warned that there would be a crash in house prices and that the decline would be in double digits:

> Reinforcing the shift from housing boom to bust is the rapidly-exiting investor. Higher borrowing costs, more cautious lenders, and, most importantly, the realization that house prices were no longer headed higher have induced flippers to stop buying, and if possible, to sell. Longer-term investors are also re-evaluating their strategies. Even if they were willing to look through the likely near-term weakening in housing values, it is difficult to justify such an investment as the cash or income return on housing has fallen sharply in recent years. (Zandi 2006, p. 16)

In 2007 the five investment banks seemed to be in a hurry to shift a number of loans which they still held on their balance sheet to securitized CDOs. Issuers were putting increased pressures on the CRAs to conclude ratings in shorter time spans, despite the fact that the ratings agencies did not have the additional staffing to meet the extra demands and were therefore becoming more dependent on the hiring of less experienced analysts. A series of emails from within Standard & Poor's, published as exhibits at the enquiry on 23 April 2010 reinforced the concerns of the analysts on staff shortages:

> From Ernestine Warner Director of Finance Surveillance writing about her concerns on staff shortages and the pressure on ratings of RMBS. [There were

something like 5900 transactions and the Director was losing key members of staff because of promotions]:
Unfortunately, the timing could not be worse. RMBS has an all time high of 5900 transactions. Each time I consider what my group is faced with, I become more and more anxious. The situation with Lal, being off line or out of the group, is having a huge impact. Ernestine Warren
Sent: Friday, April 28, 2006 2:11 PM **To**: Chun, Roy Subject: **RE**: Discussion with Lal Ernestine Warner, Director, Standard and Poor's Structured Finance Surveillance

In addition to the project above that involves some 863 deals, I have a back log of deals that are out of date with regard to ratings. When Steve and Kristie join the group as research assistants, they will take on the responsibilities of Jessica Rivera and some from Ash Rao so that Jessica can review the deals full time and Ash can review them maybe 50% of the time. This will help cover the void Lal left when he became the business analyst for the initiative, but again, does not move us any closer to FTS in the short term. We recognize that I am still understaffed with these two additional bodies. Lal being offline clearly exacerbates this problem and we may be falling further behind at the rate the deals are closing. If we do no not agree on the actual number, certainly we can agree that I need more recourse if I am ever going to be near compliance.
Sent: Thursday, June 01, 2006 11:46 AM **To**: Chun, Roy Coyne, Patrick. (United States Senate 2010)

THE SECURITIZATION PROCESS

The process of securitization has been described as being a major financial innovation that has contributed to faster economic growth. Major industries were increasingly using derivatives to finance their borrowings and since OTC derivatives were highly customized large companies were resorting to derivatives, which was also a cheaper way to fund investment (Stulz 2009):

For instance, a recent study that examines the use of derivatives by non-financial firms investigates 6,888 firms from 47 countries during 2000 and 2001. These firms constitute 99% of the world market capitalization. It finds that 60.5% of these firms use derivatives. The sample includes 2,076 U.S. firms and 65.1% of these firms use derivatives. The study concludes that using derivatives makes firms less risky and worth more. In 2009, ISDA conducted a survey of derivatives usage by the world's largest corporations, those corporations in the Fortune Global 500. The survey finds that 94% of the world's largest corporations use derivatives. (Stulz 2009, p. 7)

Derivatives had also facilitated home ownership, as the process of securitization allowed for grater lending, spreading risk and thus making mortgage loans cheaper and so increasing efficiency in financial markets in the allocation of savings and easing the use of collateral such as housing to increase household consumption (Greenspan 2010). It is estimated that securitization has funded between 30 and 75 per cent of lending in various markets, including an estimated 59 per cent of outstanding home mortgages. Furthermore, securitization played a critical role in non-mortgage consumer credit, including credit card purchases, and in the car industry where a substantial portion of sales were being financed through asset backed securities. The CDO ABS collated pools of mortgages, credit card debt and auto sales. Securitization had become a means for facilitating over 25 per cent of outstanding US consumer credit:

Housing assets as a class were worth approximately $22 trillion within a context of total household wealth of $65 trillion. There were over $12 trillion of outstanding securitized assets, including mortgage backed securities (MBS), asset backed securities (ABS), and asset backed commercial paper.

The securitization of mortgages represented a shift from the traditional originate and hold mortgage process to an originate and distribute model. The originate and hold model meant that banks had to carry out due diligence in the lending of money to mortgage applicants since the lender would hold the mortgage until the mortgage had been repaid. Careful documentation on employment, salaries and income tax returns ensured that mortgage holders were able to meet their monthly payments. By contrast, the originate and distribute model created by securitization meant that there was little downside for those originating the mortgages since their main concern was the making of fee income, being paid the fee being paid immediately when the transaction was completed, and then moving the mortgages to brokers for securitization, who in return were also paid fess for collating mortgage pools.

The process of pooling loans and turning these into investment bonds facilitated a process that allowed the easy movement of savings into consumer demand. It is estimated that during the peak of the securitization process about $3 trillion a year was being securitized. Due to the process of securitization banks and mortgage brokers were able to sell mortgages they held to investors, thus realizing new forms and additional income to offer new mortgages. Furthermore, a climate of low interest rates that started in 2000 meant cheaper loans. Savings arriving from China and other emerging economies meant a high demand for US Treasury bonds, which in turn continued to provide a low interest rates environment. Banks were now awash with savings and investors seeking higher yields. Securitization of thousands of mortgages into bonds provided stable repayments for a long period. The payment of principal and interest rate payments could be sold, providing steady incomes for investors. Investment banks holding large pools of mortgages now securitized the pools as asset backed bonds. Within a pool containing about one million mortgages issuers of potential bonds rated the mortgage pool in terms of default. One million mortgages were less likely to default than 100 mortgages, and since the mortgage would contain a representative sample from all regions the assumption was that there would be low correlations within a mortgage pool. Detailed analysis of each mortgage entry in terms of documentation, for example pay slips, income tax returns, evidence of employment, was left to the mortgage originators.

Analysts at both Moody's and S&P used various models to forecast the levels of default within a mortgage backed security. The rating agencies in processing the forecast were not responsible for due diligence in the content with an RMBS. Their duty was not to analyse individual entries to explore documentation or mortgage testing. These were assumed as being correct. Modelling was done using traditional 30-year mortgages that had little history of default. MBS securities were made up of pooled mortgages. An arranger or issuer of an MBS bond would seek to pool about 1000 mortgages worth an equivalent of $1 billion. The mortgage repayments defined the worth of the bond. The bond will be diced and sold in tranches with senior tranches being the safest and making the first claims on the repayments and mezzanine tranches which received higher rates of interest but which also faced the higher risks of default.

THE DEVELOPMENT OF COLLATERALIZED DEBT OBLIGATIONS

Ratings of CDOs increased from $10 billion a month in 2004 to $40 billion a month in 2007, despite a number of early warnings in 2006 that the housing market was already peaking and showing signs of stress. Collateralized debt obligations (CDOs) were made up of already securitized MBS and ABS. Within a CDO, therefore, there were already a number of rated bonds. However, since a CDO could be worth billions of dollars there would be millions of individual mortgage entries, car loans, credit card and student loans all pooled within the CDO. Rating a CDO was complex. However, during the peaks in the numbers of CDO transactions analysts were expected to take only a couple of weeks to rate a CDO.

Synthetic CDOs and CDOs squared were one step removed from mortgage based securities. Synthetic CDOs were often made up of a number of indices including the ABX index and also included CDS (credit default swaps) on respective CDOs. A credit default swap sought to imitate a CDO that contained MBS. The CDS was actually a forecast that certain

CDOs were likely to default. The arranger and investor in the synthetic CDO had to tailor and customize it to the needs of the buyer and the seller, with the investment bank usually acting as the market maker. A prime example was the ABACUS CDO that was arranged between Goldman Sachs and John Paulson, who selected the CDOs to be included in the synthetic CDO before the CDO was rated by Moody's. Hedge funds that wanted to short the ABX index were attracted to the purchase of synthetic CDOs. The increased use of synthetic CDOs was thus leading to a correlation creep, since most CDOs contained the same mortgages and these MBS were being recycled into new CDOs.

CDOs of asset backed securities were analysed with a different mathematical method (Monte Carlo simulations/Gaussian Copula). This new technique was introduced in early 2000. The default probability and correlation assumptions used with this new (Monte Carlo/Gaussian Copula) approach were more 'relaxed' than the assumptions used with the Binominal Model. Arturo Cifuentes, an ex Moody's analyst and now Professor at the Department of Industrial Engineering at the University of Chile, in giving evidence to the Senate Committee on 23 April 2010, described the modelling of the MBS as being in three stages:

First Stage: The Input of Data. Each mortgage entry is part of the input data showing default probability of the assets in the pool to be securitized, in essence as an estimate of the credit risk associated with the assets. At this stage the analyst depended on the issuer to input on a spreadsheet the soundness of each mortgage, assuming that each mortgage had proper due diligence. Things could therefore go wrong in the input process, especially if the data was erroneous or did not represent the real risk of each entry.

Second Stage: Model Building. Furthermore, in the building of the model there was sometimes a problem of insufficient historic data points to test the robustness of the model. Sub-prime and Alt-A mortgages were new products and therefore there was insufficient historical data to predict how the new mortgages were likely to behave. Sub-prime loans were different from traditional loans and more historic data was needed to predict how the sub-prime mortgages were behaving and how they were likely to behave in the event of increases in interest rates and falling house prices.

Third Stage: The Correlation Score. The role of the model was to predict the rate of correlation in the pool and the likelihood that all the assets in the pool might default together. A high correlation score indicated that the assets in the pool were highly clustered, that is coming from the same mortgage family issued by the same originator or being clustered in the same geographical area. Low correlations were therefore desirable, which meant more diversity in the input data to deliver lower correlation scores. The modelling of the data aimed to capture two things: the structural characteristics of the pool and a probable forecast of future trends. The model could produce misleading results if the assumptions built into the process were no longer relevant, that is the context and environment had changed while the model remained static, which meant that models needed to be updated and reviewed to capture changing contexts.

Cifuentes pointed out to the enquiry that he started to feel uneasy about the modelling process from 2000 when model builders started to make frequent modifications to the Moody's model. The analyst argued that this process reflected concern at Moody's with market share and the need to modify models to ensure that the ratings remained within the triple-A category, and so the model builders were using assumptions which were more forgiving when it came to modelling sub-prime mortgages (Cifuentes 2010).

> One might be tempted to suspect that they were 'improving' their methodologies (making them more flexible or forgiving) to maintain or increase their market share. In any event, any back-of-the-envelope analysis of some of the transactions rated in that time-frame [2001–2006] leaves one with the impression that more 'forgiving' assumptions were being introduced in terms of the key input data used in the rating process. Finally, it is fair to conclude that the result of all these changes in the methodologies that were implemented in the 2001–2006 period were behind the dismal performance of the ratings. In fact, all the corrections to their assumptions that the rating agencies have incorporated lately validate this perception. (Cifuentes 2010, p. 7)

S&P used a model called the Loan Evaluation and Estimate of Loss System (LEVELS) Model. S&P collected from the arranger of a securitization up to 70 different data points related to each underlying mortgage loan, including the amount of equity a borrower had in the home, the loan type, the extent of income verification, whether the borrower occupies the home, and the purpose of the loan. The analysis of this data allowed S&P to quantify multiple risk factors and assess the increased default probability that is associated with each factor. Based on the individual loan characteristics, the LEVELS model calculated probabilities of default and loss realized upon default. S&P also made its LEVELS model available on licence to investors and publicly announced any changes to the LEVELS model.

Raiter (2010) outlined the problem of delays at S&P to introduce a new computing model that would have taking into consideration the changing housing market. S&P had been working on a model with a sample of 260,000 households while the new module sought to capture a sample of 2 million. Raiter argued that resources were not made available to allow the model to be put on stream, that there was a fear that the new model will show that a number of securities would need to be downgraded and that introducing a new computing model would create uncertainty for issues and that the clients would move to competing ratings agencies. The study of internal emails within S&P confirm that S&P delayed the decision to deploy version 6 because of concerns that the revised model with a large sample that reflected the new mortgages and their rates of default would require existing CDO securities to be downgraded, disrupt the CDO market, and reduce public confidence in its CDO ratings.

> The version of LEVELS model developed in 1996 was based on a data set of approximately 250,000 loans. It was, I believe, the best model then used by a rating agency. Analysts continued to collect larger data sets for the next versions of the model. In late 2002 or early 2003, another version of the model was introduced based on approximately 650,000 loans. At the same time, a data set of approximately 2.8 million loans was collected for use in developing the next version of the model. That analysis suggested that the model in use was underestimating the risk of some Alt-A and subprime products. In spite of this research, the development of this model was postponed due to a lack of staff and IT resources. (Raiter 2010, p. 2)

HISTORY AND CHANGING CONTEXTS

Credit ratings have for over a century been dominated by a very small number of ratings agencies. The first credit ratings were recorded in 1909 when John Moody rated US railway bonds, followed by the Poor Publishing Company in 1916, the Standard Statistics Company in 1922 and Fitch Publishing Company in 1924. After the stock market crash of 1929 the CRAs went into decline. The ratings agencies were perceived as not important since information on companies was publicly available. In 1975 the SEC officially recognized S&P, Moody's, and Fitch as NRSROs (Nationally Recognized Securities Ratings Organizations). The SEC, through a series of no-action letters, established the three CRAs as qualified for NRSRO designation. This shift in regulatory reform corresponded to a change in the economics of the credit rating industry. CRAs abandoned their historical practice of charging investors for subscriptions and instead began charging issuers for ratings on the basis of the size of the issue. As additional regulations came to depend more on NRSRO ratings, those ratings became more important and more valuable.

The CRAs are odd beasts: They are private firms with public purposes – hence the term credit rating *agencies*, not credit rating firms. They are fully private in terms of ownership, employees and, in general, revenues. Still, some analysts argue that the CRAs are 'more properly viewed as quasi-government entities' because they serve the public function of determining (under existing regulations) which securities can (or cannot) be held by other regulated businesses. (Rom 2009, p. 643)

During the 1980s the business of rating bonds continued to expand. In 1980, there were approximately 30 professionals working in the S&P Industrials group while in 1986 there were still only 40. By the mid-1990s the landscape of the CRA started to change dramatically. By 1997, Moody's was rating 20,000 public and private issuers in the United States and about 1200 non-US issuers, including both corporations and sovereign states. S&P rated slightly fewer in each category. Moody's rated $5 trillion worth of securities; S&P rated $2 trillion. In 2000, after a number of mergers and restructuring, the three major rating agencies remaining were Moody's, Standard & Poor's (S&P), and Fitch. These three ratings agencies now dominated global markets. Standard & Poor's had 40 per cent of global ratings, Moody's Investors Service had 39 per cent, and Fitch, 16 per cent (Whithead and Mathis 2007). The CRAs could be described as a hybrid in that they were private firms but at same time they were seen as performing a public function, hence the term credit rating *agencies*, not credit rating *firms*. The CRAs were more properly viewed as quasi-government entities' (Macey 2002, p. 1)

Institutional investors including pension funds, local governments, charities and mutual money funds have all come to increasingly depend on the ratings defined by the ratings agencies. The role of credit rating agencies is therefore the rating of the creditworthiness of financial instruments, including corporate bonds, mortgage backed securities and CDOs with the aim of providing a forecast on the likelihood that debt will be repaid, with triple-A ratings defining the safest instruments while ratings below designated investment level at greater risk of default. Investments with triple-A ratings have historically had an expected loss rate of less than 0.05 percent, while the expected loss rate for triple-B investments was under 1 percent. Triple-A credit rated bonds are estimated as holding to that rating for a period of at least seven years. Gordy and Willemann's (2010) study for the Federal Reserve took the specific case study of the Constant Proportion Debt Obligation (CPDO) bonds which appeared at the peak of the market for structured credit products. The CPDO represented 'the poster child' with its complexity and its vulnerability to market volatility. Moody's rated one such CPDO (issued by UBS in March 2007) as triple-A; the issue was downgraded to below investment grade in November

2007. The model used by Moody's to rating this issue must have been that of a 1 to 250,000 chance of default:

> When credit markets came under stress in 2007, CPDOs were among the first to unravel. The first CPDO default, on a financial-only CPDO issued by UBS, arrived in late November 2007.The defaulted notes had been rated AAA by Moody's at issuance in March 2007. To have met this rating standard, the modeled likelihood of default within a year must have been less than 1 in 250,000. Since 1920, no AAA rated corporate bond has ever defaulted within a two year horizon. (Gordy and Willemann 2010, p. 2)

Standard & Poor's defined the status of its rating process as follows:

> Standard & Poor's issuer credit rating is a current opinion of an obligor's overall financial capacity (its creditworthiness) to pay its financial obligations. This opinion focuses on the obligor's capacity and willingness to meet its financial commitments as they come due. The issuer credit rating is not a recommendation to purchase, sell, or hold a financial obligation issued by an obligor, as it does not comment on market price or suitability for a particular investor. (Standard & Poor's n.d.)

Furthermore, the CRAs had also made clear in their declarations that they were not responsible for carrying out due diligence on the contents that defined a bond or security. Due diligence was assumed to be the obligation of the issuer to ensure the accuracy of each entry. Accuracy therefore depended on the issuer or on the originators of the mortgage entry. The new computerized system provided a limited analysis of FICO (Fair Isaac Corporation) credit scores: the concentration of mortgages in one region, the type of mortgages. There was no room for soft information gathering on mortgage holders.

> Unlike other gatekeepers, the credit rating agencies do not perform due diligence or make its performance a precondition of their ratings . . . the credit rating agencies do not make any significant effort to verify the facts on which their models rely. Rather, they simply accept the representations and data provided them by issuers, loan originators and underwriters. The problem this presents is obvious and fundamental: no model, however well designed, can outperform its information inputs – Garbage, In; Garbage Out. (Coffee 2009, p. 3)

On their part, the issuers structured the transactions, identified potential buyers for the securities, and underwrote those securities. For the system to function properly, the assumption was that participants would fulfil their roles and obligations to verify and validate information before they passed it on to the rating agencies. The role of the ratings agency in the process was to reach an opinion as to the ability of the underlying loans to generate sufficient proceeds to pay the purchasers of the securities. The Chairman and Chief Executive, Raymond McDaniel, outlined the due diligence process in his testimony to Congress on 23 April 2010 as follows:

> Registered securities have named underwriters who are expected to perform the due diligence function on the security to be issued. Moreover, every structured product that securitizes underlying loans has a primary lender or seller who performs a loan underwriting function. A common practice is for a securitization's underwriter to hire a due diligence firm (or to have an internal team) to investigate whether the underlying loans are in compliance with the originator's stated underwriting criteria; the originator is generally required to buy back loans that are subsequently revealed to be in violation of its stated criteria. Accounting firms are charged with verifying that the summary information of the loan pools in the prospectus matches the underlying characteristics of the pool. (McDaniel 2010, p. 7)

Between 2000 and 2006, investment banks sought ratings for nearly $4 trillion in mortgage backed securities, 36 per cent of which were backed by sub-prime mortgages. All of those securities needed ratings. It is estimated that Moody's and S&P each rated about 10,000 RMBS securities (Levin 2010). In the meantime the three ratings agencies also doubled their revenues from $3 billion to over $6 billion. The CRAs charged fees ranging between $50,000 to $1 million, depending on the complexity of the structured product. From 2004 to 2007, S&P issued ratings for more than 5700 RMBS transactions and 835 CDO transactions, while Moody's issued ratings for nearly 4000 RMBS transactions and 870 CDO transactions. Between 2000 and 2007, Moody's rated $4.7 trillion in RMBS and $736 billion in CDOs (Angelides 2010). Moody's was charging fees of 4.75 per cent for securities rated as triple-A and 3.5 per cent for those rating below AA. Furthermore, for rating a CDO Moody's was charging fees of 9 per cent.

> I want to make sure it's true, that, for many years, Moody's, in charging issuers on RMBS analysis, you charged a certain rate, in this instance 4.75 basis points for the dollars that were in the senior tranches, and 3.75 basis points for the dollars that were put in subordinate tranches, which strikes me as an incentive, creating a financial incentive for Moody's to put a greater percentage of the dollars in the senior, superior tranches. (Georgiou 2010, p. 451)

Eighty-three per cent of these bonds were downgraded as below investment grade, starting in July 2007. In July 2007 S&P downgraded 612 sub-prime RMBS with an original value of $7.3 billion, and Moody's downgraded 399 sub-prime RMBS with an original value of $5.2 billion. Moody's calculated that, overall in 2007, 8725 ratings from 2116 deals were downgraded and 1954 ratings from 732 deals were upgraded. In January 2008 S&P downgraded over 6300 sub-prime RMBS securities and over 1900 CDO securities, an unprecedented mass downgrade. In 2006, $869 billion worth of mortgage securities were triple-A rated by Moody's.

> Moody's was a Triple-A factory. In 2006 alone, Moody's gave 9,029 mortgage backed securities a Triple-A rating. That means they put the Triple-A label on more than 30 mortgage securities each and every working day that year. To put that in perspective, Moody's currently bestows its Triple-A rating on just four American corporations. Even Berkshire Hathaway, with its more than $20 billion cash on hand, doesn't make that grade. (Angelides 2010, p. 2)

THE ISSUE OF CULTURE

Understanding the ratings process requires an analysis of structure. Usually this means exploring the decision-making processes, the professional ethics and the prevailing culture within the rating agency and how that environment is shaped and defined. In a study of the evidence given at the Committee enquiries into the rating agencies, one common theme that emerges is the conflict between a business model of the ratings agency that gave priority to market share and the perceptions of the analysts who saw their role as making sure that they provided accurate ratings. Froeba (2010) described the drive towards market share as a cultural revolution at Moody's when a new managerialist ethic became ascendant, with managers sending messages through emails about the importance of maintaining market share.

> First, they 'reeducated' Moody's rating analysts – primarily structured finance analysts – that cooperation with the new culture would be rewarded and opposition punished. Essentially, they used intimidation to create a docile population of analysts afraid to upset investment bankers and ready to cooperate to the maximum extent possible. Second, they emboldened investment bankers, gave them confidence that they could stand up to Moody's analysts and gave them reason to believe that Moody's management would, where necessary, support the bankers against its own analysts. (Froeba 2010, p.1)

Analysts involved in the ratings process saw their role as providing accurate ratings. The ratings process therefore involved research and building more robust models to try to understand the changing macroeconomic context and readings of research papers. Analysts therefore saw their role as ensuring the ratings were accurate and that they would not jeopardize Moody's historic reputation:

> When I joined Moody's in late 1997, an analyst's worst fear was that he would contribute to the assignment of a rating that was wrong, damage Moody's reputation for getting the answer right and lose his job as a result. When I left

Moody's, an analyst's worst fear was that he would do something that would allow him to be singled out for jeopardizing Moody's market share, for impairing Moody's revenue or for damaging Moody's relationships with its clients and lose his job as a result. (Froeba 2010, p. 10)

The concept of culture is interesting since culture is not something which is tangible or solid but rather a feeling of a prevailing climate. Raymond McDaniel (2010), the CEO at Moody's, disputed the evidence given by the Moody's analysts and argued that there was no conflict between Moody's business model and the culture of analysis. Analysis, he argued, always prevailed. The CEO pointed out that data collection was stringent and that there was no interference with the impartiality and objectivity of the analysts. By contrast, the analysts' argument was that while no one said explicitly that market share was paramount, the pressure was that unless they rated the security their competitors would step in and do the rating. Market share was therefore about not losing a transaction, and if an analyst argued about revising a computation model the anxiety this would have created meant that the pressure was to stay with existing models even when signals starting showing that the models did not hold for the new types of mortgages.

Mr Frank Raiter, who from 1995 until his retirement in 2005, had been a Managing Director and Head of the Residential Mortgage Rating Group at Standard & Poor's, in his testimony and oral evidence described the analysts as the soldiers in the trenches who were getting little support and guidance from their managers. It was the analysts who tried to maintain standards in their ratings – 'keeping up the good fight': 'Analytical managers were driven by the desire to create and implement the best risk analytical models and methodologies possible. Senior management, on the other hand, was focused on revenue, profit and ultimately share price' (Raiter 2010, p. 4).

The continuous pressure of market share meant that rating agencies were reluctant to walk away from a rating, since a rating meant fees and the maintenance of market share. Kolchinsky (2009), also a former Moody's CDO analyst, pointed out that the market share culture meant that analysts felt unable to walk away from a rating and that analysts felt intimidated by threats of redundancy or were silenced:

> The conflicts of interest which ail the ratings industry remain unmanaged. Senior management still favors revenue generation over ratings quality and is willing to dismiss or silence those employees who disagree with these unwritten policies . . . the Credit Policy Group at Moody's remains weak and short staffed. The group's analysts get routinely bullied by business-line managers and their decisions are over-ridden in the name of generating revenue. (Kolchinsky 2010a, p. 3)

Kolchinsky's dissenting testimony did not go unanswered. In his testimony, Cantor (2009) referred directly to Kolchinsky:

> Finally, let me briefly turn to the allegations raised by Mr. Kolchinsky. In his August 28 memorandum, Mr. Kolchinsky restated his views that certain rating decisions were improper because Moody's should have applied a new and different methodology to assess certain aspects of certain transactions. Mr. Kolchinsky has raised an evolving series of claims of misconduct. As our counsel has informed the Committee, Moody's Compliance Group had reviewed such allegations when they were raised and had determined them to be unsupported. (Cantor 2009, p. 9)

However, the Chairman of the Committee, Edolphus Towns, admonished Moody's response to Kolchinsky's testimony, especially their approach to an outside firm, Kramer Levin, investigating Kolchinsky's allegations, by only giving oral instructions to Kramer Levin and supplying no written report or contract. The absence of written contracts or written reports prevented any attempt to compile a written record. Towns called this process as 'leaving no fingerprints'. In addition, Towns in his closing statement welcomed the courage of Kolchinsky in giving evidence to his committee:

> This culture of secrecy extended to companies outside Moody's as well. Moody's tells us they retained an outside law firm, Kramer Levin, to investigate Mr. Kolchinsky's allegations of illegal conduct at Moody's. But this morning we learned that this outside firm was given only oral instructions. Moody's says there is no written statement of work and no contract specifying the work to be done . . .
>
> I want to thank our two witnesses, Mr. Kolchinsky and Mr. McCleskey, who had the courage to come forward to testify about what they saw at Moody's. I am aware that testifying before Congress is never easy. We appreciate your participation. (Towns 2009, p. 4)

MARKET SHARE AND SHORT-TERM PERSPECTIVES

Investment banks were the issuers of the securities that needed to be rated. Issuers put pressure on analysts to complete ratings within periods of between one and two weeks, when, normally, complex ratings would have taken two months. At the peak of the ratings process CDO teams and MBS teams were often understaffed. Investment banks also put pressure on the managers at Moody's and S&P not to send what they described as difficult analysts on some ratings. Richard Michalek and Kolchinsksy in their evidence pointed out that they had been removed from their posts they felt because they had been awkward. Yoshizawa, a manager at Moody's, in her evidence suggested that she did not remove analysts from deals because of pressures from the issuers but rather to safeguard the analyst from harassment. Levin, the Chairman, concluded from this evidence that the investment banks were still getting what they wanted.

Investment banks could also put pressure on the ratings agency suggesting that the failure to approve a rating meant that the client, being the client, could always go to a rival rating agency and get a rating. The drive to maintain market share meant that ratings agencies could not 'walk away from a deal'.

Pressures of Maintaining Market Share and Concern with the Short Term

Chairman Levin presented a series of emails reminders from senior mangers as to the importance that Moody's maintain market share, and when market share for some ratings fell from 98 per cent to 94 per cent middle managers were asked to provide explanations. Some analysts argued that the priority of market share was undermining the due process of qualitative analysis. Fees depended on completions of ratings.

The acronym, IBGYBG, standing for 'I'll be gone, you'll be gone', was outlined by Richard Michalek (2010), a Former Creditor Officer at Moody's, in his testimony on 23 April 2010 to the Permanent Subcommittee on Investigations. In his evidence, Michalek explained the discussion that he had had with an issuer at Deutsche Bank. The phrase epitomized the culture of the securitization process. Issuers collating CDOs and seeking ratings, and ratings agencies providing the ratings, were seen as short-term preoccupations where the concern was fees, bonuses and maintaining market share without thinking of future implications. That short-term approach reflected the process from mortgage origination to the making of loans to investment banks, collating pools and putting these into tranches, to lawyers fees, with actors at each stage looking at the moment rather than at the wider macro context.

> The incentives for the 'fee-based' structuring investment bank were clear: get the deal closed, and if there's a problem later on, it was just another case of 'IBGYBG' – 'I'll be gone, you'll be gone.' (First quoted to me by an investment banker who was running out of patience with my insistence on a detailed review of the documentation.) (Michalek 2010)

THE ISSUER PAY MODEL AND CONFLICTS OF INTEREST

The 'issuer pay' model, which has been in use since 1970, is a process where the issuer of the security seeks the rating, and pays the rating agency for the rating. The potential conflict of interest inherent in this model is of the rating agencies having an interest in generating business from the firms that seek the rating, which would conflict with providing objective ratings, as well as a guarantee of the independence of the process and the integrity of the rating agency. The SEC rules do specify that it is a conflict of interest for an approved ratings agency to be both the underwriter and the rating agency of a security. The priority of a ratings agency is to exhibit integrity and impartial judgement in the ratings process. Analysts are therefore not allowed to participate in discussions about fees with the issuer. These policies are designed to separate those individuals who set and negotiate fees from those employees who rate the issue, in order to mitigate the possibility or perception that a rating agency would link its ratings with its fees (for example, that an analyst could explicitly or implicitly link the fee for a rating to a particular rating).

The two major ratings agencies increased their incomes from $3 billion to $6 billion during the period 2000–2007. As opposed to the procedural framework, the reality of the day-to-day process confirms that the issuer pay model made it difficult for the ratings agencies to walk away from a rating. Furthermore, issuers of securities could also go to a competing agency and secure a rating. Issuers who complained about the strictures imposed by some analysts were indirectly listened to, since managers at the ratings agency would always send an alternative analyst to rate a security. The concern to maintain market share with the rating agency conflicted with the concept of independence of analysis. Analysts who proved difficult in the ratings of securities were often taken away from the analysis of certain banks. In some cases awkward analysts were asked not to do ratings with certain banks, lost compensation and even their roles with the ratings agency.

Chairman Levin outlined three case studies highlighting the problems of conflict of interest to illustrate the point that ratings agencies did not walk away from a security, even when analysts were suggesting that the security might not perform.

Case Study One: Vertical ABS CDO 2007-1 – UBS and Pursuit Partners

This involved the rating of a CDO known as Vertical ABS CDO 2007-1. UBS was the major bank and they had asked both S&P and Moody's to rate this CDO. It would seem that the UBS banker failed to cooperate with the rating analysts in the supply of information. The S&P analyst recorded that the CDO was not likely to perform. However, in April 2007, despite the analyst's judgement, both S&P and Moody's gave triple-A ratings to the CDO's top four tranches. Six months later, both agencies downgraded the CDO, which later collapsed. One of the purchasers, a hedge fund called Pursuit Partners, sued over the CDO's collapse. The court found probable cause to sustain the claim by Pursuit that UBS sold the Notes to Pursuit without disclosing that the security would soon no longer carry an investment grade rating, as the ratings agencies intended to withdraw these ratings as a result of a change in methodology, and that once the investment grade rating was withdrawn, the CDO sold by UBS to Pursuit, would thereby become worthless.

In one email detailed by the court, a UBS analyst described the transaction between UBS and Pursuit as 'Sold some more crap to Pursuit' (email Malik Evans, 27 August 2007).

Case Study Two: Fremont Ratings

Correspondence on mortgage bonds issued by Fremont and which were part of an issue being compiled by Goldman Sachs became a concern for one analyst at S&P. The analyst had been reading a number of intelligence reports on Fremont which showed that Fremont was an 'outlier' in mortgage defaults and was producing unsafe mortgages. Fremont had recently broken ties with 8000 mortgage brokers:

> In January 2007, S&P was asked to rate an RMBS being assembled by Goldman Sachs using subprime loans from Fremont Investment and Loan, a subprime lender known for loans with high rates of delinquency. On January 24, 2007, an analyst wrote seeking advice from two senior analysts: 'I have a Goldman deal with subprime Fremont collateral. Since Fremont collateral has been performing not so good, is there anything special I should be aware of?' One analyst responded: 'No, we don't treat their collateral any differently.' The other asked: 'are the FICO scores current?' 'Yup,' came the reply. Then 'You are good to go.' (Levin 2010)

It would seem that the analyst did not have to factor in the history of Fremont as a possible credit risk and that mortgages issued under the Fremont label posed a question for the rating. In the spring of 2007, Moody's and S&P provided triple-A ratings for five tranches of RMBS securities backed by Fremont mortgages. By October, both companies began downgrading the CDO. Today all five triple-A tranches have been downgraded to junk status.

Case Study Three: RMBS Delphinus

In the third study the issuer of the RMBS produced 26 dummy loans to the securitization process. Furthermore, there was a problem between the closing date portfolio the issuer gave for analysis and the effective closing date. The 26 dummy assets they had included in the closing date portfolio were then replaced with 26 assets that would have made the rating worse. The SDR would have gone up and they would not have been able to close since the bond would not have passed the triple-A, but because the assets were provided after the closing date the security had already been rated.

The three case studies exhibit different worries about the ratings process but the message from all three was that, despite reservations, all the three securities were rated as triple-A and were all downgraded within six months of the rating. Management teams at the CRAs did not seem to heed the reservations of the analysts. In the case of Delphinus, the ratings agency accepted dummy mortgages at the closing date which then the issuers replaced with assets that would not have passed the ratings process and would have delayed the rating. In terms of Fremont the analyst was told to stick with the narrowness of the computation model and not to take into account the delinquency rate of mortgages originated by Fremont. Finally, in terms of UBS and Pursuit there was evidence that Moody's was sharing knowledge with their client UBS, while at the same time UBS knew that they were selling an investment to Pursuit that would soon be downgraded.

CONCLUSIONS

The concern of this chapter has been the role of the CRAs and their rating process and how the process influenced the financial crisis. While some advocates have argued that the CRAs, as with other market participants, did not anticipate the financial crisis, in this chapter the analysis has pointed to institutional failures. The CRAs' mathematical models for instance did not capture the new mortgages but the modellers continued to use the traditional 30-year mortgages to predict levels of default. Yet mortgages after 2004 have shifted towards non-documented adjustable rate mortgages dependent on FICO scores. Secondly, even when analysts expressed concern about the soundness of a rating their analysis was often ignored or marginalized. The CRAs showed little concern for the investors; the primary concern was always to maintain market share and rate bonds that were presented to the CRA by issuers. The CRAs rated about $4.7 trillion worth of asset backed securities between 2004 and 2007. Bonds that had been rated as triple-A were downgraded to below investment grade within a period of 18 months.

REFERENCES

Angelides, P. (2010) Opening Remarks of Chairman Phil Angelides at the Financial Crisis Inquiry Commission Hearing on the Credibility of Credit Ratings, the Investment Decisions Made Based on Those Ratings, and the Financial Crisis, 2 June.

Buffett, W. (2010) Chairman and Chief Executive, Berkshire Hathaway, Evidence to the FCIC Inquiry on the Credibility of Credit Rating Agencies, 2 June.

Cantor, R. (2009) Testimony of Richard Cantor, Chief Credit Officer Moody's Investors Service before the United States House of Representatives Committee on Oversight and Government Reform, 30 September.

Cifuentes, A. (2010) Testimony of Arturo Cifuentes, PhD, Department of Industrial Engineering University of Chile Santiago, Chile, U.S. Senate, 23 April, Washington, DC.

Coburn, T. (2010) Statement of Senator Tom Coburn Wall Street and the Financial Crisis: The Role of Credit Rating Agencies, 23 April.

Coffee, J. (2009) Testimony of Professor John C. Coffee, Jr. Adolf A. Berle, Professor of Law, Columbia University Law School, Before the United States Senate Committee on Banking, Housing and Urban Affairs, 5 August.

FCIC (2010) *Preliminary Staff Report: Credit Ratings and the Financial Crisis.* Financial Crisis Inquiry Commission, 2 June.

Froeba, M. (2010) Testimony of Mark Froeba Before the Financial Crisis Inquiry Commission, 2 June.

Georgiou, B. (2010) Commissioner Byron Georgiou, FCIC, Official Transcript, Hearing on Credibility of Credit Ratings, the Investment Decisions Made Based on Those Ratings, and the Financial Crisis, 2 June.

Gordy, M. and S. Willemann (2010) 'Constant Proportion Debt Obligations: A Post-Mortem Analysis of Rating Models', Finance and Economics Discussion Series, Divisions of Research & Statistics and Monetary Affairs, Federal Reserve Board, Washington, DC.

Greenspan, A. (2010) Testimony of Alan Greenspan, Financial Crisis Inquiry Commission, 7 April, Washington, DC.

Hennessey, K. (2011) Dissenting Statement of Commissioner Keith Hennessey, Commissioner Douglas Holtz-Eakin, and Vice Chairman, Bill Thomas, *The Financial Crisis Inquiry Report.* New York: Public Affairs.

Kolchinsky, E. (2010a) Statement of Eric Kolchinsky Before The Senate Permanent Subcommittee on Investigations. Hearing on Wall Street and the Financial Crisis: The Role of Credit Rating Agencies, 23 April.

Kolchinsky, E. (2010b) 'Hearing on Credibility of Credit Ratings, the Investment Decisions Made Based on Those Ratings, and the Financial Crisis', Financial Crisis Inquiry Commission Official Transcript, 2 June, New York.

Levin, C. (2010) Opening Statement of Senator Carl Levin, Wall Street and the Financial Crisis: The Role of Credit Rating Agencies, U.S. Senate Permanent Subcommittee on Investigations, 23 April.

Macey, J. (2002) Testimony before the U.S. Senate Committee on Governmental Affairs, 20 March. In *Rating the Raters: Enron and the Credit Rating Agencies, Hearings Before the Senate Committee on Governmental Affairs.* Washington, DC: Government Printing Office.

McDaniel, R.W. (2010) Testimony of Raymond W. McDaniel, Chairman and Chief Executive Officer of Moody's Corporation and Yuri Yoshizawa, Senior Managing Director Moody's Investors Service, Before the United States Senate Permanent Subcommittee on Investigation, 2 June.

Michalek, R. (2010) Statement of Richard Michalek, Former VP/Senior Credit Officer, Moody's Investors Service, Submitted to Permanent Subcommittee on Investigations, Committee on Governmental Affairs, United States Senate, 23 April.

Partnoy, F. (2006) 'How and Why Credit Rating Agencies are not like other Gatekeepers', Legal Studies Research Paper Series Research Paper No. 07-46, May.

Raiter, F. (2010) Written Statement of Frank L. Raiter On 'Wall Street and the Financial Crisis: The Role of Credit Rating Agencies' Before the Permanent Subcommittee on Investigations, United States Senate, 23 April, Washington, DC.

Rom, C. (2009) 'The Credit Rating Agencies and the Subprime Mess: Greedy, Ignorant, and Stressed?, *Public Administration Review*, **69**(4): 640–50.

Securities and Exchange Commission (SEC) (2003) *Report on the Role and Function of Credit Rating Agencies in the Operation of the Securities Market.* Available at: http://www.sec.gov/news/studies/credratingreport0103.pdf (accessed December 2010).

Securities and Exchange Commission (SEC) (2008a) *Proposed Rules for Nationally Recognized Statistical Rating Organizations.* Available at: http://www.sec.gov/rules/proposed/2008/34-57967.pdf (accessed 14 December 2010).

Securities and Exchange Commission (SEC) (2008b) *Summary Report of Issues Identified in the Commission Staff's Examinations of Select Credit Rating Agencies.* Available at: http://www.sec.gov/news/studies/2008/craexamination 070808.pdf (accessed 14 December 2010).

Standard & Poor's (n.d.) 'Standard & Poor's Issue Credit Rating Definitions'. Available at: http://pages.stern.nyu.edu/-iddy/ABS/sandpratings.htm (accessed July 2010).

Stulz, M. (2009) Testimony of René M. Stulz to the House Committee on Financial Services Over-the-Counter Derivatives Markets Act of 2009, 7 October.

Towns, E. (2009) Closing Statement, Chairman Edolphus Towns, Committee on Oversight and Government Reform Hearing: Credit Rating Agencies and the Next Financial Crisis, 30 September, Washington, DC.

United States Senate (2010) Permanent Subcommittee On Investigations Committee on Homeland Security and Governmental Affairs, Additional Exhibits, Hearing on Wall Street and the Financial Crisis: the Role of Credit Rating Agencies, 23 April.

Whithead, J. and H. Mathis (2007) 'Finding a Way Out of the Rating Agency Morass', statement submitted to the U.S. House Financial Services Committee. Subcommittee on Capital Markets, Insurance, and Government Sponsored Enterprises, 27 September.

Witt, G. (2010) Statement of Gary Witt, Former Managing Director, Moody's Investors Service. Submitted by request to the Financial Crisis Inquiry Commission, 2 June.

Yoshizawa, Y. (2010) Testimony of Raymond W. McDaniel, Chairman and Chief Executive Officer of Moody's Corporation, and Yuri Yoshizawa, Senior

Managing Director, Moody's Investors Service, Before the United States Senate Permanent Subcommittee on Investigation, 23 April.

Zandi, M., C. Chen and B. Carey (2006) *Housing at the Tipping Point: The Outlook for the US Real Estate Market*. West Chester, PA: Moody's.

6. Possible Keynesian explanations and responses

This chapter's major concern is how Keynesians would seek to explain the present financial meltdown. While there are many Keynesians and many different Keynesian traditions, the aim here will be to outline a series of arguments that are consistent with the 'Keynes' who made the case that his General Theory represented a revolution in economic thought and a departure with market liberal thinking. The financial meltdown, therefore, cannot be explained within that cluster of New Keynesian perspectives which sought a synthesis between Keynes and market economics, that is, seeking explanations around issues of market failure such as the issue of externalities or asymmetric information, as has been outlined recently by Summers (2010), Stiglitz (2010) and Haldane (2010). There is always a problem in seeking to explore what constitutes a Keynesian perspective; after all, not all those who declare themselves to be Keynesians are necessarily agreed on the central principles that define a Keynesian perspective. Attempts to define the core assumptions that shape a Keynesian perspective will always either ignore or attempt to homogenize some major and very important differences and areas of disagreements between economists who see themselves as Keynesians or post-Keynesians (Arestis and Skouras 1985). The problem is that there may be there many different types of Keynesians. As Harcourt has suggested:

> I certainly do not think that the approaches that come under this heading, though they provide important and substantial insights, have yet reached a coherent steady-state . . . the people who come under this umbrella (Keynesians) are a heterogeneous lot, sometimes only combined by a dislike of orthodox or neoclassical economics. (Harcourt 1985, p. 125)

Keynes wanted to claim that his work sought to make a break with classical economic thinking and demonstrated major flaws in the assumptions associated with classical (market) economics; and his major ambition was to replace classical economics with a superior alternative:

> I shall argue that the postulates of classical theory are applicable to a special case only and not to the general case, the situation which it assumes being a

limiting point of the possible positions of equilibrium. Moreover the characteristics of the special case assumed by the classical theory happen not to be those
of the economic society in which we actually live. (Keynes 1971, p. 3)

Keynes's starting point was to explore the nature of a capitalist
economy – not a market theory abstracted from reality, but rather how
to explain the dynamics of a capitalist economy, an economy based on
private ownership that was, therefore, inherently flawed and always likely
to be cyclical and so one that could not guarantee full employment:

> Keynes constructed a theory to explain the behavior of a capitalist economy
> which is sophisticated in its financial institutions. Such an economy is inher-
> ently flawed because it is intractably cyclical, that is such a capitalist economy
> cannot by its own processes sustain full employment, and each of a succession
> of cyclical states is transitory in the sense that relations are built up which
> transform the way in which the economy will behave. (Minsky 2008, p. 54)

In investment decisions, entrepreneurial animal spirits led to major
upswings and downswings, reflecting the sentiment and uncertainty of
optimism and pessimism. Investment decisions were not extrapolated
from the data related to past performance as a way of predicting the
future. Equally, consumers changed their sentiments about their liquidity
in terms of their levels of uncertainty. While the propensity to consume
was related to income, levels of consumption did not rise at the same rate
as rising levels of income; there was an inbuilt tendency for the savings
ratio to increase as income increased. According to Keynes this process
was likely to result in the depression of demand because of a leakage into
savings, so that even an income elasticity of 0.9, as income increased at
3 per cent a year, was likely to lead to increased savings by 3 points. The
paradox of thrift, therefore, represented a process where the individual
decision to increase savings was different from the aggregate decisions to
increase savings.

So, within a Keynesian tradition, explaining the financial crisis must
therefore include the following contributory factors.

First would be the issue of regulation and deregulation and the role of
government. Central to the theory established by Keynes was his argument that government had a central role in stabilizing economic cycles.
The repeal of Glass-Steagill, the Commodity Futures Modernization
Act, and the liberalization of financial markets would therefore be events
central to a Keynesian explanation of the financial meltdown. The shift
to a more laissez-faire policy framework after the 1980s would be the
major explanation in Keynes. The ascendance of rational expectations
and efficient markets theories provide the intellectual frameworks for

governments, starting with Mrs Thatcher in the UK and President Reagan in the US initiating a process of deregulating the financial markets

Secondly, utilizing the concept of the propensity to consume, Keynesians can explain how consumption changed as house prices changed. While house prices were rising, consumers felt their net worth was rising, which meant their savings were rising, which in turn increased consumption. Equally, the financial meltdown and the declines in household incomes meant that households now had to repair their savings, which in turn reduced consumption and aggregate demand, which then in turn resulted in unemployment.

Thirdly, Keynesians would also argue that the financial meltdown was related to the growth in income inequality and stagnant wages. While take home pay for 90 per cent of the population had remained unchanged for the past 20 years the increase in house prices allowed households to take out equity against their homes and use the additional finance to purchase consumer goods.

Economic policy making represents political choices. Embracing a market liberal economy creates different economic outcomes when compared with a Keynesian strategy. Krugman (2007) has called the years between 1950 and 1972 the year of compression. By contrast, the period since 1980 has been associated with the great divergence. The age of compression is correlated with continuing low levels of unemployment, low inflation, continuing growth rates in GDP and also rising wages. In the UK between 1950 and 1970 the number of unemployment was about 250,000. When unemployment increased to 1 million during 1972 this was seen as a major setback and the Heath government was forced, through a series of policy U-turns, to show that his government was still committed to full employment. The age of Keynes therefore created full employment and also rising wages. It was also the age of compression because of the narrowing of inequality. Higher wages and high levels of employment created a climate where the growth of the economy was also spilling over into higher take home pay. This was the post-war settlement of full employment and growing public expenditure.

The 1980s were characterized by high levels of unemployment. Unemployment in the UK averaged 2 million during the Thatcher decade, compared with 250,000 of the previous two decades. Wages as a ratio of GDP stagnated. Trade union reforms resulted in fewer strikes and fewer attempts at wage resistance. The monetarist counter-revolution aimed at dissolving the Keynesian institutional approach to policy making. The election of the Thatcher government in Britain in 1979 and that of President Reagan in the USA in 1980 seemed to confirm, for some commentators at least, the end of Keynesian thinking and the influence of

Keynes on economic policy making. Both these governments were often seen as reflecting the new mood of the market liberal counter-revolution of the 1980s, set against the Keynesian corporatism of the 1960s and the 1970s. In contrast the 1980s are associated with the rights of the individual, as against the vested interests which dominated the Keynesian era. The Thatcher decade and the impact of Margaret Thatcher's brand of market liberalism was assessed in November 1989 in a *Financial Times* editorial as follows:

> She believes in self-reliance, enterprise, thrift, law and order and a limited state. She abhors trade unions, spongers and left wing intellectuals. The triumph of these attitudes was no accident. It reflected the failure of socialist corporatism to deliver acceptable economic performance or social harmony. Her government is criticised for over-centralisation of power . . . Only a powerful state, Mrs Thatcher believes, can protect the people from the barons of corporatism. Within society more is now in the hands of the individual: but within government more is in the hands of the Prime Minister. (*The Financial Times*, 21 November 1989)

The concern was now inflation, lower levels of public expenditure and reducing the tax burden. This was the age of divergence that creating increased income inequality and contributed to the financial meltdown in 2007.

Keynesian and market liberal economy policy frameworks create different landscapes of winners and losers. Keynesian economic strategies result in narrowing inequalities and generating high wages. Workers in a context of full employment feel more secure about their jobs and seek to improve their take home pay, looking to share in the increased prosperity generated by economic growth. Market liberal strategies result in the concentration of income towards the top earners. There is a retreat from the narrowing of inequalities towards the dynamics of inequality. During the years of compression the Gini coefficient for the UK was around 0.25. Since the mid-1980s the Gini coefficient has risen to 0.34. In the USA the coefficient has risen from 0.34 in the mid-1970s to 0.44 in 2005. While the policy priority of Keynesians is full employment, market liberals' chief concern is inflation. Trade union reforms and removing trade union immunities are important to a market liberal perspective. Market liberals blame unemployment on institutional rigidities.

The UK coalition government elected in May 2010 outlined their economic policies in the June 2010 budget and the Comprehensive Spending Review of 2010 has further constructed an economic strategy that can be described as returning the economy to pre-Keynesian days. The decision to reduce public expenditure by around 80 billion by 2015 and seek a balanced budget is founded on an argument that at present government spending is crowding out the private sector. Reducing public expenditure, therefore, would allow the private sector to take the lead to produce future growth and prosperity. While the government has accepted that decisions to reduce public expenditure would create unemployment this would be of a short-term duration because the growth in the private sector would be able to absorb the unemployment rate. However, in setting a pathway for public expenditure the coalition government had implicitly accepted that the UK economy contracted by approximately 4 per cent of GDP during the period 2007 to 2009 and that this loss of GDP will be permanent. The UK economy is forecast to grow at 1.2 per cent a year between 2010 and 2015, compared to a growth trend of 12 per cent between 1989 and 2007. Public sector deficits are therefore described as being structural, in that expenditure is rising faster than potential GDP growth:

> It is essential to understand the assumptions made by the UK government in deciding its fiscal strategy. First, the government has decided that a substantial part of the GDP lost in the crisis would never return . . . In 2015 GDP is just 9.6 per cent higher than in 2007 – a compound rate of growth of just 1.2 per cent per year . . . almost 12 per cent below the 1989–2007 trend. (Wolf, 2011)

The UK coalition government has been criticized for not having a growth strategy, although there is agreement that Britain became too dependent on the financial sector and the housing market after the mid-1980s. From the mid-1980s Britain lost the highest number of jobs amongst the advanced economies in manufacturing. UK manufacturing experienced the highest rate of decline, losing some 3.2 million jobs between 1980 and 2007. Compared to the interventionist policies of Germany and Japan, the UK Government under Mrs Thatcher argued the case that the decline in manufacturing was a non issue because the New Economy of value added in finance, marketing, and insurance would replace the manufacturing sector. Now, in 2011, as the UK seeks to ask the question where does growth come from, the focus on export and manufacturing seems to be the new vogue.

The coalition strategy rests on the implicit assumption that reductions in public expenditure will provide the room for increased private sector investment. Obviously, this policy approach relies on the argument that public expenditure is crowding out the private sector, even though interest rates are around 0.5 per cent. Also it relies on the Bacon and Eltis (1978) thesis which said that public expenditure was non marketable and therefore did not contribute to GDP. Public expenditure just redistributed resources and it was only private investment that generated growth, an argument recently echoed by Eugene Fama:

> The problem is simple: bailouts and stimulus plans are founded by issuing government debt (the money must come from somewhere). The added debt absorbs savings that would otherwise go to private investment. In the end, despite the existence of idle resources, bailouts and stimulus plans do not add to current resources in use. They just move resources from one use to another. (Fama, quoted in Skidelsky 2009, p. 48)

Obviously such an argument can only hold if it is accepted that health care and education and other infrastructure expenditures do not contribute to GDP growth. It is more ideology to argue that only the private sector expenditure contributes to GDP growth. Teachers do educate a future generation of people to give them the skills to seek employment. The relationship between the private and public sector has become more interdependent, with public sector contracts being procured by the private sector. The concept of an economy divided between a marketable and non-marketable sector is rather misleading and out of date in a modern economy.

In the meantime, the Obama stimulus package of $870 billion has been criticized because it has failed to reduce unemployment to 8 per cent, as was forecast by the Obama advisory group. In 2011 US unemployment is still around 9.4 per cent. The Obama fiscal stance has recently been heavily criticized by the Chairman on Oversight and Government Reform, the Republican Representative Darrell Issa, for returning to failed Keynesian economics:

> The abysmal results came as no surprise to those who knew that the Keynesian doctrine of spending your way to prosperity had been discredited decades ago . . . In response to the stimulus package Prof Barro said: 'It would be unfortunate if the best Team Obama can offer is an unvarnished version of Keynes' . . . the financial crisis and possible depression do not invalidate everything we have learnt about macroeconomics since 1936. (Issa 2011)

The Chairman of the Oversight Committee provides an argument which is expunged of historical context, an argument that does not acknowledge the condition of the US economy in 2008 and early 2009, the sharp declines in GDP and the argument that the financial meltdown was creating a situation in which the US economy was falling off a cliff in those early days of the financial crisis. By 2009 US GDP had contracted by 6.4 per cent and unemployment had been rising by 600,000 a month; unemployment expanded from 4.6 per cent in 2007 to 9.4 per cent in 2009 – the highest jump in US unemployment since the depression of 1929. Issa and his supporters do not evaluate the countervailing argument of whether without the Obama stimulus unemployment would have been even higher.

THE KEYNESIAN REVOLUTION

In 1984, reflecting on both the 50th anniversary of the publication of Keynes's *General Theory of Employment*, and the impact that the economics of Keynes had on the thinking of other economists and also of government, Lord Kaldor suggested that, 'Nearly 50 years after [*General Theory*'s] appearance controversy still rages around its basic ideas and prescriptions, and I do not think that any major economist in the West would regard the issues raised by Keynes as finally settled' (Kaldor 1984, p. 1).

Nixon's 1972 declaration that we are all Keynesians now was correct (Davidson 2009). Keynes's argument for government intervention was always going to be more than a technical economic argument about the fiscal stance or the budget deficit – it was about the long-term role of government within the economy. In 2011 most of the advanced economies can be defined as Keynesian economies in the sense that public expenditure is a permanent part of the economic landscape, with government averaging around 40 per cent of GDP – that includes social expenditures on health, education and social security, as well as infrastructure expenditures on roads, railways, and communications. Approximately 20 per cent of the workforce work directly in the public sector or are dependent on the public sector for procurement. It is important to state at the outset that public expenditure in the advanced economies has played the role Keynes predicted of being the stabilizing role within the market economy.

The arguments outlined by Keynes in the *General Theory* represented a departure from the classical economists' arguments that had dominated economic thought for the previous 150 years. It was, as Keynes suggested, a fundamental challenge to how to think about economic problems. Keynes asserted that he was constructing a theoretical framework that was anchored in reality to solve economic problems now, in contrast to the marginalist economists who had created an economics that was highly abstracted from reality. Keynes therefore confronted market liberalism at the level of assumptions, including the principles of rational individuals, the concept of competitive markets, and equilibrium theory. At a second level, Keynes disagreed with a prevailing philosophy that suggested that markets represented scientific laws and therefore economic outcomes had to be accepted as a form of inevitability, with no room for policy alternatives or policy choices. The argument that financial markets were efficient in the allocation of capital and that market participants in pursuing self-interest were in the best position to produce voluntary codes of regulation meant that government had a limited role to play, namely to provide a regulatory framework that ensured markets worked efficiently. In contrast, Keynes provided a series of policy options and choices which were continuously available to governments.

Finally, Keynes provided arguments that moved beyond economics and showed individual self-interest was not a sufficient ethic to guide economic policy – there were also issues of civic virtue, social justice, and democracy, which were inextricably related to the wider concerns of creating a civilized economy. Keynes was therefore well aware that his commitment to full employment spilled over into issues of policy making, and the democracy dialogue issues of income distribution and politics:

> The great thinker that he was, Keynes freed his mind from the binds of the classical analysis that was the conventional wisdom of economists of his (and our) time, he was able to reorient economic analysis in his mind toward a realistic analysis of the economic world in which we actually live. By so doing, Keynes was the best trustee for a stable, peaceful, and civilized global economy available for all mankind. (Davidson 2009, p. 3)

According to Keynes, therefore, his theory could not accommodate the postulates of market economics. Instead his major aim was to show that his theory was closer to reality and had therefore to replace a body of knowledge which did not address the observed world. Market liberal and Keynesian discourses were therefore incommensurate because they interpreted the world in different ways, and because they were incommensurate it was not possible to accommodate both theories. The Keynesian perspective is constructed as a separate and alternative way of seeing the world. Keynesianism represents a discursive society with a different series of beliefs which seek to challenge and replace the conventional wisdom of market economics. A Keynesian discourse is associated with the argument that markets cannot be left to themselves, that markets do not clear and that prices do not adjust according to supply and demand. Skidelsky (1977) in his book *The End of a Keynesian Era* wrote:

> He [Keynes] had, seemingly, bequeathed to politicians the economic equivalent of the Philosopher's Stone – the ability to turn slumps into booms and so create general and permanent abundance for the first time in history . . . and his name deserves to be given to an era which created at any rate the 'possibility of civilisation' for the people of the West. (Skidelsky 1977, p. 1)

On New Year's Day 1935 Keynes wrote to George Bernard Shaw reflecting on the possible intellectual contribution the General Theory would make to economic thought. Keynes was convinced that the concepts he was putting forward represented no less than a revolution in economic thinking:

> I believe myself to be writing a book on economic theory which will largely revolutionise – not, I suppose, at once but in the course of the next 10 years – the way the world thinks about economic problems ... I can't expect you or anyone else to believe this at the present stage, but for myself I don't merely hope what I say. In my own mind I am quite sure. (Harrod 1951, p. 642)

Furthermore, in the preface to the *General Theory* Keynes also reflected on the emotional and intellectual journey he experienced to make the shift from the taken-for-granted knowledge outlined in the classical economic paradigm, 'The composition of this book has been for the author a long struggle of escape ... from habitual modes of thought and expression' (Keynes 1936, p. viii).

KEYNES AND THE THEORY OF SCARCITY

Keynes challenged Say's Law that supply would create its own demand. According to this assertion there will always be demand and the problem is always supply. Within a theory of scarcity, markets had to deal with the three questions of what to produce (production), how to produce (allocation) and for whom (distribution). Keynes wanted to point out that on the demand side of the economy there was likely to be a leakage in that while it was true that people consumed in relation to their income, as incomes grew the rate of consumption was not the same as the rate of income growth. People saved and hoarded money.

> The fundamental psychological law, upon which we are entitled to depend with great confidence ... is that men are disposed, as a rule and on the average, to increase their consumption as their income increases, but not by as much as the increase in their income ... These reasons will lead, as a rule, to a greater proportion of income being saved as real income increases. (Keynes 1936, pp. 96–7)

The theory of scarcity implied there was never a problem of a lack of demand. Population growth and changing expectations would always ensure that demand outstripped supply. There was therefore never a problem of unemployment because the dynamics of unmet demand assumed there was always a need for additional supplies of labour. Wages were determined in the labour market. The demand for labour depended on labour supply and the number of workers willing to work for a given wage. Unemployment was therefore voluntary. People stayed unemployed as they waited for better and higher wages. Welfare payments allowed for longer periods of job search as workers stayed in between jobs for longer. Market economists argue that because we are rational agents we continuously make decisions as consumers, as suppliers of goods and services, and as investors and savers. As rational individuals we meet in the goods market, the labour market, and markets for investment and savings. Each market works according to the processes of supply and demand; each market obeys the price mechanism; and each market adjusts around an equilibrium price and quantity. The goods market determines the price and quantity of goods to be produced, which in turn determines the levels of employment and wages. The demand for money is described as being stable because it represents the number of transactions in the good markets. Savers and investors meet around the rate of interest. Savings are influenced by the rate of interest, with savers increasing savings if interest rates are high in contrast to investors whose investment decisions are inversely related to the rate of interest.

Keynes focused on the problem of aggregate demand as the way of breaking out of the scarce resources syndrome associated with market economics. The concept of aggregate demand pointed to problems of equilibrium between levels of demand and potential economic capacity and the possibility that economic capacity could outstrip effective demand, which in Keynesian economics represented a deflationary gap.

The financial meltdown of 2007 has created a capacity gap. The UK economy has shrunk by 4 per cent and there is, therefore, spare capacity. Inflation is not the problem. The concern is deflation and falling prices. So while it is true that inflation in early 2011 had risen to 4 per cent, that increase is mainly in imported inflation through increases in commodity prices and the VAT rises announced in the government budget of June 2010.

Market economists have constructed models on a narrow concept of rational agents, making careful calculations from the past and correctly forecasting the future. The efficient markets theorists, who developed financial models, used data that was expunged of context. Data sets did not included periods of recession. Keynes argued that because the future was uncertain, decisions about the future tend to be based on 'impulse' and 'sentiment'. Decisions are more likely to represent a series of wild fluctuations between excessive optimism and unwarranted pessimism. Decisions tend to follow more of the herd instinct of rushing forward in large numbers and also retreating, which means that economies would fluctuate between unsustainable booms and slumps.

Within the framework of Walrasian equilibrium, prices were the signal for both suppliers and consumers to adjust their expectations, so that if the price increase was too high then goods would be left on the shelf. Suppliers seeing the unsold goods would reduce the price to meet the new demand. Keynes argued that reducing the price was only one among other decisions available to suppliers. In contrast to reducing the price, suppliers could reduce the level of output. With unchanged demand and a falling supply, suppliers would be able to clear their shelves without reducing their prices. According to Keynes, therefore, a fall in demand was not necessarily addressed through flexible prices, but through a fall in output. Suppliers could therefore make choices between their levels of output and the level of demand for their product. Even if demand fell suppliers could still aim to maintain the level of profitability. Keynesian economists including Kalecki (Sawyer 1985), Robinson (1972) and Kaldor have all pointed to the problems of monopolies in different sectors of the economy. According to Kalecki, for example, it was more likely that the competitive markets were present in areas of the economy concerned with primary commodities such as agriculture, coffee growing, coal mining, and other raw materials. In the world of manufacturing and added value, Kalecki suggested that these industries are characterized by a system of administered costs. These industries do not calculate the value of the marginal costs of their labour or their marginal revenue but the mark-up price of their product by inputting the cost of materials, labour and capital, and adding an administered rate of profit. According to the world of administered prices, therefore, firms do not adjust their output according to prices but rather start off with their administered price as given and then allow output to meet changes in demand at the mark-up price.

According to the theory of administered prices, a fall in demand is not met by a change in price but by changing the levels of output. Firms can shut off parts of their productive capacity and also shed labour. For this reason, Keynes, in 1929, opposed the market liberal argument of reducing wage rates as a way of reducing the level of unemployment. Keynes argued that wages could not be separated out from aggregate demand. If wages were allowed to fall, aggregate demand was likely to fall and firms would be left with unsold goods on their shelves. Their response, because of administered prices, would be to reduce output which would increase unemployment further. The new unemployed also depressed the level of aggregate demand because there was now less income in the economy.

The response to the financial meltdown in 2007 was for suppliers to reduce their demand for additional products and instead run down inventories. This resulted in the first wave increase in unemployment. Secondly, employers utilized the new context of unemployment to increase the productivity of their existing workforce. So, during the financial meltdown starting in June 2008 the unemployment rate in the USA was rising by 600,000 a month, and eventually reached 15 million unemployed in mid-2009.

Keynesian analysing of the present recession would point out that the major declines upheavals that started in the financial sector would spill over into the real economy in terms of a sudden fall in output. Corporations faced with sharp declines in consumer demand reduced their existing inventories; which in turn explained the rising levels of unemployment. A fall in demand did not result in a decline in prices. The economy has contracted by 6.4 per cent in the USA and for the OECD countries by an average of 4 per cent.

In response to falling demand, household savings in the USA have shifted from 0.5 per cent of GDP in 2006 to 5.6 per cent in 2010. Keynes argued that future decisions on investment were, by their nature, unpredictable and uncertain. Investment decisions were therefore likely to be swayed by current news and emotions about the present state of the market rather than rational forecasts. Future investment was not founded on historic data to predict the future. Once the premise of uncertainty and risk were included into the markets for investment and savings then it was likely that there would be discrepancies between the levels of savings and investment. Since deflationary gaps were likely to occur between the levels of investment and savings it was imperative for government to shorten the lags between investment and savings.

To deal with the present crisis, therefore, Keynesians would argue that the only viable consumer is the government. In a context of declining propensities to consume the only consumer with a high propensity to consume is the government. Keynesians would therefore support President Obama's stimulus package, and also the major increases in public expenditure in China. By contrast the UK coalition government's declaration to make the deficit their priority would suggest a government that seeks to return the economy to pre-Keynesian arguments.

Dealing with the question 'why do investors invest?', it was not just the rate of interest which was the determining factor, but also sentiment about the future of the economy and future levels of demand. Decisions in the car industry to invest in robotics, for example, do not just depend on interest rates but also on forecasts about future trends in car ownership, costs of materials, costs of petrol, and decisions by government to build new roads. The rate of interest is one factor which influences investors' future investment decisions, but the forecast of future economic trends and the stability of demand are sometimes more crucial.

The important lesson to be emphasized by Keynesians from these observations was that the problem of unemployment was always to be associated with a lack of demand and underutilized economic resources. Since industries were likely to de-stock as demand fell this meant that on the supply side of the economy there was always likely to be underutilised capacity. The supply side was therefore always likely to be more elastic and respond that much faster to changes in demand. This view completely challenged the thesis put forward by Marshall and other market liberal economists who have tended to argue that, in the short term at least, supply was likely to be inelastic since firms could not change their production process or their levels of output in the short term. Keynes suggested that completely the reverse was true.

KEYNES AND THE POLITICS OF FULL EMPLOYMENT

Keynes was sure in his own mind that both his theory and his policy prescriptions represented a departure from market liberal thinking. Keynes's main economic argument was that the classical theory of money was misleading, that the world of investment was highly speculative and uncertain and that it was, therefore, this process that created a capitalism which was cyclical, and so unable to guarantee full employment. Secondly, Keynes made the cure of unemployment his major policy concern. For Keynes slumps were an unnecessary evil that led to the waste of human resources. It was just not good enough to say that markets would adjust. The unemployment rate of 14 per cent of the UK workforce that came out of the Great Depression in 1929 was a human tragedy. Keynes had argued at the Macmillan Committee that the government should aim to reduce unemployment by 500,000 through increases in public expenditure totalling some £100 million which was a stimulus package equivalent to 2.5 per cent of GDP. Keynes had been drafted to the Macmillan Committee by the UK Treasury in the hope that his views would become marginalized and irrelevant and yet during the hearings of that Committee Keynes found allies in Lord McKenna, a Chancellor of the Exchequer during the Asquith Government, and Ernest Bevin the leader of the UK's largest trade union.

The impact of Keynes on policy making was seen in the 1944 Employment White Paper which committed the British Government to a 'high and stable level of employment'. Other countries, including the USA, Germany, Japan and Sweden, made similar commitments in 1946. In all of these countries the commitment to full employment became a deliberate political choice. The implication of this policy choice was stated quite clearly in a *Times* editorial: 'Such a commitment means the loss of authority for the owner who could always say – if you do not want to work for the wage I am paying you there are plenty more who would – full employment has altered those relationships' (*The Times*, 23 January 1943).

The rates and levels of unemployment do represent a threat to those in work. Unemployment does act as a form of discipline in wage setting, a point recognized by Kalecki in 1943. Kalecki was aware that a commitment by governments to embrace a policy of full employment represented a political choice because, '"the sack" would cease to play its role as a disciplinary measure. The social position of the boss would be undermined and the self-assurance and class consciousness of the working-class would grow. Strikes for wage increases and improvements in conditions of work would create political tensions' (Kalecki in Sawyer 1985, p. 151).

Keynes was aware of the repercussions of full employment and the lack of agreement between government and trade unions on wages, and he equally accepted that this was a political rather than an economic problem. Keynes had argued that his concern was with economic problems – unemployment was an economic issue. Whether full employment was compatible with holding down wage inflation represented a different problem:

> I do not doubt that a serious problem will arise as to how wages are to be restrained when we have a combination of collective bargaining and full employment. But I am not sure how much light the kind of analytic method you apply can throw on this essentially political problem. (Keynes, in Kahn 1974, p. 371)

The commitment to full employment was altering the power relationships between employers and workers. While previously employers could make workers redundant if they did not accept the going wage and go out and hire new labour, full employment meant that such a pool of the willing unemployed no longer existed. This was therefore the Keynesian revolution – to create a context of full employment, and that context of full employment created the moral virtue of a civilized economy and democracy. The threat of unemployment left people vulnerable to poverty, to having to accept the authority of the employer and to offer no resistance. This inequality of relationships hindered democracy. So, for Keynes his economics carried a moral and ethical dimension:

> Of course I do not want to see money-wages soaring upwards . . . It is one of the chief tasks ahead of our statesmanship to find a way to prevent this. But we must solve it in our domestic way, feeling that we are free men, free to be wise or foolish. (Keynes 1944, p. 429)

For Keynes dealing with the implications of a context of full employment was a political issue. As Keynes argued, in a democracy people were free to make choices. That freedom provided a context for trade unions to push for higher wages, which, in turn, would be inflationary. Equally, government, employers and trade unions had the capacity to create institutional frameworks that would provide a climate of full employment and also wage moderation. In a democracy people had choices. The process

of institutionalizing wage settlements created the possibilities for dialogue, which was an essential element of democracy. While neoclassical
economists argued that such institutions represented major obstacles to
the working of the markets and contributed to unemployment, Keynes
pointed out that a civilized economy becomes possible when unemployment is not used as a tool to discipline the labour force, but rather to
utilize the process of dialogue as the means to reach civilized agreements
on employment and inflation.

During the depression years from 1929 Keynes's main concern was the
high levels of unemployment which had reached 1.14 million, equivalent
to 20 per cent of the UK workforce. Keynes had criticized the Chancellor
of the Exchequer Winston Churchill's decision to return to the Gold
Standard in 1925, arguing that the decision would lead to high unemployment. The Treasury view at the time was the one advocated by market
economists that markets would adjust, wages would fall, responding to
the challenge of competition, and there would be no unemployment. With
unemployment rising the Treasury advocated that there should wage
reductions of 10 per cent. Keynes in making the case against wage reductions did not argue the case of wage stickiness but rather that declines in
money wages would affect aggregate demand.

KEYNES, THE SAVINGS GLUT AND GLOBAL IMBALANCES

Keynesians would support the Bernanke thesis that there was a 'savings
glut'. In discussing the propensity to consume, Keynes pointed out that
consumption was related to disposable income and could be a stable function that could be disturbed by sudden changes in income, 'the propensity to consume may be considered a fairly stable function . . . Windfall
changes in capital values will be capable of changing the propensity to
consume and substantial changes in the rate of interest and fiscal policy
may make some difference' (Keynes 1936, pp. 95–6).

The rapid increases in house prices between 1990 and 2007 did create
a form of windfall in capital assets. Consumers felt that the higher house
prices increased their net worth. They were now able to withdraw equity
on their homes and increase consumption even though disposable income
was not rising. A second windfall came in the form of the lower interest rates being offered by the financial sector. The higher global savings
pushed down interest rates. Keynes's case was that there was no guarantee that savings would equal investment. Rather the possibility was
that savings would always be greater and higher than investment. Money

was not just for transaction purposes but was also important to satisfy an immediate insurance need in times of contingency and people needed money to cope with a rainy day. This meant that people would prefer to hold assets that were highly liquid and could be readily turned into cash to meet contingencies.

The growing economies of China and India and other emerging economies have generated surpluses and high levels of global savings. Export-led countries including China, India, Japan and Germany, as well as the oil producing countries, have generated major trade surpluses. By contrast, the USA, the UK and other advanced economies have become deficit countries. These savings were channelled to the US financial sector in search of yield. However, rather than being utilized for new productive investments, the savings were used to keep interest rates low and drive up US consumption. So, while the Federal Reserve was seeking to increase interest rates, the high global savings kept interest rates low.

The free unfettered market will not deal with global imbalances. When Keynes was reflecting on the limits of the gold standard and how gold was flowing into the United States and France with no natural forces that could have corrected the flow, Keynes identified the unequal relationships between creditor and debtor nations. The creditor nations with growing surpluses had choices of how to invest the surplus. The debtor nations had no choice but to open their markets to competition and hope that through open markets they could restore exports. Likewise in 2011 the creditor nations have the choice to continue with their export-led growth policies. The debtor nations, including the USA and the UK, have to structure their economies away from consumption and towards exports.

Dealing with global imbalances requires the input of government. China needs to be persuaded to increase consumer demand. At present China has a high savings ratio because of the absence of a welfare safety net, which means that people save for dealing with personal insecurity. An improved welfare safety net would allow for increased personal consumption and therefore for the expansion of imports from countries like the US and the UK.

In the present financial crisis, market economists have predictably blamed the government housing policy for encouraging home ownership for those with high risk of defaulting, or, secondly, blamed the Federal Reserve and its failed monetary policy. For market economists, therefore, the problem has been of a monetary glut rather than a Keynesian savings glut. This of course represents a return to Friedman's helicopter syndrome of the government showering the economy with newly printed money. Since within a market model all agents are fully rational, it is government policy that distorts the workings of efficient markets.

However, market economists cannot have it both ways. In the context of explaining why fiscal policy does not work, market economists had resorted to the concepts of Ricardian Equivalence theory. This proposition suggests that any attempt by government to increase public spending will be negated – the multiplier effect will be zero because, as government increases spending, rational agents will increase their savings to pay for future tax increases. However, when it comes to explaining the present recession Taylor (2010) has blamed Alan Greenspan and the low interest rates regime that fell below the Taylor rule. Low interest rates lead to increased borrowings. So, in the second explanation, the rational agent suffers from monetary illusion, while with fiscal policy the rational agent is a fully informed perfectly rational agent.

Economics is not like Newtonian physics. There are, therefore, no laws of supply and demand and no guarantee of equilibrium. The financial system combined with entrepreneurial spirit generated demand for investment that contained the potential for runaway expansion powered by an investment boom. This investment boom was eventually halted because the financial system become fragile. Stability creates its own instability.

Skidelsky (1977, 2009) has suggested that Keynes not only offered governments the context for intervention in national economies but also a form of international Keynesianism so they could intervene strategically to ensure that the prosperity and welfare of societies were guaranteed. Rather than accepting a limited role for government as suggested by the market economists, Keynesians argued that the role of government needed to be extended. The idea of leaving markets to themselves, of not being able to influence the external pressures of the marketplace, needed to be replaced by the idea that the marketplace could be influenced so that government could offer hope rather than resignation: Keynesians argued that the markets could be reformed. Markets did not produce optimal outcomes, yet governments were always in a better position to analyse these outcomes and embark on policies which produced better results. The market liberal argument – that in the long term markets would find their own equilibrium – was not a solution to people's daily lives:

> But this long run is a misleading guide to current affairs. In the long run we are all dead. Economists set themselves too easy, too useless a task if in the tempestuous season they can only tell us that when the storm is long past the ocean is flat again. (Keynes 1971, IV, p. 65)

The argument that at the end of the day markets would adjust at some level did not offer any objective criteria for evaluating the conduct of economic policy. The observed rates of unemployment in the 1920s and early 1930s, wild fluctuations in unemployment in the 1890s and 1900s and the levels of unemployment in the 1980s all represent different histories of unemployment, yet within each of those periods the levels of unemployment and duration of unemployment were different. The unemployment of the 1920s was concentrated in certain industries, especially those industries directed at export markets. During the decade of the 1920s the number registered as unemployed was always above the 1 million mark, some 18 per cent of the total labour force. Unemployment reached its peak of 3 million in 1929. The market solution to the problems of unemployment in the 1980s also seems to be found in the long run. Unemployment rose steeply, from 1.3 million in 1979 to a peak of 3.2 million in 1982. Unemployment remained at over 3 million until 1987 – a much longer duration this time than in the 1920s. For over a decade in the 1980s registered unemployment did not fall below 2 million. It is in this context that Keynesians question the discrepancy of history and the theory of equilibrium. The theory of markets and the flexible price mechanism do not offer indicators as to when and how markets will clear.

According to the rational expectations view, rational agents have perfect information and are able to predict the relationships between supply and demand. The rational expectations model suggests that unemployment is voluntary – the unemployed, as rational agents, choose to be unemployed, hoping to re-enter the labour market as wages increase. The welfare safety net provides the necessary income for those who exit the labour market.

FROM THE ECONOMICS OF SCARCE RESOURCES TO THE ECONOMICS OF PROSPERITY

The central concern of market economics is to resolve the problem of how to allocate limited resources in the context of unlimited demand. Market economists argued that the market was the best method to allocate resources. Markets were always more efficient and more flexible than any central authority. Furthermore, the marketplace was less likely to be discriminatory in deciding who gets what. The way to growth and continuous prosperity was for government to create a framework in which enterprise could flourish, enterprise being the ability to take risks, to see opportunities and take advantage of them. Enterprise could only flourish in the spirit of free markets. Governments had therefore to create an enterprise culture where people could be encouraged to take risks and have the incentives to take those risks. Since the endowment of resources available to a 'community' was supposed to be determined exogenously, the welfare of the community could be maximized (or its misery minimized) only by the free play of market forces under an enterprise system with the minimum of government interference and regulation. 'Keynes asserted the contrary. His main proposition was that in normal circumstances production in general was limited by effective demand which determined *how much* of potential resources were effectively utilised. Here therefore was scope . . . for securing greater material welfare through the purposeful direction of the economy' (Kaldor 1984, p. 2, original emphasis).

The main criticism directed by Keynesians against the market liberal approach to economic growth and prosperity was that it depended too much on the enterprise of the individual. Within market economics the possibility of government being able to influence the level of aggregate demand was not entertained since demand was stable. Government, according to market economists, could only influence demand through increases in the supply of money, as in Friedman's helicopter thesis of the money supply. However, such an increase was only a short-term solution. Increases in the money supply would, in the short run, lead to price increases which were higher than wage increases; this increase in prices would lead to expansion in output and employment. However, in the long run workers would match increases in prices with increases in wages, which would cancel out the price advantage and also the increases in output. Unemployment would, in the long run, return to the natural level. Market economists see government as having, at best, a neutral effect in influencing output, growth and employment. Furthermore, any such government interference was more likely to lead to higher prices and inflation.

In contrast, Keynes argued that the level of aggregate demand could be changed by government either seeking to influence the level of individual demand or by changing the level of its own demand on resources. Personal consumption could be changed by governments altering the states of taxation and improving personal disposable income. Also, governments could influence aggregate demand through changes in public expenditure by either deciding to build roads or hospitals, or by employing more teachers or doctors. Government expenditure was more likely to change the levels of effective demand. Government tends to consume all resources while tax changes are likely to lead to both consumption and savings. Changes in aggregate demand depend on the ability of government to target consumption on groups with a high marginal propensity to consume, which includes those on low incomes. It is for this reason that Keynesians see policies which seek to redistribute income through fiscal measures as not being purely social policies but also as policies which have a direct impact on the economy.

The attempt to influence aggregate demand meant that government had a key role to play in the redistribution of resources. In his pamphlet *How to Pay for the War* Keynes showed that government, without resorting to deficit financing, could re-channel existing taxation and public expenditure to fund armaments (Harrod 1951). Keynes argued that government had a high propensity to consume and that by increasing the level of taxation and reducing personal consumption, the new taxation was to be spent on defence, which in turn produced the equipment required, but also employed people, who, in turn, spent their income in the commercial sector, thus generating through the multiplier effect new income and taxation. Keynes argued that this form of redistributing income could influence aggregate demand within a balanced budget.

However, Keynesians also advocated that deficit financing could be used as a fiscal stabilizer, arguing that when savings were outstripping investment because of 'sentiment' about investment decisions, government could 'mop' up the unused savings and re-input these otherwise idle resources back into the economy as government investment, which was likely to influence demand and private sector investment. The increased demand and higher levels of investment would result in increased levels of sustainable employment. In his 1929 pamphlet *Can Lloyd George Do It?* Keynes advocated that government should direct investment into export industries, implying that he was in favour of government-directed investment. Furthermore, Keynes was also sufficiently political to recognize that a policy of cheap money was likely to produce conflicts of interest between the financial and the manufacturing sectors of the economy. A cheap money policy implied that government should conduct a policy which would lower the rate of interest for the manufacturing sector, which was more important than protecting high interest rates which benefited the financial sector. The interests of banking, therefore, had to be subordinated to manufacturing.

The attempt by one country to pursue a cheap money policy, however, was likely to fail in the international context. If one country did decide to go it alone and reduce interest rates than this action was likely to lead to an exodus of foreign holders as they searched for higher interest rates. The priority was, therefore, for countries to come together and co-ordinate their monetary policies, which meant that countries were not competing with one another on interest rates. A co-ordinated approach to currency and interest rates meant that governments could deal with financial interest rates together. The alternative policy of restricting imports and extending protection by individual governments was likely to lead to a beggar-my-neighbour policy with each government seeking to export their national unemployment to another nation. Protectionist policies were likely to lead to a contraction of world trade and a decline in prosperity.

The possibility and willingness of governments to construct supranational institutions which could influence national economic policies meant that by surrendering some of their national interest to the international context, governments were actually contributing to international stability and also to the prosperity of the people they sought to represent. Governments could no longer ignore the fact that economies were becoming more interdependent and that national economic policies have to be made in an international context.

CONCLUSIONS

Keynes recognized that full employment requires a political arrangement which allows government to maintain a commitment of full employment without the threat of inflation. Inflation and unemployment in a Keynesian sense were, therefore, political decisions in that governments needed to create institutions and arrangements to deal with the trade-off of employment and inflation. Keynes is therefore often associated with tripartite and corporatist politics as deliberate arrangements to resolve economic problems in a political context. Equally, a large public sector, public investment in capital goods, and public services, including health and education, are also associated with the influence of Keynesian thinking.

Keynes produced a revolution because he pointed out that people did not have to live with the outcomes of the marketplace, but that it was essential for humanity and civilized societies to change the nature of the circumstances in which they found themselves. The perception of having to live within the market and not being able to influence market forces because they represent immutable laws implied that people and their governments had little or no autonomy in the conduct of economic policy, but had to live with the constraints of the marketplace. By contrast, Keynes showed that the aim of any community was to discover ways of improving welfare and general prosperity. Economic policy alternatives always represented deliberate political choices. Living within a classical market liberal model represented a political choice of living with the status quo: accepting income inequalities as being the natural outcomes of markets, that unemployment was voluntary and that a welfare safety net distorted the marketplace. The market liberal argument for lower taxation confirmed their position that the problem was the supply side and that reducing taxation would increase labour supply and would increase the willingness of speculators to invest. Public expenditure because of Ricardian Equivalence had no impact on the economy.

By contrast, policy making that embraced the thinking of Keynes committed governments to full employment, to higher levels of public provision and towards better redistribution of income. A Keynesian strategy implied the concept of the civic virtue of mutuality and democracy. Making civic virtue an integral part of Keynesian economics implies that Keynesians take a wider view of human nature. The individual is an integral part of the community, deriving dignity and well-being from being a member of society who participates as part of the wider community. Civic virtue means the rights and expectations of individuals to be treated as equals – not just as consumers in the marketplace, but also as members of communities.

Keynesian economics is therefore seen as belonging to the tradition of collectivism, where individual self-interest has been rejected as the main motivating force in society. Instead, the encouragement of self-interest has been associated with promoting greed and a fractured society, where the material prosperity of some and the experiences of deprivation of others are seen as divisive and offering no opportunity for constructing contracts which could actually improve general welfare:

> personal liberty without the full employment of all our national resources is still uncivilised. Less-than-full employment of resources is not only wasteful but it also strikes at the heart of community values and the spirit of excellence. Jobs provide people with the basis for the practice of excellence in a very important sphere of their lives. For our society and others, occupations also play a part in creating individual roles and developing personal dignity . . . for it is barbaric to require that certain people in society be denied employment . . . A nation which thrives on the hardships of its members cannot be called civilised. (Davidson and Davidson 1988, p. 20)

REFERENCES

Arestis, P. and T. Skouras (eds) (1985) *Post Keynesian Economic Theory*. Sussex: Wheatsheaf Books.

Bacon, R. and W.A. Eltis (1978) *Britain's Economic Problem: Too Few Producers*. London: Macmillan.

Davidson, G. and P. Davidson (1988) *Economics for a Civilised Society*. London: Macmillan.

Davidson, P. (2009) *John Maynard Keynes*. Basingstoke: Palgrave Macmillan.

Haldane, A.G. (2009) 'Rethinking the Financial Network', speech delivered at the Financial Student Association, April, Amsterdam.

Harcourt, G.C. (1985) 'Post Keynesianism: Quite Wrong/Nothing New?', in P. Arestis and T. Skouras (eds) *Post Keynesian Economic Theory*. Sussex: Wheatsheaf Books.

Harrod, R.F. (1951) *The Life of John Maynard Keynes*. Basingstoke: Macmillan.

Issa, D. (2011) 'Obama's Keynesian Failures Must Never be Repeated', *The Financial Times*, 8 February.

Kahn, (Lord) J. (1974) 'On Re-Reading Keynes', *Proceedings of the British Academy*, **LX**: 361–92.

Kaldor, (Lord) N. (1984) 'Keynesian Economics after Fifty Years', in D. Worswick and J. Trevitchick (eds) *Keynes and the Modern World*. Cambridge: Cambridge University Press.

Kalecki, M. (1943) 'Political Aspects of Full Employment', *Political Quarterly*, **4**: 322–31.

Keynes, J.M. (1935) 'Letter of 1 January 1935 to George Bernard Shaw', reprinted in the *Collected Writing of John Maynard Keynes*, 13 (1971). London: Macmillan.

Keynes, J.M. (1936) *The General Theory of Employment, Interest and Money*. London: Macmillan.

Keynes, J.M. (1944) 'A Note by Lord Keynes to *The Economic Journal*', *The Economic Journal*, December.

Keynes, J.M. (1971) *The Collected Writing: The Economic Consequences of the Peace*. London: Macmillan.

Krugman, P. (2007) *The Conscience of a Liberal*. New York: W.W. Norton and Company Ltd.

Minsky, H.P. (2008) *John Maynard Keynes*. London: McGraw Hill.

Robinson, J.V. (1972) 'What Has Become of the Keynesian Revolution?', Presidential Address, reprinted in Robinson J (1979) *Collected Economic Papers*, Vol V. Oxford: Basil Blackwell.

Sawyer, M.C. (1985) *The Economics of Michal Kalecki*. London: Macmillan.

Skidelsky, R. (1977) *The End of a Keynesian Era*. London: Macmillan.

Skidelsky, R. (2009) *Keynes: The Return of the Master. Why Sixty Years After his Death, John Maynard Keynes is Still the Most Important Economic Thinker in the World*. London: Allan Lane.

Stiglitz, J. (2010) *Free Fall, America, Free Markets and the Sinking of the World Economy*. London: W.W. Norton and Company.

Summers, L. (2010) 'America's Sensible Stance on Recovery', *The Financial Times*, 18 July.

Taylor, J. (2010) 'The Financial Crisis and the Policy Responses: An Empirical Analysis of What Went Wrong', paper to the Financial Crisis Inquiry Commission, 2 September, Washington, DC.

Wolf, M. (2011) 'Britain's Experiment with Austerity', *The Financial Times*, 9 February.

7. Structural explanation of the financial crisis

The financial crisis has confirmed the contradictions between capitalism and democracy. Capitalism needs democracy since the process of democracy gives legitimacy to the economy. The revolutions in the Middle East of 2011 confirm the limitations of autocratic capitalism, of a concentration of elites and growing income inequalities. The financial crisis is also evidence of growing income inequalities in the advanced economies: of stagnant incomes for 99 per cent of the population and a skewed income distribution towards the top 1 per cent of earners. The dual ethics of a capitalism of one dollar, one vote, and a democracy of one person one votes has resulted in the ability of those on high incomes to hire lawyers and accountants that ensure tax breaks for a few, and also a process that is shaped by financial donations and lobbyists and which undermines the democratic process.

In the context of these contradictions this chapter seeks to explore social structures, ideology, power and influence and how these processes provide a framework for analysing the nature of the financial meltdown. It is therefore an attempt to provide an interdisciplinary approach, borrowing concepts from sociology, politics, economics and anthropology to try and locate the financial crisis in wider social, political and economic landscapes. Social structures, including institutions of government and private sector entities, by their nature create issues of power and influence. Looking at the financial sector, with investment banks worth twice UK GDP and in the USA the top five Banks amounting to 65 per cent of GDP, there is inevitably an issue of the concentration of power and influence (Johnson 2009). Equally, public sector institutions are guided and shaped by philosophies. Economic theory founded in rational expectations and efficient markets ideas have become an integral part of the thinking and the policy processes of financial institutions (Foley 2010; Turner 2010).

Secondly, and connected with issues of power and influence, are the arguments that point to increased income inequalities, the concentration of income with an elite that in turn seeks to influence and shape the policy process, and indeed are defining and shaping the policy process (Atkinson et al. 2010). The new plutocracy and the concentration of income is subverting the democratic process, with these elite providing campaign contributions to lawmakers that seek to protect their vested interests. Hedge fund managers have, for example, been able to persuade lawmakers that their earning should be taxed as capital gains rather than as income tax which means an income tax payer is paying a higher rate of tax then a hedge fund manager. The hedge fund managers have reported earnings of $598 million, which is about 19,000 times the median wage.

Between November 2008 and November 2009 Wall Street firms and executives gave $42 million to lawmakers, mainly to members of the Finance and Banking Committee and also to the House and Senate leaders. As part of the lobbying process the finance industry spent another $300 million on lobbying members of Congress. Campaign contributions totalled $1.44 billion in 1998 but this had accelerated to $3.48 billion in 2009. As elections become more expensive and advertising costs increase, politicians become more dependent on financial contributions if their voices are going to be heard.

There are sharp contrasts when asking whose voices are likely to be heard in the context of the increased concentration of wealth and income within the top 0.01 per cent of households? In December 2010, in spite of the rhetoric about the government's deficits, policy makers in the USA allowed the Bush tax cuts for higher earners to stay in place until 2012. By contrast there has been a deafening silence about the concentration of wealth and income and the increases in income inequalities. Recent studies confirm the degree to which people have misleading conceptions about income inequalities. The concentration of wealth in the top 0.01 per cent of earners is creating a context where democratic countries like the USA and the UK start to resemble a banana republic, with wealth concentrated in few hands and vulnerable to corruption and crony capitalism. Thirdly, the processes of social structures confirm the concentration of financial markets in fewer and larger banks. The top five banks in the USA have assets equivalent to 60 per cent of US GDP (Ferguson and Johnson 2010). Further, the concentration of income has also allowed for these banks to hire lobbyists and for these institutions to become directly involved in shaping the policy process.

Ferguson and Johnson (2010) have used the metaphor of the myth of the 'Danaid Jar' to argue that one effect of the financial crisis was the re-distribution of income from the majority of the population to the few very rich. The financial meltdown not only necessitated a series of bank bail-outs to the major investment banks in order to stabilize the financial sector, but also had major spill-over effects on increased rates of unemployment and falling house and equity prices. Households saw their net worth diminish by approximately $10 trillion while their retirement pensions fell by 18 per cent. In addition, the financial crisis created major problems for government finances, with steep declines in GDP and tax revenues, which forced governments to seek reductions in social provision for education, health, social security payments and pensions.

> The Myth of Danaid Jar thus seems a perfect departure point for our reflections on comparative bank bailouts.
> The myth recounts the sad story of the daughters of Danaus. Forced to marry against their will, all but one murdered their husbands on their wedding night. As punishment, they were sent to Hades and condemned forever to try to fill with water a jar that was really a sieve.
> Systemic banking crises strikingly resemble the jar in the myth . . . ordinary citizens pour tax dollars into banks owned mostly by people far richer than they are, while enduring higher rates of unemployment . . . Public deficits mushroom while government spending on everything else gets crimped. Just as in the *La Caricature*'s little gem, however, in the final analysis the broad flow of resources is upward, from the poor and middle classes to the rich. (Ferguson and Johnson 2010, p. 2)

Between the fourth quarter of 1996 and the peak quarter of 2006 house prices in the USA increased by 86 per cent. Akerlof and Schiller (2009) pointed out that the magnitude of house prices did not reflect economic fundamentals. House prices were rising at an average of 15 per cent per annum between 2003 and 2007. The movements in asset values between stocks and housing were qualitatively different, while the stock market did behave as a random walk in that future movement in S&P or the FTSE 100 could not be predicted, however house price movement was predictable and moving upwards. Materials and building costs as well as wages in the construction industry had remained relatively stagnant. Furthermore, there was a major discrepancy between aggregate take home pay and house prices. While for long periods in housing history there was a stable correlation between median wages and median housing prices, representing a ratio of 3.6 times house prices to wages, by 2004 this had jumped to 4.6 times. Housing is the most important asset for the majority of households. In terms of household net worth, housing assets amount to $22 trillion compared to $9 trillion in the equity markets. Housing assets are therefore the major assets for the majority of households. The increases in the value of housing provided the context for major steep increases in household net worth. In the USA household net worth peaked at $67 trillion in 2006. In 2008 it was estimated that net worth had declined by $15 trillion to $52 trillion. Households interpreted the increase in the price of their homes as representing an increase in their portfolio and personal wealth which meant that they needed to save less. Studies of the savings ratio confirmed that in 2000 the savings ratio in both the USA and the UK fell to less than 1 per cent. Household were therefore consuming more. The issue was whether the increases in house prices were real or inflationary. Did the increase in house prices represent real wealth or was this a purely paper increase? Households interpreted the increase in house prices as something real. Mortgage brokers encouraged people to unlock their equity and households responded by surrendering any equity they had in their homes for ready cash liquidity, which then was used to buy consumer durables. Stiglitz (2010) estimates that households were withdrawing about \$975 billion in equity during any one year, which was equivalent to 7 per cent of GDP. In total, households extracted some \$2.3 trillion of equity.

This refinancing contributed to overall GDP growth through increases in personal consumption expenditure. The increases in house prices were global. House prices were rising in the USA, the UK, France, Ireland and Spain. Historically, the relationship between house prices and household income had held steady at 3.5 times household incomes. However during the period 2000 to 2007 that correlation started to breakdown. The relationship between median wages and median house prices had spiked at 4.6 times household incomes.

House prices increases were a bonus for policy makers. There were no pressures for increases in wages as households felt they were becoming more prosperous. There was therefore a reluctance by policy makers to point out that the increases in house prices could also go into decline. Households also used their newfound wealth for consumption purposes, buying new consumer goods and doing major alterations to their homes. The new housing wealth increased households' marginal propensity to consume.

The economic theories of the efficient markets hypothesis (EMH) and rational expectations hypothesis (REH) created the intellectual argument that there were good economic reasons as to why house prices were accelerating and that the increases reflected the intrinsic values of housing investment. Furthermore, market participants were rational agents. According to EMH, therefore, the acceleration in house prices from 2000 to 2007 reflected a good estimate of the intrinsic value of housing. Alan Greenspan argued that housing reflected increases in demand because of rising incomes, low interest rates and a general shortage of housing caused by planning rules and restricted land spaces. There was, therefore, no housing bubble. Siegel (2010) has pointed out that the study of housing confirmed that over a period of 60 years the cumulative losses in housing costs were around 2.5 per cent, so housing was seen as a safe asset. Even if some borrowers defaulted, house prices were sufficiently robust to absorb losses.

[I]n the 61 years from 1945 through 2006, the maximum cumulative decline in the average price of homes was 2.84% in 1991. If this low volatility of home prices persisted into the future, a mortgage security composed of a nationally diversified portfolio of loans comprising the first 80% of a home's value – the so-called 'first tranche' – would have never come close to defaulting. The credit quality of home buyers was secondary because if historical volatility held, the underlying collateral – the home – could always cover the principal in the event the homeowner defaulted. (Siegel 2010, p. 7)

As house prices started to decline in late 2006 households were faced with lost equity and higher mortgage repayments. In 2011 approximately 23 per cent of US households were underwater, where the collateral of their homes was below the money they are borrowing. House prices have declined by 30 per cent (FCIC 2011). It is estimated that households have lost some $8 trillion in their net worth. The response has been for households to repair their savings. Savings shifted from less than 1 per cent of GDP in 2005 to 5.4 per cent in 2011. This shift in savings also meant a sharp decline in consumer demand. In 2006 household borrowing had reached $1 trillion. In 2009 households were now savings $279 billion, a reversal of approximately $1.3 trillion in aggregate demand.

Overall mortgage indebtedness in the United States climbed from $5.2 trillion in 2001 to $10.5 trillion in 2007. The mortgage debt of American households rose almost as much in the six years from 2001 to 2007 as it had over the course of the country's more than 200-year history. The amount of mortgage debt per household rose from $91,500 in 2001 to $149,500 in 2007. With a simple flourish of a pen on paper, millions of Americans traded away decades of equity tucked away in their homes. (FCIC 2011, p. 180)

An alternative explanation outlined by Akerlof and Schiller (2009) suggested that the increase in house prices reflected exuberance irrationally based on stories that house prices would always rise and that housing was a good investment. Secondly, the authors look at the dimension of confidence, with its roots in the Latin word 'fido', meaning trust. Home owners trusted that institutions would protect their interest; home owners trusted the brokers to advise them on what type of mortgage was suitable for them, yet the broker model was broken because brokers were not just acting on behalf of the borrower but were also getting a fee from the lender to channel the borrower towards a higher cost mortgage, in return for which the broker received fees from the lender. Investors also trusted the Credit Rating Agencies for the triple-A ratings of asset backed securities and relied on the CRA for due diligence. Thirdly, Akerlof and Schiller introduce the concept of snake oil – that capitalism sells you things that you might think you want rather than things that you actually want or need – and that the snake oil products which are on the market might not necessarily be good for the home owner. Adjustable rate 2/28 teaser mortgages could be defined as being a snake oil product.

THE GREAT MODERATION

In outlining the thesis of the Great Moderation, Bernanke (2004) pointed to the success of Chairman Paul Volcker at the Federal Reserve during the period 1976 to 1980 in bringing inflation under control and creating a macro-economic landscape of low inflation expectations. This meant that in future governments, through monetary policy, would always create a low inflation environment which in turn meant that negotiating agents were bargaining for wages within a context of low inflation expectations. By the end of 2000, the US economy had grown in 39 straight quarters.

The Thatcher government elected in the UK in May 1979 published its Medium Term Financial Strategy with the budget statement of 1980, outlining pathways for inflation, the money supply and government deficits. The UK central bank was the given the macro-economic task of sustaining an inflation target of 2.5 per cent. In the period 1997 to 2005 inflation targets and the independence of the central bank were essential to the Blair government macro-economic policy. At this time the government felt able to pronounce that the cycle of boom and bust had been conquered.

The Great Moderation was also linked to the 'Quiet Period' in the financial sector (Gorton 2009). During the years 1934 to 2007 there had been no systematic banking crisis to compare with the continuing runs on banks in the 1880s, the great panic of 1907 and the Great Depression of 1929. To stabilize the financial markets, major bank reforms including Glass-Steagill and the Securities Act of 1933, together with the establishment of the Federal Deposits Insurance Corporation (FDIC) to guarantee bank deposits, had created a stable environment for depositors, who knew their money was safe. The FDIC insured bank deposits up to $2,500 – an amount that covered the vast majority of deposits at the time; that limit was revised to $100,000 in 1980, where it stayed until it was raised to $250,000 during the crisis in October 2008.

Thirdly, the Great Moderation was also associated with the process of globalization that started in the early 1980s. That process of globalization was shaped and defined by the Washington consensus of greater liberalization of financial markets, privatisation of state enterprises and contracting out of services. Free trade opened markets, which in turn resulted in lower global prices that brought increases in prosperity for consumers without the pressures of increases in take home pay.

During this period the advanced economies had also become increasingly dependent on increases in house prices and the growth of the financial sector as the major factors of economic growth. Increases in house prices were therefore celebrated as confirming the success of the economy. Higher prices reflected strong fundamentals of economic growth – rising incomes and prosperity, and therefore the willingness of people to pay more for their homes. Housing became a savings portfolio. As housing prices increased, households were encouraged to take out the equity on their homes and use it to finance consumption. As house prices grew, households extracted equity, while at the same time the savings ratio fell. When the US Federal Reserve cut interest rates in 2000 and the cost of mortgages fell, mortgage equity withdrawal increased to a total of $2 trillion between 2000 and 2007, while housing debt surged, climbing from $460 billion in 2000 to $2.8 trillion in 2003, allowing people to withdraw equity built up over previous decades and to consume more, despite stagnant wages.

SOCIAL STRUCTURES

In the following sections the concern will be to explain the financial crisis as located within the structural properties that define and shape issues of power and influence. Structural properties define relationships between individuals and organizations as well as relationships between and within institutions. Buildings have outlines that are highly visible where the structures create recognizable shapes. We know a bridge is a bridge by its span and its structure. Some parts of social structures are also highly recognizable, including the offices of government, the headquarters of corporations and factories. We easily recognize an industrial town when we see one. Chimneys and smoke dominate the landscape. Towns that depend on high-tech pharmaceutical research have buildings that define the shape of the economy. People come to railways stations and bus stations at peak times of day, commuting to and from work, and that pattern repeats itself daily in many cities and towns and in different countries.

Social structures create patterns and routines that both enable and act as a constraint on individuals. Structures cannot be changed overnight. People learn to live and adapt to changing economic structures. Industry migrates and stable industrial communities go into decline. As steel making migrated from Sheffield in the UK, new steel plants emerged in China. The wool industry, so important to Yorkshire, has been replaced with new high-tech fibres that do not need flowing waters to wash wool nor large spinning factories. The internet has changed work patterns. For some, there is no necessity to be at their geographic place of work – they can use new technology to perform their jobs – and so commuting patterns have changed.

Minsky (1976) defined capitalist society as a specific social structure which is founded on the private ownership of property, decentralized economic decisions and private enterprise existing alongside government provision. Within that capitalist economy there are markets and these markets are also structured. Some markets are dominated by small business while others markets are shaped by large corporations. Shopping malls are equally structured. There are those containing shops that aim to attract high income earners with expensive jewellery and clothing boutiques, while there are also shopping malls that aim to capture a wider consumer market. Markets are structured to reflect structured consumers. Consumers are not homogenous, since they reflect different income groups with different tastes and different levels of income.

Social structures also create issues of power and influence. The centres of government attract the lobbyists and those who seek to shape the policy process and who feel they need to have access to the policy makers. In this system some have ready access to government while the majority are on the outside, voiceless, making their protests through megaphones in the hope of being heard. By contrast those who can sit, be photographed and drink coffee with a policy maker do not need the aid of the megaphone to be heard. Corporations are willing to hire professional lobbyists and pay fees because the lobbyists have access to the corridors of government. Some organizations are sufficiently large and influential that they do not need the lobbyists. Financial contributors to policy makers provide a ticket of access.

The structure of government creates processes that reinforce inequality of access in the shaping of the policy process. The geographical locations of government are in themselves a declaration of where power is located. Lobby groups rent offices in close geographic spaces to government. Those who want to influence and shape the policy process need to maintain a presence on a day-to-day basis; ensuring the voices of their clients are articulated becomes essential in the policy formulation stage:

> The point is that a staggering amount of money from big corporations, executives, and other wealthy individuals lies like a thick fog over the nation's capital, enveloping everyone and everything. Not only has it enriched Washington lobbyists, lawyers, and public relations professionals and seduced thousands of ex congressmen but it has also transformed Washington into a glittering city of high end restaurants and exquisite hotels. (Reich 2010, p. 111)

Washington, London, Berlin, Paris, Beijing, Moscow and Mumbai are declarations of where power resides. These cities have all become economically prosperous because high-income professionals demand residences in these locations. Lobbyists want to be close to the White House in both Moscow and Washington and to the seat of the government of India and China and the UK parliament in London. Property prices reflect that process. London and Washington have exquisite hotels and restaurants to meet the tastes of highly paid lobbyists who entertain their customers and also bring customers and policy makers together.

Government and public institutions are visible structures. The electoral process defines the structures of accountability and transparency of public sector institutions. The legislative process and regulatory framework also govern the behaviour of the private sector. Market economies exist within structures. The market economy is therefore a social construct as defined by the policy process, by regulations that are defined and shaped by government. The market therefore does not exist in vacuum. The idea that markets create quasi-scientific laws of supply and demand and that these laws are pervasive to the extent that government has no choice but to observe the laws of markets, makes humanity a servant of the market rather than the market being a factor that can be utilized to further human welfare.

Social structures are not static – they are human defined and therefore reflect the changing landscapes of expectations. Governments have visions and those visions very often mean major institutional reform. The 1948 Labour Government established the NHS, nationalized major industries and redefined the boundaries between the public and private sectors. President Roosevelt, elected in the aftermath of the Great Crash in 1933, sought to structure the finance sector through the Glass-Steagill reform and the Securities Act of 1933. Roosevelt also tried to boost wages as a way of increasing aggregate demand. This was a major departure from the policy priorities of Presidents Hoover and Calvin Coolidge and their policy perspective of allowing free markets to define the shape of the US Economy. President Reagan's major priority was to push back the interventionist state, which he argued was the problem rather than the solution. Alan Greenspan's priority as Chairman of the Federal Reserve was therefore to liberalize the financial sector. During the Roosevelt presidency inequality had narrowed. The period 1941 to 1970 was a period of low unemployment and the narrowing of wage differentials. By contrasts the tax reductions under the Reagan budget in 1981 represented a reversal of trends established in the Roosevelt years. Prior to the election of 1980 the top income tax bracket stood at or above 70 per cent, where it had been since the Great Depression. President Reagan dropped the top bracket from 70 per cent to 50 per cent, and eventually pushed it all the way down to 28 per cent. Since then, it has hovered between 30 and 40 per cent. The tax composition reveals some more shifts. At the federal level, progressive taxes made up 60.8 per cent of the total tax in 2000. By 2005 this had declined to 56.4 per cent. Meanwhile, regressive taxes increased from 38.9 per to 43.1 per cent. Corporation taxes under Roosevelt amounted to 5.6 per cent of GDP. During Truman and Eisenhower this had declined to 4.5 per cent, while under Nixon and Ford the tax declined further to 2.7 per cent, then under Clinton to 2.4 per cent and in 2007 to 1.3 per cent which became the lowest level of corporate tax since 1940. Between 1980 and 1984 the real disposable income of the poorest fifth declined by 8 per cent, while the real disposable income of the wealthiest 5 per cent jumped by 9 per cent.

THE STRUCTURES OF INCOME INEQUALITY

The mapping of incomes and who gets what are a product of social structures. Governments make decisions on tax reform which influence the distribution of income. Governments create legislative processes on trade unions and pay policy that influence take home pay. Governments come to power not as empty vessels but with held beliefs, and those beliefs need to be developed into a policy framework. Thirdly, there are issues of power and influence: how government responds to the pressures of finance; which interests to listen to; and how various interests influence the policy process.

Studies by Piketty and Saez (2003) and Atkinson, Piketty and Saez (2010) have focused on the top 1 per cent and 0.01 per cent of income earners by studying their tax returns. The focus on these earners confirms that education does not explain income inequality. With the top 10 per cent of earners educational qualifications tend to be similar, so the issue is how to explain the major widening of incomes between the top 1 per cent the other 9 per cent, but, more importantly, how to explain the differences with the top 1 per cent. Atkinson, Piketty and Saez (2010) conducted a study of 22 countries that included, in Europe, the UK, Italy, France, Germany and The Netherlands, in North America, the USA and Canada, in Latin America, Argentina, and then Japan, India, China, Australia and New Zealand. All these countries confirm that that during the period 1970 to 2007 the top 1 per cent of earners saw their income increase by 10 per cent of GDP. The top 1 per cent accounted for 8.9 per cent of GDP in 1976 and by 2007 this had increased to 23.3 per cent. For the top 0.01 per cent, income increased from 2.8 per cent of GDP to 12.3 per cent of GDP. In the meantime, during the same period, incomes for 99 per cent of the population were growing at 0.60 per cent per annum. This meant that in terms of GDP growth between 1976 and 2007 the top 1 per cent captured 58 per cent of GDP growth. While for the period 2000 to 2007 the top 1 per cent had captured 65 per cent of GDP growth.

The study of wages and income equality can be divided into two distinct periods: (1) the years 1950 to 1974, defined as the era of the Great Compression; and (2) the years 1980 to the present, which is categorized as the Great Divergence. Between 1945 and 1973 both productivity and family incomes doubled. Median income in 1947 amounted to some $21,700, which by 1973 had increased to $44,380 – an increase of 2.8 per cent per annum. While productivity had increased 103.7 per cent during the period, wages had also increased 103.9 per cent. Inequality as measured by the Gini coefficient was narrowing, people were in full time employment and experiencing annual wage increases. In the UK the Gini coefficient narrowed from 0.32 in 1948 to 0.25 in the 1970 while in the USA the Gini also fell from 0.38 to 0.34 during the same period. Public provision including health care, education and social protection were also contributing to the reduction of inequalities.

By contrast, between 1973 and 2000 wages increased at the rate of 0.7 per cent per annum, so while productivity increased by 102 per cent incomes increased by 20 per cent. So for the period, for 90 per cent of the population, incomes increased by 12.5 per cent while the top 10 per cent experienced increases of 40 per cent and the top 1 per cent increases of 75 per cent. However, the study of the top 1 per cent needs to be broken down further, with the top 0.1 per cent experiencing an increase of 117 per cent and the top 0.01 per cent an increase of 156 per cent. The period 1980 to 2007 became the age of divergence. The narrowing of inequalities had been reversed by 2007. The major tax breaks for high income earners contributed to the growing inequalities. Industrial relations entered an era of quietism. Trade union membership went into a steady decline. UK trade union membership peaked in 1975 at 50 per cent of the UK workforce, by 2007 trade union membership had fallen to 30 per cent. In the USA trade union membership also declined sharply – to 7 per cent of the total workforce, with the public sector being the one major area of trade union membership. The collectivist ethics of industrial communities that shared experiences and collective memories were replaced by a new individualism. The decline of manufacturing also meant the retreat of industrial communities in coal mining, steel making and engineering. The new jobs were more individualist.

Stiglitz (2010) has argued that the Reagan/Thatcher era created a 'moral deficit', a context in which the chief executives of companies felt free to appropriate the fruits of success of their companies for themselves and other senior managers. So while chief executives of companies were earning 40 times the income of the average worker in 1970, this had increased to 480 times in 2007. From 1975, therefore, there was a major moral shift. Executives of companies and senior managers used their compensation policies to ensure that the financial successes of their companies were reflected in the rewards given to a few. These few defined themselves as the superstars of the company and they were rewarded for the uniqueness of their talents that made the company a success. In the global economy these talented people were few and in high demand and their salaries reflected their endowments. The adage applied to David Beckham as an exceptional football player, 'there's only one David Beckham', was extended to business: the CEOs of the major investment banks now demanded compensation packages that reflected their star quality. In the meantime the workforce shared the fruits of that success by having continuity of employment and stable wages. Their employment depended on the success of their leaders. During the Thatcher and Reagan years the sense of fairness in compensation was replaced by how much the executives could appropriate for themselves. In 2010 the S&P 500 CEO averaged incomes of $105 million,344 times the pay of a typical worker. In the meantime the top 50 hedge fund managers averaged incomes of $588 million each, which was more than 19,000 times the average income.

> As the United States slipped into crisis, I worried that what I had seen so often in developing countries would happen here. Bankers who had in large part pre-cipitated the problem, took advantage of the panic that resulted to re-distribute wealth – to take from the public purse to enrich their own. (Stiglitz 2010, p. 41)

In their study, *Winner-Takes-All Politics*, Hacker and Pierson (2010) point out:

> From 1979 until the eve of the Great Recession, the top one percent received 36 percent of all gains in household incomes . . . Economic growth was even more skewed between 2001 and 2006, during which the share of income gains going to the top one percent was over 53 per cent. That's right: More than 50 cents of every dollar in additional income pocketed by Americans over this half decade accrued to the richest 1 in 100 households. (Hacker and Pierson 2010, p. 3)

STRUCTURAL INEQUALITIES AND THE FINANCIAL CRISIS

Housing Investment and Household Incomes

As Chairman of the Federal Reserve, Alan Greenspan's decision to reduce interest rates after 2001 was an attempt to deal with the fear that the terror attacks on the World Trade Centre would create a loss of consumer confidence. The terrorist attacks on the United States followed the bubble in the dot-com companies that had seen major decline in equities amounting to $10 trillion. In seeking to avoid a deflationary spiral, Greenspan felt it was appropriate to keep interest rates low from 2001 to 2003. The policy of low interest rates together with the global savings glut provided the context for households to realize previously tied-up capital in their homes, either to buy new and bigger homes or to use some of the equity to satisfy pent up consumption drives. The promise of low interest rates made borrowing cheaper and households became more willing to take on the increased risks of borrowing. Households were spending the acquired capital on consumer goods, which in turn increased overall consumption by 3 per cent. Between 1980 and 2007 two-thirds of GDP growth was related to housing, with people either buying or modernizing their homes, with the financial markets providing the finance for households to refinance their mortgages.

The financial crisis of 2007 has redistributed income from the bottom 99 per cent to the top 1 per cent of income earners. The re-distribution of income has involved two processes. First in the context of increases in house prices and low interest rates, households with traditional mortgages and who had equity in their homes decided to turn the financial wealth tied up in their home into liquid assets that allowed them to increase consumption. In 2011 the landscapes of savings and equity has shifted. Households no longer have wealth in their homes; instead they have higher levels of debt. As house prices have declined by around 20 to 30 per cent, so have households' net worth. Equities have also declined by 20 to 30 per cent, which in turn has reduced the values of retirement schemes and pensions by around 18 per cent.

Rajan (2010) has utilized the concept of structural fault lines in the US economy in his explanation of the financial meltdown. Included in Rajan's list of fault lines are: (1) the increase in the concentration of wealth and the growth in income inequality; (2) the decline in the number of students attaining degree qualifications; (3) the problem of stagnant wages; (4) the weak safety net to deal with long-term unemployment; and (5) political paralysis. These fault lines, according to Rajan, were making the USA less able to meet the challenges in global markets from emerging economies including China and India. Political paralysis generated by partisan politics was creating a situation in which the USA government was unable to provide a policy framework for dealing with future investment in education and infrastructure, coupled with an inability to provide a welfare safety net. The lack of a welfare safety net meant that governments were under increased pressure to reduce unemployment, especially when compared with countries that had safety net to deal with unemployment. These factors, Rajan argued, explain how the US government was willing to allow house prices to increase and also to encourage easy credit as a 'form of panacea' – this was a policy of least resistance compared with alternative attempts to increase taxes and re-distribute income through the tax system and through improvements in social provision:

> Politicians have therefore looked for other ways to improve the lives of their voters. Since the early 1980s the most seductive answer has been easier credit. In some ways, it is the path of least resistance. Government-supported credit does not arouse as many concerns from the Right at the outset as outright income redistribution would . . . Politicians love to have banks expand housing credit, for credit achieves many goals at the same time. It pushes up house prices, making households feel wealthier and allows them to finance more consumption. (Rajan 2010, p. 31)

Geisst (2009) has also taken up the connection between stagnant wages and rising house prices. Credit card debt and taking out equity on homes as housing prices were rising provided the avenue to higher consumption, even if this was not warranted when wages and household income are taken into consideration. 'The increase in house prices and the heightened use of credit cards were accompanied by low growth in real wages, as had been the case for two decades. To achieve the American Dream average American families were going into more debt given the low growth in incomes' (Geisst 2009, p. 166).

Easy credit, the expansion of credit cards and more affordable mortgages created the possibility for higher levels of consumption that benefited households and the economy. It was a strategy that, at least in the short term, only seemed to create winners. The equity and housing bubble confirmed that the strategy of consuming wealth while increasing household debt was, in the long run, not sustainable. The drawing out of equity was directed to consumption without increasing investment.

Financial Markets and the Emergence of New Elites

Tett, in her evidence to the FCIC enquiry and subsequent writings (2009, 2010), has argued that market participants involved in the securitization process were an elite within the financial sector. This tribe used language that was often opaque, founded on complex mathematical models, and based their arguments on risk dispersion and market completion, which were one step removed from public scrutiny. Only when the bubble burst was there any attempt to explain the process of securitization. Tett has argued that her training in anthropology gave her the necessary tools to study financial markets as a system and how systems create ideologies and social silences. Tett argues that this social silence benefited the world of finance as the ideology was taken for granted as being beneficial to the economy. Financial instruments including MBS, CDS, CDOs and synthetic CDOs were welcomed as being enablers in creating market liquidity. Yet these instruments were so complex that they were not actually being traded in markets, although the prices were modelled to markets. Tett used the concept of social silences to explain how the process of securitization was not being discussed in the media where what was happening seemed to be too complex and too abstract to attract a storyline, a human face, or even data, since the derivatives market was mainly over the counter and data was difficult to find:

> However, a second, related, problem is a pattern of social 'silence'. As Pierre Bourdieu, the French anthropologist and intellectual, observed in his seminal work *Outline of a theory of practice*, the way that an elite typically stays in power in almost any society is not simply by controlling the means of production (i.e. wealth), but by shaping the discourse (or the cognitive map that a society uses to describe the world around it). And what matters most in relation to that map is not just what is discussed in public, but what is *not* discussed because those topics are considered boring, irrelevant, taboo or just unthinkable. Or as Bourdieu wrote: 'The most successful ideological effects are those which have no need of words, but ask no more than a complicitous silence. (Tett 2010, p. 7)

The process of securitization and the structuring of mortgage backed securities, CDOs and synthetic CDOs, provided the new asset class as all these securities were rated as triple-A. On Wall Street, as these loans were repackaged and turned into bonds to be sold to investors around the globe a, a new term was coined: IBGYBG, 'I'll be gone, you'll be gone'. This referred to deals that brought in big fees up front while risking much larger losses in the future. And, for a long time, IBGYBG worked at every level. These mortgages were very quickly securitized and issuers, including investment banks such as Merrill Lynch, Bear Stearns and Lehman Brothers, together with commercial banks and thrifts including Citibank, Wells Fargo and Wachovia, ensured that these bonds were rated as triple-A and then sold off to global investors through Special Investment Vehicles.

> [W]e follow the profound changes in the mortgage industry, from the sleepy days when local lenders took full responsibility for banking and servicing 30-year loans to a new era in which the idea was to sell the loans off as soon as possible, so that they could be packaged and sold to investors around the world. New mortgage products proliferated, and so did new borrowers. Inevitably, this became a market in which the participants – mortgage brokers, lenders, and Wall Street firms – had a greater stake in the quantity of mortgages signed up and sold than in their quality. (FCIC 2011, p. 56)

Johnson's (2009) central argument was that the financial sector has had a major influence on the policy process in America. The finance industry in the USA has gained prominence because of what Johnson calls cultural capital as a belief system. The financial sector over the past two decades has grown from 4 per cent of GDP to 9 per cent of GDP and its contribution to corporate profits have increased from 16 per cent to 40 per cent:

> these various policies – lightweight regulation, cheap money, the unwritten Chinese-American economic alliance, the promotion of homeownership – had something in common. They *all* benefited the financial sector. Policy changes that might have forestalled the crisis but would have limited the financial sector's profits – such as Brooksley Born's now-famous attempts to regulate credit-default swaps at the Commodity Futures Trading Commission, in 1998 – were ignored or swept aside. (Johnson 2009, p. 7)

Ideas and Ideologies

Finally, there is the influencing factor of ideology as a system of held values and beliefs. Theories of rational expectations and efficient markets (EMH) that had become the paradigm of university academic departments had also become the mode of thinking within the structures of the policy process. Opinion formers, policy makers and those who implemented policy, steered their organizations and departments to incorporating the concept of free unfettered markets into their mission statements. The ideas of rational expectations and efficient markets became part of the DNA for governments, for Ministries of Finance and central banks. The Medium Term Financial Strategy (MTFS), launched by the Conservative Chancellor of the Exchequer, Nigel Lawson, outlining pathways for the money supply, government borrowing and inflation, came straight from the rational expectations textbook. The MTFS outlined future pathways that would provide transparency for market participants on expected rates of inflation and the relationship between government borrowing and the money supply.

Evidence that agents had different views of the futures, that there was divergence and heterogeneity, was ignored by the rational expectations modellers (REH). The representative agent was as defined by the theory not by the evidence of research. The argument was that markets were efficient in the sense that all prices reflected intrinsic values, and that the prices of all assets had real fundamental reasons for being at a level as announced by markets. Neither REH or EMH has any explanation for the financial meltdown, since in rational markets there are no possibilities of bubbles, and bubbles, if they exist, represent irrational reasons.

Market liberals want to argue that markets exist in their own right, obeying the laws of supply and demand, using mathematical models as sound as those utilized in theories of gravity. Yet, as Lawson has explained, in the natural sciences the observation of particles takes place within a laboratory that seeks to look at the intrinsic properties of the particles while controlling for extrinsic factors. The study of economics cannot allow for such experimentation: the variables that are studied are connected and cannot be isolated.

Turner (2010) commented that when he was appointed to head the FSA he felt he had become the high priest of the ideology of the liberalization of financial markets. The role of the FSA was confined to making sure that financial markets worked smoothly: the FSA's priority was to deal with market imperfections. It was therefore the job of the FSA to ensure greater transparency in the market and that there were no information asymmetries, and to focus on areas of market failures. It was outside the remit of the FSA to ask whether market liquidity was actually beneficial or whether derivatives were serving a social purpose. The free market was therefore an inherent part of the FSA's DNA, as it was for other institutions involved in financial markets – including the IMF, which even on the eve of the financial meltdown was extolling the role of derivatives in the global economy. Turner argued that while within the world of economics there existed many approaches, the dominant conventional wisdom was defined by the efficient markets and rational expectations economic models:

> we should also not underplay the importance of an ideology in itself – of a set of ideas complex and internally consistent enough to have intellectual credibility, but simple enough to provide a workable basis for day-to-day decision-making. Complex human institutions – such as those which together form the policy-making and regulatory system – are difficult to manage without guiding philosophies – and guiding philosophies are most compelling when they provide clear answers. (Turner 2010, p. 9)

The importance for Turner was therefore understanding the transmission process of ideas and the policy process. Institutions need guiding philosophies and free market thinking served the policy process well because it offered simple guidance for policy makers: markets worked best with minimum intervention and it was better to leave it to the market participants to make the rules rather than regulators. Rational expectations suggested a minimum role for fiscal policy.

Reinhart and Rogoff (2008, Reinhart and Reinhart 2010), in their historical studies of financial crisis, have pointed out that most crises start in the banking or housing sector where bubbles are formed because of high leverage and increased risk exposure. Reinhart and Rogoff associate the financial crisis with the policy of liberalization and deregulation in financial markets that started with the years of President Reagan in the USA and Prime Minister Thatcher in Britain, when both governments committed themselves to deregulation and a retreat of the state. The repeal of Glass-Steagill in 1999 and the Commodity Futures Modernization Act of 2000 were among a series of a policies that created the climate of deregulation:

> While each financial crisis no doubt is distinct, they also share striking similarities in the run-up of asset prices, in debt accumulation, in growth patterns, and in current account deficits. The majority of historical crises are preceded by financial liberalization. While in the case of the United States, there has been no striking de jure liberalization, there certainly has been a de facto liberalization. New unregulated, or lightly regulated, financial entities have come to play a much larger role in the financial system, undoubtedly enhancing stability against some kinds of shocks, but possibly increasing vulnerabilities against others. (Reinhart and Rogoff 2008, p. 4)

Ideology is an inherent part of economic modelling. A system of held beliefs influences discourse and assumptions. The concept of the rational individual is an assumption that seeks to countervail the argument of government and bureaucracy as to who is best at making decisions on how to distribute scarce resources. The debate of the interwar years and during the Cold War was therefore between Soviet planners and the Friedman and Hayek arguments of a market that was decentralized and where it was better for individuals to make decisions because of their diversity. These myriad possible decisions could not be captured by the bureaucratic central planners. Paradoxically, the rational expectations model, and the concept of the representative agent as defined by the model, leaves no room for diversity or heterogeneity. Instead, the model of rational expectations creates a mechanical individual who is purely calculative – who has all the information and therefore invests in the same portfolio balance of equities that reflect risks and riskless assets. Rational agents have full information and they cannot beat the market.

Ideology does play an important role. Economic theory is developed in the laboratory of academic economics departments. Theory and evidence are published in economic journals. However, the definition of what constitutes economics has become severely restricted. Only those who write equations are deemed to be legitimate economists. It is always better to write a model, no matter how abstract and how well it fits with the reality of economic data – it is the model that is most important. The elegance of models therefore has come to define what constitutes economics.

> Economists wish to convince each other. Economists wish to receive each others' attention. Attention is given to new and novel ideas, to arguments that

have not been raised, to insights that run counter to conventional wisdom. More likely, existing theories are abandoned because a newer theory is more convincing. Theories are abandoned because its well of novel insights and therefore its resulting steady stream of exciting new discovery and the resulting publications is drying up. Theories are abandoned because the new is sexy and the old is not. This is a theory of scientific revolution . . . but with a caveat: the revolutions happen out of boredom with the old and the promise the new territory holds, its a priori appeal. There may be something wrong with that old theory – but the merits lie elsewhere than in cleaning that up.

As a byproduct, old theories are never really discarded. Economists love to hang on to beliefs once formed and they once thought to have learned as correct. Despite the excitement for new ideas that may turn over conventional wisdom, economists cling to it anyhow. One can never take a first look a second time. To take a fresh new look at the facts is difficult individually, and it may be impossible for the science as a whole, perhaps with the exception of the next generation of researchers. As a result, old ideas often have a remarkable staying power. (Uhlig 2010, p. 7)

However, the relationship between the theorist and the policy practitioner is essential. The economic theorist has no power or influence – the aim of the theorist is for her ideas to be adopted by the policy maker or policy practitioner. Economists do become engaged in the policy process as advisors to government, selling their ideas and hoping that the policy makers take ownership of them. Institutions of government do need philosophies and EMH and REH offered a simplistic analysis of how the economy works and what needs to be done. Don Kohn, Vice Chairman of the Federal Reserve, in a speech in November 2008 reflected on the limitations of economic modelling, especially the impact of REH and EMH:

The challenge is to improve our understanding of the linkages between the financial sector and real activity. The recent experience indicates that we did not fully appreciate how financial innovation interacted with the channels of credit to affect real economic activity – both as credit and activity expanded and as they have contracted. In this regard, the macroeconomic models that have been used by central banks to inform their monetary policy decisions are clearly inadequate.

These models incorporate few, if any, complex relationships among financial institutions or the financial-accelerator effects and other credit interactions that are now causing stresses in financial markets to spill over to the real economy. Rather, these models abstract from institutional arrangements and focus on a few simple asset-arbitrage relationships, leaving them incapable of explaining recent developments in both credit volumes and risk premiums. Economists at central banks and in academia will need to devote much effort to overcoming these deficiencies in coming years. (Kohn 2008, p. 1)

So while there were pluralities of economic models and disagreements, the ascending paradigm continued to be the commitment to deregulation.

It was the ideas of EMH and REH that produced the intellectual framework for the legitimizing of the deregulatory process of the 1980s. It was also the ideas of free unfettered markets that created the context for the OTC derivatives, which in turn helped to fund the credits cycle in the housing market, which then resulted in the financial meltdown.

The argument between Keynesians and market liberals has always been an argument of competing ideologies. Keynesian economists were concerned with aggregate demand, the distribution of income unemployment, uncertainty and the unpredictable nature of a capitalist economy. By contrast, market liberal economists had their starting point in the market economy arguing that markets were neutral and had nothing to say about income distribution or unemployment, since these processes were the natural outcomes of markets. The ideas that market are neutral therefore fitted well with those interests that seek to resist government intervention and seek to advocate minimum government and low taxation since it is markets that are deciding entitlements. The rich become rich because of their specific talents that need to be rewarded. Inheritance and how passing on family incomes perpetuates inequality becomes a non-issue.

> The sudden triumph of rational expectations theories rested in an important way on their presentation of macroeconomic policy, particularly monetary policy as 'neutral', that is, by implication, without impact on distribution. From this point of view it is easier to see why the balance of power in disposing of theoretical speculation shifted from econometricians to the theorists themselves. Even a relatively crude examination of macroeconomic data reveals the central importance of distribution (between wage and non-wage incomes, for example) in the dynamics of business cycle fluctuations. To those who share the tendency of neo-liberal economic policies to accept and encourage increasing inequality in the distributions of wealth and income, research on the actual dynamics of wage setting and its relation to unemployment is as irrelevant as it is unwelcome (Foley 2010, p. 9)

Foley (2010) has argued that market liberal economists have marginalized the concerns of unemployment and income inequality. Research in these areas has become positively unwelcome in the ascendant paradigm of rational expectations. Unemployment is voluntary because rational agents are constantly choosing between work and leisure. Secondly, within efficient markets distribution of incomes represent the efficient distribution of resources and entitlements. Markets are competitive and compensation reflects rewards to those with specific skills and knowledge.

The context for the ideological departure is important. RHE and EMH gained ascendancy in the mid-1970s during the debate on the causes of stagflation when the issues were unemployment and income distribution. Governments were at a watershed, debating whether to surrender their commitment to full employment. Incomes policy as a means of dealing with inflation was proving to be unwelcome to market liberal advocates who saw governments having to increase social provision and entitlements in order to secure incomes policy. Thirdly, the period 1950 to 1974 had seen the narrowing of income inequalities because of full employment and rising incomes.

Keynesian arguments during the mid-1970s were that stagflation could be resolved by the recycling of savings from the oil producers to the advanced economies and that the problem of inflation was imported inflation. Keynesians still argued that the problem remained a problem of aggregate demand to resolve the problem of unemployment and that the government should not use unemployment to curb inflation:

> This is emphatically not to argue that other points of view in macroeconomic analysis are free of ideological motivation. Those economists who see business fluctuations as an expression of inherent instabilities in market organization, and who focus their attention primarily on the distributional dynamics of the business cycle clearly start from their own values and vision. As you can imagine, no matter how much they share an interest in the details of financial institutions or macroeconomic fluctuations it is not easy for people who instinctively see the capitalist market economy as a miracle of efficiency, freedom, and coordination of information to interact constructively with others who regard it as an exploitative, unstable, irrational, historically limited system. I hope the story of economics, however, alerts us all to the pervasive influence of ideology in the choice and framing of scientific problems, as well as in the systematic strengthening and weakening of various elements of scientific method and procedure. (Foley 2010, p. 13)

CONCLUSIONS

A structural explanation of the financial crisis seeks to locate the causes of the present recession in relation to issues of power, ideology, the policy process and structures that define and shape social relationships. The influence of money in politics, of financial donations to policy makers and political parties, together with the financing of lobbyists, distorts both the policy process and democracy. Money creates a context of unequal access in the formulation of policy. Policy makers co-opt selected experts to help draft regulations which means that those effected can help shape the complexity and the outcomes of policy. Policy practitioners and institutions of government need a guiding philosophy. The influences of rational expectations and efficient markets theories have dominated the thinking of how financial markets work. Economic theory provided the necessary science that facilitated a climate of deregulated financial markets.

There is now an increasing disconnect between policy formulation, policy implementation and the repercussions of policy making for individual lived lives. Issues of structures are at one remove from people's daily experiences. Lobbyists and policy experts are connected within narrow social networks in the offices of government. Most people only experience the implementation phase and how this then impacts their daily lives. By then of course it is too late to bring about policy change. Those who are affected are not invited to the policy formulation stage.

Governments would argue that it is the people who have the power because come election times they can change the government. That is a limited choice because during a period of five years people are not involved in the shaping of policy; they are reduced to the mute audience in the auditorium, sitting in the dark watching the political actors on the stage and then being asked to clap at the end of the performance. Barber (1984) pointed to the differences between thin and thick democracy, where thin democracy is limited to the electoral process while thick democracy represents the commitment to a democratic culture. The financial crisis confirms the presence of thin democracy as opposed to thick democracy.

REFERENCES

Akerlof, G. and R. Schiller (2009) *Animal Spirits: How Human Psychology Drives the Economy, and Why it Matters for Global Capitalism.* Oxford and Princeton, NJ: Princeton University Press.

Atkinson, A.B., T. Piketty and E. Saez (2010) 'Top Incomes in the Long-run of History', in A.B. Atkinson and T. Piketty (eds) *Top Incomes: A Global Perspective.* Oxford: Oxford University Press.

Barber, B. (1984) *Strong Democracy: Participatory Democracy for a New Age.* Berkeley and Los Angeles, CA: University of California Press.

Bernanke, B.S. (2004) 'The Great Moderation', speech before Eastern Economic Association, Washington, 20 February. Available at: *www.federalreserve.gov/boarddocs/speeches/2004/20040220/default.htm#f1*

FCIC (2011) *The Financial Crisis Inquiry Report: Final Report of the National Commission on the Causes of the Financial and Economic Crisis in the United States.* New York: Public Affairs.

Ferguson, T. and R. Johnson (2010) 'When Wolves Cry "Wolf": Systemic Financial Crises and the Myth of the Danaid Jar', INET Inaugural Conference, King's College, Cambridge University, April.

Foley, D. (2010) 'Mathematical Formalism and Political-Economic Content', paper presented at the inaugural conference of the Institute for New Economic Thinking, Session 6, 23 March. Available at: http://ineteconomics.org/sites/inet.civicactions.net/files/INET%20C@K%20Paper%20Session%206%20-%20Foley_0.pdf

Geisst, C. (2009) *Collateral Damage: The Marketing of Consumer Debt to America.* New York: Bloomberg Press.

Gorton, G. (2009) 'Slapped in the Face by the Invisible Hand: Banking and the Panic of 2007', paper prepared for the Federal Reserve Bank of Atlanta's 2009 Financial Markets Conference: Financial Innovation and Crisis, 11–13 May.

Hacker, J. and P. Pierson (2010) *Winner-Takes-All Politics: How Washington Made the Rich Richer – and Turned its Back on the Middle Class.* London: Simon and Schuster.

Johnson, S. (2009) 'The Quiet Coup', *The Atlantic Monthly,* May.

Kohn, D. (2008) 'The US Economy and Monetary Policy', speech at the University of North Carolina at Wilmington North Carolina, 26 February.

Minsky, H. (1976) *John Maynard Keynes.* London: McGraw Hill.

Piketty, T. and E. Saez (2003) 'Income Inequality in the United States, 1913–1998', *Quarterly Journal of Economics,* **118**(1): 1–39.

Rajan, B.G. (2010) *Fault Lines: How Hidden Fractures Still Threaten the World Economy.* Oxford and Princeton, NJ: Princeton University Press.

Reich, R. (2010) *After-Shock: The Next Economy and America's Future.* New York: Alfred A Knopf.

Reinhart, C. and V. Reinhart (2010) 'After the Fall', paper presented at the Federal Reserve Bank of Kansas City Economic Symposium, Jackson Hole, Wyoming 27 August.

Reinhart, C. and K. Rogoff (2008) 'Is the 2007 US Sub-Prime Financial Crisis So Different? An International Historical Comparison', *American Economic Review,* **98**(2): 339–44. Available at: http://www.aeaweb.org/articles. php?doi=10.1257/aer.98.2.339

Siegel, J.S. (2010) 'Efficient Market Theory and the Recent Financial Crisis' paper presented at the inaugural conference of the Institute for New Economic Thinking, King's College, Cambridge, UK, 9 April. Available at: http://www. scribd.com/doc/30612159/Efficient-Market-Theory-and-the-Recent-Financial-Crisis-Jeremy-Siegel

Stiglitz, J. (2010) *Free Fall: America, Free Markets and the Sinking of the World Economy.* London: W.W. Norton and Company.

Tett, G. (2009) *Fool's Gold: How Unrestrained Greed Corrupted a Dream, Shattered Global Markets and Unleashed a Catastrophe.* London: Little, Brown.

Tett, G. (2010) 'Silos and Silences: Why So Few People Spotted the Problems in Complex Credit and What That Implies for the Future', *Banque de France Financial Stability Review, Derivatives – Financial Innovation and Stability,* **14**(July): 121–9.

Turner, A. (2010) 'Economics, Conventional Wisdom and Public Policy', paper presented at the inaugural conference of the Institute for New Economic Thinking, Cambridge, UK April. Available at: http://ineteconomics.org/sites/ inet.civicactions.net/files/INET%20Turner%20%20Cambridge%2020100409_0. pdf

Uhlig, H. (2010) 'How Empirical Evidence Does or Does Not Influence Economic Thinking and Theory', paper presented at the inaugural conference of the Institute for New Economic Thinking, Cambridge, UK, 8–11 April. Available at: http://ineteconomics.org/sites/inet.civicactions.net/files/INET%20C@K%20 Paper%20Session%205%20-%20Uhlig_0.pdf

8. The politics of recession: power and politics

Making the statement 'recessions are political' suggests that recessions are not exogenous events. Recessions are human made and therefore reflect deliberate policy choices. The metaphor of the ship of the state being guided by the ship's captains to weather the storms of the global economy implies that governments have no choice but to respond to events that are always beyond their control. Recessions being defined as being inevitable suggest that these economic events are like earthquakes or floods, events that cannot be predicted or controlled, and that the role of government is about cleaning up the mess. The earth has shifting plates, volcanoes that generate tsunamis, floods and human tragedies. Recessions are described as equally tragic events, but are also seen as an inherent part of a market economy. However, the argument of 'a politics of recession' points to the view that recessions are human made and reflect the outcome of a series of policy decisions.

The Thatcher government's monetary policies adopted in the 1980 budget contributed to the recession of 1981 and 1983. High interest rates, high sterling and reductions in public expenditure were aimed at changing the UK economic landscape. Growth and employment were no longer the policy objectives. The Thatcher government made inflation the number one macro-economic objective. Paul Volcker, the Chairman of the Federal Reserve, also made the conquering of inflation the policy priority of the Carter Presidency. Unemployment in both the UK and the USA climbed to post-war heights. In the UK, unemployment jumped from over 1 million in 1979 to 3 million in 1982, while in the USA the unemployment rate increased from 4 per cent to 7 per cent. In both countries the policy objective was to reduce inflation expectations. By the government showing leadership in the control of monetary policy, it was argued, various bargaining agents, including trade unions, would seek moderate wage settlements within a stable economic environment. However, policy choices between employment and inflation were political choices. The control of inflation was favoured by business and by high-income earners. The argument that inflation eroded the incomes of those on pensions or social security were always misleading since governments could protect groups on fixed incomes by linking their incomes to the Consumer Prices Index (CPI) or the Retail Prices Index (RPI). The control of inflation also widened income inequality. Inflation targeting by the central bank created a permanent incomes policy. Wages no longer kept pace with rates of growth in productivity. Unemployment acted as a threat for those in work. By contrast, a policy commitment to full employment had reduced income inequalities because of trade union resistance and the shift towards labour in pay bargaining.

Likewise, the UK coalition government is equally involved in making political choices in responding to the present recession. The government has made the case that they have no choice but to tackle the UK deficit, otherwise the bond market would impose its own terms and conditions for lending to the UK government. However, UK interest rates have remained at 0.5 per cent and Treasury yields have remained stable at around 3.4 per cent. The UK is not Greece or Ireland. First, the UK has a debt structure that matures after a ten-year period. Secondly, there is a room always for the Bank of England to buy Treasury Bonds. Thirdly, there are different ways of tackling the deficit – a series of policy choices between expenditure reductions and tax increases. There is also the issue of speed in achieving the reductions. At all these levels there are policy choices that reflect political priorities and political ideologies. The financial crisis has provided the government with a window of opportunity to bring about a longer-term change of expectations between public and private provision. The reductions in public expenditure are not aimed at dealing with the deficit as a short-term problem, but, rather, the government has approached public expenditure as a structural issue that has long-term implications. Proposals on pension reforms, retirement, pension contributions, student tuition fees, eligibility to social welfare, health reforms: all these represent major policy changes.

Inherently, there is always the political choice of policy instruments. The preference for monetary policy to deal with inflation is political since there are alternatives, including incomes policy and price controls. Inflation is not always a monetary phenomenon. Increases in the money supply reflect wider structural pressures. Monetary policy and inflation targeting through the central bank are an implicit rather than an explicit incomes policy. With the central banks responsible for meeting inflation targets, at the first sign of inflation pressures the response of the central banks is to increase interest rates. So, if there are signs of increases in wage settlements, the increase in interest rates, which increases interest payments on mortgages and other household debts, negates wage increases. The preference for a monetary approach is political since the policy is implicit. By contrast, an explicit income policy involves wage bargaining and trade-offs. Trade unions seek compensation from the government for agreeing an incomes policy, which often involves prices controls.

Policy responses in a recession create a context for a series of policy alternatives reflecting political priorities and political choices. Recessions are not shared experiences. Recessions create winners and losers in the context of time and geographic spaces. During the major labour shake-outs in UK manufacturing during the 1980s, men who lost their jobs in steel making and coal mining and who were then aged 50 or above never worked again. The jobs that were created in retail parks did not match the skills of steel workers or coal miners. Industrial communities experienced high rates of unemployment. Britain of the 1980s was de-industrializing (Bazen and Thirwall 1989; Martin and Rowthorn 1986). Some 2 million jobs in manufacturing were lost during the period 1983 to 1987, while a further 1.5 million were lost in the mid-1990s. Manufacturing in Britain had amounted to 46 per cent of GDP in the mid-1950s; this ratio had declined to 22 per cent of GDP in the mid-1980s and to 16 per cent by 2009.

A series of initiatives to regenerate economies have taken decades. Manchester and Liverpool have succeeded in redefining their identities, as have Leeds and Glasgow, but Bradford and Hull never recovered their former levels of prosperity. Studies of the UK coalition government's planned expenditure have pointed out that some of the proposed reductions are more likely to impact northern towns. The attempts to bring regeneration to these cities could again be halted. London continues to be the major generator of UK economic growth. In the USA the decline of car making, coal mining and steel making meant major jobs losses in Pittsburgh, Illinois, Detroit and Michigan. In the meantime, the sunshine states of Florida and California flourished. The resistance to the Obama administration's decision to provide funds for Chrysler and General Motors reflected the fragmented experiences of the financial meltdown.

Recessions are not collective shared experiences or collective histories, but instead reinforce a landscape of policy winners and policy losers. Identifying the politics of recession requires the process of peeling the onion – that is, studying the various layers of the policy process. The contents of policy statements are often benign in content, with government making the case that the policy serves the national interest. Furthermore, this outer layer is usually founded on a narrative that implies there is no alternative to the policy being followed by the government. Dissenting discourses are marginalized. Policy statements are also usually emptied of political ideology.

Policy is not benign. It does not necessarily serve the public interest. There are always political choices and those choices create a map of winners and losers. Sacrifices are not shared. In the context of recession there is always the argument that dealing with a recession needs a policy framework that creates incentives for some through tax breaks and reductions in social security payments for others. Recessions provide windows of opportunity for policy change and the layering of policy with ideology. Governments reduce taxes on corporations and business so that these enterprises can compete and restore lost jobs. Equally, there is a demand for deregulation and the removal of burdens on business. Reductions in public expenditure on social programmes always receive the support of the business community, who argue that reducing the deficit would reduce interest rates. Public provision is perceived as crowding out the private sector, both in terms of financial resources and employment resources. National pay bargaining in the public sector is blamed for wage setting in the economy, when within the private sector there is a need to create more flexible wage settlements that reflect local markets.

Britain experienced seven different recessions after 1945 and the response to each recession reflected changing expectations and possibilities. Dealing with the recession of 1947 the Attlee government had to deal with the issue of devaluing sterling, and yet that government still felt sufficiently in control of events to ignore the demands of the financial sector to increase interest rates and instead maintained the cheap money policy advocated by Keynes. During the recessions of the 1950s and early 1960s the Conservative government's response was to increase the budget deficit, reduce taxes and improve aggregate demand. The recession of 1974 was a watershed in that the experience created a number of challenges for the government. At an intellectual level, the stagflation of 1974 created the context for monetarists to challenge the Keynesian conventional wisdom. The recession of 1974 therefore created the intellectual watershed which allowed the ascendance of a monetarist counter-revolution.

The following sections seek to analyse three policy phases in UK macro-economic policy. The first phase includes the period 1948 to 1970 and has been categorized as the Butskellite consensus. The twin concepts of Butskellism and consensus are important because the aim is to show that, while there were changes in government between Labour and Conservative administrations, there was the shared view that the objective of macro-economic policy was to preserve full employment, and, secondly, that in dealing with inflation governments needed to secure wage moderation with the trade unions. This was the post-war settlement of full employment, social provision through public expenditure, and incomes policies for dealing with inflation. The economic record for the period shows that unemployment stayed at a very low level of 240,000, which was approximately a 2.5 per cent unemployment rate. Economic growth rates of 3 per cent per annum might have been lower than for France or Germany, but in terms of UK economic history these growth rates were the most stable since 1880.

The second period represents the watershed years of 1970 to 1979. These years were a watershed in the sense that the Heath government elected in 1970 had promised a quiet revolution of bringing order to industrial relations, removing subsidies to the nationalized industries and creating a series of welfare reforms aimed at creating a welfare safety net and reducing a series of universal benefits. However, as the unemployment rate reached the 1 million mark Prime Minister Heath and his government reversed their policies on public expenditure and returned to more orthodox fiscal policy. Equally, the Trade Union Act of 1971 was abandoned. The Labour Government initially came to office in 1974 on the promise that through the social contract they would create a more stable industrial relations environment. However, the oil price shocks, the devaluation of sterling and large public sector deficits forced the Labour Government to seek financial assistance from the IMF. The year 1976 was a watershed year in the sense that the Labour Government adopted a policy of reducing public expenditure while unemployment had reached 1.7 million. Labour had abandoned the commitment to full employment.

The third phase seeks to explain the Thatcher Revolution and how in 2011, three decades later, the Thatcher years had changed the UK economic, political and social landscapes. In embracing the argument that governments cannot buck markets, the growth of income inequalities, dislocation and unemployment and the concentration of incomes towards the top 1 per cent of earners can be attributed to the Thatcher Revolution. Trade union legislation, the experience of the steelworkers, and the miners strikes were landmarks in the decline of the trade unions. Finally, the policy priority of curbing inflation resulted in major increases in unemployment. Throughout the years 1979 to 1992 UK unemployment averaged over 2 million, reaching peaks of over 3 million in 1982 and 1987.

THE BUTSKELLITE CONSENSUS

The period 1948 to 1974 has been described as the Butskellite consensus of commitment to the post-war settlement of collectivism and full employment. The term Butskellism represented the amalgam of the names of two Chancellors of the Exchequer: Rab Butler, who was the Conservative Chancellor during the 1951 government, and Hugh Gaitskell who was the Labour Chancellor between 1950 and 1951. The term was used to indicate policy continuity in the post-war period:

> In one sense, therefore, the new state represented the cost of social peace, full
> employment of resources, and an expanding domestic market. The government
> now took over directly the responsibility for formulating the 'national interest'
> in economic matters, and undertook to promote by its policies, not merely full-
> employment, but stable prices, economic growth and a trade surplus. (Gamble
> 1974, p. 31)

The post-war settlement, according to Gamble, reflected an economic
policy framework that included the commitment to full employment, price
controls and a contract between the state and civil society. The post-war
settlement confirmed the break from the economic policy landscapes that
had preceded World War II, which were characterized by high levels of
unemployment and industrial conflict, as reflected in the General Strike
of 1926 and an unemployment rate of 25 per cent during the Depression
of 1929.

The priorities of the Labour Government elected in 1945 had been
outlined in two major policy statements: first in 'Labour's Immediate
Programme' published in 1937 and then in Labour's election manifesto
of 1945 – 'Let Us Face The Future'. The commitment to nationalization
was central to Labour's programme. Labour's economic thinking in the
conduct of the process of economic policy was also very much influenced
by the economics of Keynes. Hugh Dalton (1935), in his book *Practical
Socialism*, together with Douglas Jay's *The Socialist Case* (1937), provided
the foundations for combining the concept of demand management, as
outlined by Keynes, with full employment and income re-distribution.
Dalton also agreed with Keynes that Britain needed to follow the cheap
money policy of low interest rates as a means of generating investment.
However, after Keynes died in 1946 Dalton felt isolated as he came under
increasing pressures from the financial sector and economists to bring his
cheap money policy to an end. The classical economists were re-emerging
and rediscovering the arguments on balanced budgets and the danger of
the state crowding out the private sector.

The Labour Government elected in 1945 set about redefining the
boundaries between the public and the private sectors. Labour's economic
policy was more interventionist, accepting the Keynesian argument about
the role of the state in stabilizing the capitalist economy through the direction of investment in the nationalized industries. The Trade Union Act
of 1927 was repealed. Labour established a series of welfare programmes
including universal pensions, unemployment benefits and a universal
health service, together with the commitment of full employment. The
Attlee government also nationalized utilities including gas and electricity, as well as the mining industry and also steel making. The economic
priority was to restore manufacturing and move the economy towards

export-led growth, which meant holding down personal consumption. Rationing and austerity were therefore important pillars of the economy, as was the commitment to incomes policy. Furthermore, in the context of full employment the government aimed to secure its income policy as an anti-inflation policy through agreements with the trade unions.

> That Labour Government, coming out of the war-time coalition headed by Churchill, laid the foundations for a consensus which lasted until the IMF cuts in 1976 and can be seen as having ushered in, and later seen out, a new era in which there was general agreement that full employment and the welfare state were to be permanent features of British society. (Benn 1988, p. xv)

In the meantime, the Conservative Party had to change its image, to break with its past and the association of the party with the economics of laissez faire, the slump and the unemployment of the inter-war years. The 'progressive' wing within the Party was therefore in ascendancy after 1945 (Gamble 1974). Rab Butler, seen as the architect of the post-war Conservative agenda, warned the Party of

> our need to convince a broad spectrum of the electorate, whose minds were scarred by inter-war memories and myths, that we had an alternative policy to Socialism which was viable, efficient and humane, which would release and reward enterprise and initiative but without abandoning social justice or reverting to mass unemployment. (Butler 1971, p. 132)

Rab Butler and Walter Monckton set up to explore a new approach to the economy and industrial relations for a future Conservative government. The outcome was the Industrial Charter of 1947 in which the Conservatives pledged to recognize workers' rights, including the right to belong to a trade union and the right to strike. The Charter was accepted by the Conservative Party Conference in May 1947. According to Anthony Eden, who was then deputy leader of the Party, the Charter confirmed the true tradition of Toryism:

> We are not a Party of unbridled brutal capitalism and never have been. Although we believe in personal responsibility and personal initiative in business, we are not the political children of the laissez-faire school. We opposed them decade after decade. Where did the Tories stand when the greed and squalor of the industrial revolution were darkening our land? I am content with Keir Hardie's testimony: 'As a matter of hard dry fact, from which there can be no getting away, there is more labour legislation standing to the credit of the Conservative party on the Statute Book than there is to that of their opponents'. (Conservative Party 1947, pp. 42–3)

The evaluation of the performance of the British economy during the period 1951 to 1964 produced different judgements. At one level, when compared to other countries the economy's performance was seen as conforming to the view of Britain's long-term economic decline. While growth for the UK economy averaged between 2.5 and 2.9 per cent per annum, France was experiencing growth rates of 7 per cent per annum, and West Germany's rate of growth was 5 per cent per annum. However, in terms of Britain's economic history, the period represented an era of continuous growth which had produced increases in living standards, a high level of consumption, stable employment and higher wages (Cairncross 1985).

Britain in 1951 had recovered most of its export markets. Exports had risen from 50 per cent below the pre-level war to nearly 55 per cent above, and were, by 1951, paying for 85 per cent of imports. Britain by 1951 had the best economic performance in Europe, and output per person had increased faster than in the USA (Williams, 1982). The years 1946 to 1951 was also a period of continuous full employment, living standards increased by about 10 per cent and the economy was growing at 3 per cent per annum, perhaps the longest period of sustainable growth in Britain's economic history – a better record even than when Britain had claimed to be the workshop of the world.

The government's economic advisors, including James Meade and Harold Robbins, agreed with Keynes that the problem of the external deficit reflected the excess of demand and suppressed inflation in the economy. This inflationary gap, argued Keynes, could only be remedied through the budget process by reducing aggregate demand. The Chancellor, Hugh Dalton, resisted this advice throughout the period 1945 to 1947. Labour's concern was to prevent the economy falling into recession, as had happened after the First World War when the boom was followed by a slump. Dalton felt that it was better for a Labour Government to have a bit of inflation rather than deflation: 'Before the war we had deflation which was not suppressed, and which was not potential but actual, and if we must choose between a slight – and I emphasise the word slight – between a slight inflationary flush and a slight deflationary pallor, I prefer the slight inflationary flush' (Dalton, Lecture to the Fabian Society, 13 November 1946, quoted in Pimlott 1987, p. 97).

The priority of the Labour Government was its commitment to full employment (Aldcroft 1984). Any attempt to reduce demand through fiscal policy was therefore likely to be deflationary and a threat to employment. Labour's attitude to inflation was mainly guided by the view that inflation represented an increase in prices rather than excess demand and that increases in prices required controls similar to those set up by the wartime government. For this reason, therefore, Labour's anti-inflation strategy up to 1947 was the control of prices through rationing and public subsidies on food, fuel and rents.

The economic policy framework did generate stability. Britain experienced continuing growth of around 2.5 per year for a period of 20 years, which improved living standards and consumption. This led Prime Minister Harold Macmillan, at the 1960 election, to declare that Britain had never had it so good (Brittan 1964). Prime Minister Macmillan was reflecting on the experience of long-term unemployment during the Great Depression and the related increases in poverty levels. The period 1950 to 1970 did seem to be a qualitatively different landscape to that of the 1930s.

The Conservative government between 1951 and 1964 did seek to use demand management to deal with economic cycles, using exchange controls and incomes policy to deal with inflation, and then showing a willingness to increase public expenditure and reduce taxation if the economy seemed to be slowing down. UK unemployment between 1950 and 1970 remained at around 250,000, which was approximately 2.5 per cent of the UK workforce. This had to be compared with an unemployment rate of 1.4 million between 1927 and 1939, which was equivalent to 25 per cent of the UK workforce. Wages were also rising in line with productivity growth. The Gini coefficient, as a measure of inequality, confirmed the narrowing of differentials between high and median earners. The Gini coefficient declined from 0.30 in 1950 to around 0.25 in 1970. Rising wages and full employment was contributing to lower income inequalities (Addison 1975).

The period 1950 to 1970 could be described as the Golden Age of Keynes – an age of full employment and increases in wages and living standards. Both Labour and Conservative governments followed a consensus-building approach in terms of industrial relations. Incomes policy was seen as central in curbing inflation and therefore the government needed to make compromises with the trade unions in securing incomes policy. This compromise usually meant the government making the commitment to hold down prices. There was, therefore, a policy of rent control in social housing, the government also held down the prices of gas, water and electricity as a means of creating a trade-off between prices and wages.

Some voices within the Conservative Party reflected the restlessness within the Party over accepting the post-war settlement. Nigel Birch and Enoch Powell resigned from the Treasury during the 1961 budget. They felt that the government should have focused on reducing the deficit, while the Prime Minister insisted that his government would not use the tool of unemployment to deal with inflation. Macmillan therefore encouraged his Chancellor, Reginald Maudling, to announce a 'go-for-growth' budget.

THE WATERSHED YEARS, 1970–1979: THE END OF A KEYNESIAN ERA

The Heath Government: 1970–1974

Trade union militancy contributed to the ebbing of Keynesian economic thinking. Trade union reform had become a major preoccupation for the 1966 Labour Government. The Royal Commission on Trade Unions (Donovan Commission) established by Prime Minister Harold Wilson in 1964 had reported in 1968 (Clegg 1970; HMSO 1968). One major finding of the report was the growth of the informal sector in trade union activity as opposed to the formal sector. The formal sector which was represented by the elected leadership of the trade unions and had been the bridge between the government and trade union members had been eclipsed by the informal sector of shop steward committees that were able to call for strikes without seeking the approval of the formal sector. The informal sector was therefore a form of decentralized bargaining that was undermining national bargaining agreements. The Commission recommended that there should be cooling off periods before strikes were called, that there should be secret ballots and that there should limits on secondary action (Bain 1984; Clegg 1970). Barbara Castle (Castle 1980), who was the Minister responsible, published the White Paper *In Place of Strife* in 1969 (HMSO 1969). However, that White Paper never became law since there were major disagreements within the Labour Government about Labour's relationships with the trade unions (Callaghan 1987).

This context is important to understand because when the Conservative Government led by Edward Heath won the election in 1970 there was an assumption that the Heath government had been given a mandate to make a break with the post-war settlement. The Conservative Party manifesto promised to phase out subsidies to the nationalized industries, to introduce more selective principles in social policy, to reduce personal taxation and to repeal efforts on the control of wages, prices and profits. The Conservative Party also pledged to alter the balance in industrial relations. The Conservative manifesto, *A Fair Deal at Work*, pointed out that:

> There were more strikes in 1969 than ever before in our history. Already in the first three months of 1970 there were 1134 strikes compared with 718 in the same period last year, when the Labour Government said the position was so serious that legislation was essential in the national interest. This rapid and serious deterioration directly stems from Labour's failure to carry through its own policy for the reform of industrial relations ... We welcome the TUC's willingness to take action through its own machinery against those who disrupt industrial peace by unconstitutional or unofficial action. Yet it is no substitute

for the new set of fair and reasonable rules we will introduce. (Conservative Party 1970, p. 23)

On winning the election Mr Heath pointed out that the ambition of his government was to bring forward a 'Quiet Revolution'. Sir Leo Pliatzky (1982), who was the permanent secretary to the Treasury during the 1970s, made the case that it was the Heath Government which introduced the market liberal agenda associated with the Thatcher governments in the 1980s:

> in a good many respects its [the Heath Government] philosophy anticipated the brand of politics which later came to be associated with Margaret Thatcher. There was the same commitment to restore a market economy, the same aspirations to roll back the frontiers of the public sector. This was the philosophy of Selsdon Man. (Pliatzky 1982, p. 98)

The 1971 Industrial Relations Act legislated that trade unions had to register with the Certification Officer, and in registering had to submit their union rule book. The rule book had to reflect changes in the handling of disputes, including unofficial disputes, ballots and the closed shop. Furthermore, the Secretary of State through the National Industrial Relations Court was now able to compel trade unions to suspend industrial action for a period of up to 60 days. Workers had now the right to belong or not belong to a trade union, and those who joined a trade union had to join a 'registered' union; strikes which aimed to compel workers to join unions were deemed illegal. Moran (1977) has argued that the unwillingness of the Secretary of State to negotiate on any of the central pillars of the legislation increased the pressures on the TUC to break off the consultation process with the government and embark on a campaign to make the Act unworkable: 'The events of 13–15 October are of the greatest importance in understanding the final fate of the 1971 Act . . . If Carr had not insisted on the indestructibility of the eight pillars, a very different outcome could have occurred. The unions would have negotiated, though reluctantly' (Moran 1977, p. 89).

The Act remained in operation for two and half years, but little significant use was made of it. The TUC campaign of non-registration, the secret payments of fines on behalf of the AUEW and the TGWU for refusal to register and the unwillingness of the CBI to use the legislation meant that effectively the Act had been put on ice whilst the government's attention by 1972 had already turned to securing tripartite discussions with the CBI and the TUC on the problems of wage inflation.

Whilst the Heath Government had promised a Quiet Revolution and less government in 1970, the collapse of the RB211 engine at Rolls Royce, the threatened closure of the Upper Clyde Shipbuilders, and the rise in unemployment to 1 million by 1971 produced the climate for a change in policy: government was to become more interventionist, increasing public expenditure in a plan to increase growth and reduce unemployment:

> The issue of rising unemployment dealt the killer blow to the Quiet Revolution . . .
>
>   [T]he upward trend towards the one million mark evoked fears of a return to the mass unemployment and social hardships of the 1930s, fears that Mr Heath and his ministers regarded as justified. According to one close adviser, Mr Heath was emotionally concerned with unemployment – he was constantly talking about the wasteland of unemployment. (Holmes 1982, pp. 44 and 46).

Trade union resistance and the increase in unemployment to 1 million resulted in the reversal of the Quiet Revolution. The Heath Government increased public expenditure and reduced taxation during the Barber boom in response to unemployment, while the government still needed to have a policy for dealing with inflation. Incomes policy and securing an agreement with the trade unions were seen as the preferred policy choices rather than allowing unemployment to become a threat.

The problem for the government was whether it was willing to control prices in order to secure a trade union agreement. The trade unions wanted a policy of prices control in exchange for incomes policy. They therefore asked for additional subsidies on housing rents, a freeze on utility prices, and the restoration of free school meals. These demands were seen as being too political.

In February 1974 the Heath Government called an election on the platform of who rules Britain and lost.

The Labour Government: 1974–1979

The Labour Party in opposition made the point that Labour had a historic and special relationship with the trade unions, and rather than seeking confrontation a new Labour Government would, through the social contract, generate a better climate for industrial relations (Callaghan 1987). Furthermore, the Labour Government of 1974 was committed to establishing the National Enterprise Board to renationalize the steel industry, create planning agreements and provide a framework for the growth of manufacturing. Harold Wilson, then leader of the Labour Party and eventual Prime Minister, criticized Mr Heath for being committed to a free market ideology, calling him 'Selsdon Man'.

The problem for the Labour Government of 1974 was the oil price shock of 1973 which was still having major ripple effects on the global economy and the eventual devaluation of sterling. The oil prices increases had shifted global savings to the oil producing countries and there was still the unresolved issue of how these global savings could be recycled to prevent a recession in the advanced economies. In the context of these challenges, the Labour Government could not sustain the path for public expenditure outlined in 1974, and in 1976 had to seek an IMF loan to deal with a public sector borrowing requirement (PSBR) that had grown to 9 per cent of GDP. Central to the Labour Government's Letter of Intent to the IMF was the plan to reduce public expenditure year on year starting in 1976 and to reduce the PSBR to 3 per cent of GDP by 1979. The brunt of Labour's reductions package was capital expenditure and also reductions in current expenditure on education, health and housing. Labour also had to phase out the subsides to the nationalized industries, which in turn made incomes policy with the trade unions more difficult to sustain. However, decisions on fiscal policy to reduce public expenditure while unemployment was rising was seen as the defining moment when the UK government broke away from Keynesian ideas:

> We used to think that you could spend your way out of a recession and increase employment by cutting taxes and boosting government spending. I tell you in all candour that this option no longer exists and insofar as it ever did exist, it injected a higher dose of inflation and a higher level of unemployment. Unemployment is caused by pricing ourselves out of jobs quite simply and unequivocally. (Labour Party 1976, p. 188)

The Callaghan speech confirmed a paradigm shift in economic policy making. After 1976 governments were no longer committed to maintaining full employment. In addition it would no longer be taken for granted that governments would use the lever of public expenditure as an automatic stabilizer. According to the new thinking, government did not influence the level of employment – employment was determined in the labour market:

> In practice it was not the Conservatives in Government who first denounced Keynes and embraced Friedman. It was not Mrs Thatcher but Jim Callaghan as Prime Minister who declared that we could no longer spend our way out of a slump. It was Dennis Healey not Geoffrey Howe who first put monetarism onto the agenda of British politics and abandoned a Keynesian strategy. Butskellism has come and gone. (Holland 1980)

THE THATCHER REVOLUTION

The election of Mrs Thatcher as Conservative Party leader in 1975 confirmed the ascendancy of the market liberal faction within the Party.

This faction had never been comfortable with the post-war settlement and included personalities such as Jock Bruce-Gardyne, Nicholas Ridley, Keith Joseph, Nigel Lawson and John Biffen, forming a group of MPs that had continuously indicated their commitment to market liberalism during the years of the Heath government and had actually voted against the government during the policy 'U-turns' of 1972 (Bruce-Gardyne 1984; Gilmour 1983; Joseph 1975). Mrs Thatcher showed her commitment to market liberal ideas by inviting speakers from major policy think tanks, including the Adam Smith Institute and the Salisbury Review, to give talks to Conservative Party policy makers at Conservative central office. Mrs Thatcher embraced the world of market liberal ideas and wanted these ideas to be translated into policy (Jenkins 1987).

On coming to power in May 1979 the major policy departure embraced by the Thatcher Government was its commitment to monetarism and the central argument that the government would curb inflation through monetary policy. The design of the Medium Term Financial Strategy (MTFS), outlined by Chancellor Geoffrey Howe in the budget of 1980, was seen as the most explicit commitment by government to the ideas of rational expectations and a monetarist doctrine. It confirmed the degree of commitment of the Thatcher government to monetarist explanations and policies towards inflation by making clear associations between inflation, the money supply and the public sector deficit:

> The first quality [of Mrs Thatcher] was a sense of moral rectitude which accounted for the single main achievement that would not have happened without her. This was the attachment to fiscal rigour in the early years, which, whatever analysis is made of its consequences, was an extraordinary exercise in political will . . .
> [T]he determination to pursue the economics of good housekeeping, preached at the knee of her father [which] she constantly invoked and elevated above the merely political to the moral level, came mainly from within her more than anybody else. It was her special contribution. (Young 1989, pp. 543 and 544)

The politics of Thatcherism seemed to advocate the return to a market economy, yet at the same time seemed to favour a strong centralizing state (Gamble 1988): 'The state must be strong: firstly to unwind the coils of social democracy and welfarism which have fastened around the free economy; second to police the market order; thirdly to make the economy more productive and fourthly to uphold social and political authority' (Gamble 1988, p. 32).

Kaldor (1980), in his evidence to the Select Committee on Monetary Policy, had produced data which indicated that the relationship between the 'unfunded' part of the PSBR and the growth of M3 produced a poor correlation, whilst bank lending to the private sector produced a more positive relationship. According to Kaldor, it was the central bank lending to the private sector which was the major contributor to monetary growth. He suggested, therefore, that:

> [the issue of the] 'money supply' which is supposed to play such a key role in the sequence of events is really no more than a fig leaf (or at best a smoke-screen) . . . In fact the downward pressure on prices exerted by the money supply is non existent – it is a figment of the imagination. A downward pressure on prices, in so far as it exists, comes from the loss of price leadership of British firms to foreign producers in the home market and not just in foreign markets which results from the over valuation of the pound, the absence of trade barriers and the rapid fall of the home producers' share in the home market (Kaldor 1980, p. 97)

Kaldor argued that the problem of inflation was still the problem of wage resistance, but rather than the government seeking to secure an incomes policy, the government had opted for the MTFS, which in an indirect way sought to break with wage inflation by creating unemployment. He therefore argued that the government's strategy would only succeed in curbing inflation through the creation of unemployment. That would bring trade unions to heel and eventually wage settlements. The problem was whether all workers would feel equally threatened by the rise in unemployment:

> If the Government succeeds in its object, it is likely to do so by causing wages to fall behind in the 'weak sectors'. Past experience suggests that the 'tattered' wage structure that would emerge from this process is not likely to be viable and the workers in the disadvantaged sectors will take every opportunity to regain their normal status in the scale of relative earnings. (Kaldor 1980, p. 96)

Denationalization, contracting out and liberalization were also important dimensions to the Thatcher Revolution. The government had announced that they wanted to permanently re-draw the boundaries between the private and the public sectors of the economy. The programme of denationalization, which started with Amersham International and British Telecomm in 1982, eventually also led to the denationalization of the utilities of gas, water and electricity, which were all privatized by the end of 1990. Other industries, including British Freight, Rolls Royce, British Airways and British Steel, were also denationalized. The 'ratchet' of socialism had been reversed.

Mrs Thatcher won three consecutive elections in 1979, 1982 and 1986. This, in one sense, represented a paradox. Studies by Alt (1979) had suggested that changes in government represented a process of 'kicking out the rascal', which meant that governments were elected according to economic performance. Mrs Thatcher was winning general elections in spite of the persistently high levels of unemployment. Unemployment in the 1980s had become a non-issue compared with the experience of the post-war years. The increase in unemployment to 1 million in 1972 represented a watershed when compared with the previous two decades of unemployment rates at 250,000. Edward Heath had to show that he was still committed to the policy of full employment and performed a series of famous U-turns, including the Barber boom, to regenerate the economy. During the Thatcher years there were years when unemployment peaked at over 3.2 million.

It is now more that 30 years since Mrs Thatcher took office in May 1979 and quoted St Francis of Assisi on the step of Ten Downing Street – promising to bring harmony where there was disharmony. During her time in office, the defeat of the steel workers in 1982 and the one-year-long miners strike in 1984 completely changed the industrial relations landscape. After 1984 trade unions were in retreat. The numbers of days lost at work because of industrial disputes declined sharply, while trade union density also declined, from a peak of 54 per cent membership in 1976 to approximately 30 per cent in 2010.

The economic landscape has also changed over the past three decades. Industrial communities in steel, coal mining and textiles are no longer part of the economic landscape. Approximately 3.4 million jobs in manufacturing have disappeared and manufacturing output declined from 24 per cent of GDP in 1979 to 16 per cent in 2010.

Mrs Thatcher embraced the argument that governments could not buck the market, which meant that governments had to accept the laws of supply and demand. If manufacturing was in decline this was part of the global process and governments had to provide incentives for the growth of new enterprises. Mrs Thatcher argued that the role of government should be confined to reducing taxes on enterprise to attract new research and development and to attract new industry.

The Big Bang of 1986, which provided for the liberalization of financial markets, was seen as a major breakthrough in the deregulation of financial markets. The process of liberalization allowed banks to give loans on mortgages while building societies were allowed to merge and form themselves into banks. London aimed to compete with New York to become the major financial centre. Canary Wharf was to attract the major global investment banks and hedge funds.

The financial sector's ratio of GDP expanded from 3 per cent of GDP in 1979 to 9 per cent of GDP in 2010. The UK is responsible now for 43 per cent of the over-the-counter (OTC) derivatives market, compared with 24 per cent in the USA. The OTC market, according to the latest IMF figures, show derivatives worth some $580 trillion, which is approximately 10 times the size of global GDP. While in the USA the top ten banks have assets equivalent to 65 per cent of US GDP, in the UK the Royal Bank of Scotland alone was worth three times UK GDP.

During the Thatcher years there was the acceptance that Britain was in transition to a New Economy. Giddens (2001) argued that the Knowledge Economy was transforming Britain and shifting power from the hierarchy of organizations to those who sold their knowledge and concepts. Organizations were becoming democratized. There was no need for trade unions because workers now had knowledge power. Beck (2006) pointed to the new individualism of work being an individualized experience, as opposed to the collective experiences of industrial communities. Bauman (2000) referred to a new sociology of liquid modernity – liquid in the sense that there were no longer static structures and communities but liquid forms of relationships.

NEW LABOUR: 1997–2010

The Blair Government elected in 1997 was the first in Labour's history to win two consecutive elections with large majorities. On winning the election in 1997, Tony Blair made it clear in his first speech that it was New Labour that had won the election. Implicitly Blair was distancing himself from 'Old Labour', which was associated with nationalization, economic planning and strong trade union ties: it was Blair's New Labour – committed to the continuity of the Thatcher Revolution that had won the election. New Labour offered continuity with the Thatcher experiment of privatization, of strengthening financial markets and pushing reforms in health and education.

The first action of the New Labour Government was to give independence to the Bank of England, giving the Bank the major policy objective of sustaining an inflation target of 2.5 per cent. The government also created the Monetary Policy Committee that would make transparent its discussions and judgements on interest rates in consultation with the Governor of the Bank of England.

Gordon Brown as Chancellor of the Exchequer outlined two golden rules for the control of public expenditure. The first rule put the focus on continuing to reduce the national debt as a ratio of GDP, and secondly on equating current expenditure with current revenues and only borrowing to meet capital expenditure. The government also set up an annual comprehensive spending review to re-allocate expenditure in between programmes.

The period 1997 to 2004 showed UK public finances to be in good shape. The Blair Government had succeeded in reducing the debt ratio to GDP from 45 per cent to 35 per cent. Government debt repayments also shrank from 50 billion to 25 billion annually. Tax revenues were buoyant. There was no recession and Gordon Brown could claim that the Labour Government had solved the problems of booms and bust. During the Blair years unemployment fell below 1 million and the inflation rate stayed within the Bank of England limits of 2.5 per cent. Wage settlements of 3.5 per cent meant really increases of only 0.8 per cent per annum.

However, the financial meltdown of 2007 soon undermined the achievements of New Labour.

Gordon Brown as Prime Minister led the global response by taking banks into public ownership and guaranteeing their assets. While Hank Paulson, the US Treasury Secretary, sent confusing signals with the TARP programme, the Labour Government was soon able to bring stability to the financial sector. Paulson was for ideological reasons reluctant to follow the British model and be seen as nationalizing the financial sector. However, in the rescue of AIG, the Federal Reserve ended up taking up 78 per cent ownership of AIG and the $700 billion TARP programme was used to remove the toxic assets of the bank's balance sheet.

The coalition government elected in May 2010 blamed the outgoing Labour Government for the increase in public sector deficits. On the eve of the financial meltdown the UK debt to GDP ratio was at 40 per cent – below the average for the OECD countries. During 2008 and 2009 UK GDP shrank by 4 per cent while tax revenues declined by 18 per cent. These two factors contributed to the deterioration of the public finances. Debt as GDP ratio increased to 68 per cent by 2009 and the PSBR increased to 10 per cent of GDP. The second criticism by the coalition was that the Labour Government created an economy that was not sustainable in the long term. The Labour Government had put too much emphasis on the financial sector and the housing market as being the generators of growth. While it is true that the Labour Government became as mesmerized by the City, as the Thatcher Government had been, it was during the Thatcher years that the focus of the economy shifted towards finance. The process of de-industrialization had accelerated during the Thatcher years with the loss of 2.5 million jobs in manufacturing. The Thatcher government had argued that the decline of manufacturing was being replaced by the knowledge economy of value added created in such areas as advertising, and in the growth of the insurance and banking sectors.

CONCLUSIONS

The study of economic policy in the UK since 1945 confirms a major shift from the commitment to full employment, Keynesian ideas and universal welfare that dominated the period 1945–1974, to a policy framework that put the emphasis on the conquering of inflation as the major economic objective. The ascendance of market liberal ideas, both at the level of government and within institutions involved in the policy process, created a dominance in economic thinking that was difficult to challenge. While there is a plurality of approaches as to how economies work, the axioms presented by market liberalism of rational expectations and efficient markets provided policy makers with ready-made policy frameworks.

The shift at the levels of ideas also meant a shift in the balances of power and influence. In the context of full employment trade unions were in the ascendancy. While governments were committed to full employment they had to secure trade union agreements on incomes policy. In exchange for wage moderation trade unions asked for price controls and for increases in social spending as a means of benefiting their membership. The study of income inequalities confirms that inequalities narrowed between 1950 and 1974. The Gini coefficient declined from 0.30 in 1950 to 0.25 in 1974. Wages were rising in line with the growth in productivity and people were sharing in the fruits of growing prosperity. Unemployment throughout this period stayed at 2.5 per cent. However, the period beginning in 1979 saw the widening of income inequalities as the Thatcher government reduced the upper tax limits from 80 per cent to 40 per cent. Unemployment during the Thatcher years peaked at 3.3 million. Trade union membership declined from 50 per cent in 1976 to 30 per cent in 2010. The Gini coefficient grew from 0.25 per cent to 0.34 per cent.

REFERENCES

Addison, P. (1975) *The Road to 1945*. London: Jonathan Cape.
Aldcroft, D. (1984) *Full Employment: The Elusive Goal*. Sussex: Wheatsheaf Books.
Alt, J. (1979) *The Politics of Economic Decline*. Cambridge: Cambridge University Press.
Bain, G. (1984) *Industrial Relations in Britain*. Oxford: Basil Blackwell.
Bauman, Z. (2000) *Liquid Modernity*. Cambridge: Polity Press.
Bazen, S. and J. Thirwall (1989) *De-industrialization*. Oxford: Heinemann Education Press.
Beck, U. (2006) *The Cosmopolitan Vision*. Cambridge: Polity Press.
Benn, T. (1988) *Out of the Wilderness: Diaries, 1963–1967*. London: Arrow Books.

Brittan, S. (1964) *The Treasury under the Tories, 1951 to 1964*. Harmondsworth: Penguin.

Bruce-Gardyne, J. (1984) *Mrs Thatcher's First Administration*. London: Macmillan.

Cairncross, Sir Alec (1985) *Years of Recovery*. London: Methuen.

Callaghan, J. (1987) *Time and Chance*. London: Collins.

Castle, B. (1980) *The Castle Diaries, 1974 to 1976*. London: Weidenfield and Nicolson.

Clegg, H. (1970) *The System of Industrial Relations in Britain*. Oxford: Basil Blackwell.

Conservative Party (1947) *Conservative Party Conference Report, 1947*. London: Conservative Political Centre.

Conservative Party (1970) *A Fair Deal At Work*. London: Conservative Political Centre.

Dalton, H. (1935) *Practical Socialism for Britain*. London: Routledge.

Gamble, A. (1974) *The Conservative Nation*. London: Macmillan.

Gamble, A. (1988) *The Free Economy and the Strong State*. London: Macmillan.

Giddens, A. (2001) *The Global Third Way Debate*. Cambridge: Polity Press.

Gilmour, I. (1983) *Britain Can Work*. Oxford: Martin Robertson.

HMSO (1968) *Royal Commission on Trade Unions and Employers Associations 1965–1968 Report*, Cmnd 3623. London: HMSO.

HMSO (1969) *In Place of Strife*, Cmnd 3888. London: HMSO.

Holland, S. (1980) 'The Politics of Howleyism', *The Guardian*, 16 June.

Holmes, M. (1982) *Political Pressure and Economic Policy*. London: Butterworth.

Jay, D. (1937) *The Socialist Case*. London: Faber and Faber.

Jenkins, P. (1987) *Mrs Thatcher's Revolution*. London: Jonathan Cape.

Joseph, K. (1975) *Stranded in the Middle Ground*. London: Conservative Political Studies.

Kaldor, (Lord) N. (1980) *Memorandum on Monetary Policy*. London: HMSO.

Labour Party (1976) *Annual Conference: Verbatim Report 1976*. London: The Labour Party.

Martin, R. and B. Rowthorn (1986) *The Geography of De-Industrialisation*. London: Macmillan.

Moran, M. (1977) *The Politics of Industrial Relations*. London: Macmillan.

Pimlott, B. (1987) *The Diary of Hugh Dalton*. London: Jonathan Cape.

Pliatzky, Sir Leo (1982) *Getting and Spending*. Oxford: Basil Blackwell.

Williams, P. (1982) *Hugh Gaitskell*. Oxford: Oxford University Press.

Young, H. (1989) *One of Us*. London: Macmillan.

9. The politics of the Financial Crisis Inquiry Commission

The concern of this chapter is the Financial Crisis Inquiry Commission (FCIC), which was established by President Obama in January 2010 specifically to explore the causes of the financial crisis. The work of the FCIC represents at present the most comprehensive study of the crisis. The Inquiry was highly transparent in that it had open hearings with witnesses giving testimonies under oath. The FCIC started the hearings in January 2010 and produced the final report in January 2011 (FCIC 2011). The FCIC Commissioners conducted interviews with 700 participants and had available some 250,000 documents. The brief for the FCIC, created by Congress in the aftermath of the financial crisis, was to:

> examine the causes of the current financial and economic crisis in the United States ... the Commission reviewed millions of pages of documents, interviewed more than 700 witnesses and held 19 days of public hearings ...
>
> We also studied relevant policies ... [and] examined the roles of policy makers and regulators ...
>
> In that sense the Commission has functioned somewhat like the National Transportation Safety Board which investigates aviation and other transportation accidents so that knowledge of the probable causes can help avoid future accidents. (FCIC 2011, pp. xi and xii)

During the early days of the financial crisis, Nancy Pelosi, leader of the House of Representatives, called for a 'Pecora type Commission' to investigate the financial crisis. When the Senate established the FCIC the name of the Pecora Commission was again invoked. While there was no such thing as the Pecora Commission, the lawyer and judge, Ferdinand Pecora, was the Chief Counsel to the United States Senate Committee on Banking and Currency, having been brought in during the last days of the outgoing administration of President Hoover in December 1932. The original investigation had been established by the President in March 1932. In November 1932 the Commission had not still made any major recommendations and seemed to have stalled (Perino 2010). Senator Norbeck, a Republican Senator who chaired the Banking Committee, and who had survived the Democrat cyclone of November 1932, had hired Ferdinand

Pecora in December 1932 in a last ditch attempt to try and show that the Inquiry could produce some tangible recommendations. There was still a lot of public anger about the Depression, some 86 per cent of the Dow Jones had been wiped out between 1929 and 1932 and the unemployment rate had reached 25 per cent. Not much was expected since these were the dying days of the outgoing Congress. However, during a period of ten days of interviewing key witnesses, Pecora had reignited the investigation. His questioning of Charles Mitchell, Chief Executive of the National City Bank, confirmed the degree of mis-selling of securities by the City Bank, especially Peruvian bonds, which the bank had known were high risk bonds but yet had failed to advise their clients on the risk exposure of these bonds. Within a few days Mitchell had been discredited and was forced to resign his position.

It was because of Pecora's impact on the investigation that in 1932 the Commission became known as the Pecora Commission. The Commission submitted their report in late January 1933 just before President Roosevelt took his oath of office. The Commission's findings had an immediate impact on the President and during his acceptance speech he used the concept of money changers in referring to the CEO executives in the finance industry, a term that had been made possible by the Pecora hearings:

> . . . rulers of the exchange of mankind's goods have failed, through their own stubbornness and their own incompetence, have admitted their failure and abdicated. Practices of the unscrupulous money changers stand indicted in the court of public opinion, rejected by the hearts and minds of men . . . the money changers have fled their high seats in the temple of civilization. We may now restore that temple to the ancient truths. (President Roosevelt, 3 March 1933, the first inaugural lecture as reported in *The New York Times*)

Perino, in his study of the impact of Pecora on the thinking of Roosevelt, commented:

> Somewhere in Manhattan, perhaps sitting by the radio in his Upper West Side apartment, Ferdinand Pecora, must have been smiling. It was Pecora more than anyone else, who deserved credit for those lines. Though Roosevelt claimed that the lines had come to him a week earlier while he was sitting at a service at St James Episcopal Church, it was Pecora and the Senate hearings he'd wrapped up just two days earlier that had made those lines true. (Perino 2010, p. 3)

The impact of Pecora was immediate. The Glass Bill to reform the finance industry which had been defeated during the January sitting was resubmitted by Glass together with Steagill and became the Banking Act of 1933. This was followed by the setting up of the Federal Deposit

Insurance Corporation (FDIC) and the Securities Act of 1993. These reforms had been made possible by the Pecora Commission.

The findings of the FCIC were published in the *Financial Crisis Inquiry Report* in January 2011. The Commission carried out 12 public hearings and received hundreds of testimonies and some 200,000 submissions of expert documents, interviews, and archives of emails that formed the opinions and decisions on which the Commission was able to draw in providing an understanding of the crisis. Chairman Phil Angelides opened the Commission hearing on 10 January 2010 with the following comment:

> People are angry. They have a right to be. The fact is that Wall Street is enjoying record profits and bonuses in the wake of receiving trillions of dollars in government assistance – while so many families are struggling to stay afloat – has only heightened the sense of confusion.
>
> I see this commission as a proxy for the American people, their eyes, their ears, and possibly also their voice. This forum may be the only opportunity to have their questions asked and answered. This forum may be our last best chance to take stock of what really happened so that we can learn from it and restore faith in our economic system. (Angelides 2010a, p. 1)

In his statement, Angelides thus interpreted the purpose of the commission as giving a voice to the voiceless population and acknowledged the anger felt by people who were losing their jobs, their homes, their savings and their hopes for retirement. Furthermore, the Chairman highlighted the sense of unfairness that, even in the middle of recession, bank executives were receiving large compensation packages while their banks were in receipt of government finances, and therefore taxpayers' money, to help keep the banks in business. The hearings of the Commission became highly contestable as the enquiry progressed. The hearings confirmed the ideological differences between the Commissioners. The ten Commissioners appointed by Congress comprised six Democrats and four Republicans. Chairman Angelides, Commissioners Brooksley Born, Byron Georgiou, Heather Merron, John Thompson and Senator Graham were the Democrat appointees. Vice Chairman Hon Bill Thomas, Commissioners Keith Hennessey, Douglas Holtz-Eakin and Peter Wallison were the Republican Appointees. The final report was signed by the Democrat Commissioners while there were two dissenting reports from the Republican Commissioners. Wallison (2011) produced one dissenting report while the other was headed by Commissioner Hennessey (Hennessey 2011).

The majority final report (FCIC 2011) attributed the crisis to issues of deregulation, the over-the-counter (OTC) derivatives, the failure of regulators, predatory lending and the failures of the Credit Rating Agencies in the ratings of asset backed securities. The main issues raised by the majority report pointed out, firstly, that the financial crisis could have been avoided and had to be understood as being the product of human actions rather than being an exogenous event that was beyond the control of government. Even though the Federal Reserve did reduce interest rates it was not inevitable that the financial sector would introduce a series of asset backed securities that eventually had to be downgraded to below investment grade. Also there were many warnings that the increases in house prices were unsustainable. Secondly, the report pointed to widespread failure by financial regulators. Regulatory arbitrage created a context for banks to search regulators that offered minimum supervision. Regulators competed to acquire charters which increased their budgets and revenues. Some regulators did not have the capacity to supervise complex global banks and holding companies. Regulators were also fully aware that the climate was one which encouraged deregulation. Regulators lived in a climate of constant push-back by policy makers when it came to making recommendations on tighter regulation. The deregulated climate had put handcuffs on the regulators. Thirdly, there was the failure of risk management. Banks held too many asset backed securities so that when these assets were downgraded and had to be marked to market the banks were forced to write down a number of assets. Bear Stearns's failure to oversee the hedge funds meant that their collapse eventually spilled over into a crisis at the bank.

The theme of the majority report, therefore, was the context of deregulation. The climate of unfettered markets had contributed to the growth of OTC derivatives and the securitization processes of mortgages had resulted in a disavowal of responsibilities by brokers, lawyers and originators of mortgage products. Since fees were being paid up front little thought was given to long-term consequences. Hank Paulson, who had been Secretary for the Treasury during the financial crisis, explained the financial crisis as follows during his testimony to the FCIC Inquiry:

> The subprime market by itself was relatively small – relative to the U.S. economy or to the U.S. capital markets. And the problem was much bigger. There were excesses, as we've talked about, in housing and across the markets more broadly. I'll give you an analogy that's used a lot. There is a lot of dry tinder out there. Okay? And the driest tinder was subprime. That's where the fire started. But there were a lot of other excesses. And that is really what happened. And there were a whole lot of things coming together to create this crisis. (Paulson 2010, p. 25)

According to the majority report the financial crisis needed to be located in the specific context of deregulation in financial market. The shift from originate and hold to originate and distribute in banking philosophy meant there was a downgrading of standards in dealing with mortgage applications. Banks no longer held 30-year mortgages. The aim was to bundle and securitize mortgages and earn upfront fees from the securitization process. Mortgage brokers had the incentive to channel borrowers towards high interest mortgages because of fees and compensation. The Credit Rating Agencies increased their incomes from $3 billion to $6 billion through the securitization process. Some $4.3 trillion of asset backed securities were securitized during the period 1990–2007. Households surrendered their equities and remortgaged their homes, which in turn gave them the means to increase their personal consumption. The financial sector grew from 3 per cent of GDP to 5 per cent of GDP, while profits from the financial sector increased from 15 per cent to 40 per cent of corporate profits. Bank executives took compensation packages of $48 million as a reward for increasing the profitability of their banks. The OTC market increased from $23 trillion to a notional amount of $640 trillion. The OTC market was deregulated and lacked transparency; it created interconnectedness and then uncertainty. Over-the-counter derivatives were opaque, complex and difficult to understand; this created uncertainty and amplified the financial crisis:

> They were so opaque and complex and difficult to understand. Those products are hard to understand. And that is why I so strongly believe that you want to press standardization, [it] is in all of our interest. So I think the way you do this is you press – everything is standardized onto an exchange. And the over the counter you put through a central clearinghouse where you've got great oversight. And then . . . you put big capital charges so you penalize complexity. (Paulson 2010, p. 21)

Goldman Sachs adopted a strategy of going short on mortgage backed securities and yet kept selling the long side to their clients (FCIC 2011). Goldman Sachs and UBS were sued by their customers for selling asset backed securities which were downgraded from triple-A to below investment grade within a few months. In the case of John Paulson, who agreed with Goldman Sachs to select a series of portfolios within a CDO, he was able to take out insurance for $15 million against the possibility of a CDO worth $1.5 billion going to default. Paulson chose the weakest series of mortgages in the CDO. Goldman Sachs as the market maker sold the long side to IKB without telling IKB that Paulson had selected the portfolio and had gone short. The CDO was downgraded within a few weeks; Paulson made $1.5 billion for his company. By contrast, IKB had to seek a financial bail-out from the Swiss government. Evidence presented to the FCIC Inquiry confirmed that the issuers were aware they were selling bonds to their clients that were below investment grade. Investors were relying on the Credit Rating Agencies (CRAs) and their ratings of securities. The CRAs were trusted for providing accurate ratings. Some $4.3 trillion of derivatives were downgraded from triple-A to below investment grade. The CRAs were inherently involved in a conflict of interest as they were relying on issuers based fees. This relationship made it difficult for the CRAs to walk away from a rating. The processes of securitization and the shift from the originate and hold model of banking to the originate and distribute model, resulted in moral hazard, the breakdown of the trust between the borrower and the brokers.

The analysis of the near collapse of AIG in September 2008 highlighted the weaknesses created in the deregulated OTC derivatives market during 1999 and 2000. The deregulated derivatives markets had grown from $35 trillion in 2000 to $640 trillion in 2007 (BIS 2008). AIGFP was able to sell $270 billion worth of derivatives because it did not have to post collateral. AIG assumed that the triple-A ratings meant there would be no default and therefore the income received from the CDS markets was revenue. However, CDS was a pseudo insurance in the sense that the insurance company was not forced to post collateral to show that it was able to pay if there was default. AIGFP insured $80 billion of CDS for a $7 billion premium. This exposure would have not have been possible within a traditional statutory insurance. Secondly, when some mortgages started to default Goldman Sachs asked AIG to pass collateral to Goldman Sachs to balance the downside of the insurance. Goldman Sachs asked AIGFP for some $1.8 billion and AIGFP questioned the amount. AIGFP argued that there was no market for the CDO and therefore Goldman Sachs was aggressively marking down the CDO. Eventually AIG paid $1.2 billion to Goldman Sachs.

Ultimately, the US government had to provide a rescue package of $180 billion for AIG and take 78 per cent ownership in the entity. The case study of AIG showed the problems of derivatives at a number of levels. First, if these derivatives had been properly traded on exchanges there would not have been any dispute about the price levels of the CDOs. Secondly, if the CDS had been a statutory insurance AIG would have had to post daily collateral to reflect price changes. Thirdly, there is the question of whether, in the absence of a market for CDOs, Goldman Sachs was in a monopoly position to mark to market.

The minority report from Commissioners Hennessey, Holtz-Eakin and Vice Chair Thomas (Hennessey 2011) argued that the majority report had blamed too many culprits and that it lacked economic analysis. Hennessey and his group pointed out that the housing bubble was a global experience and was not confined to the USA. There were major housing bubbles in the UK, Ireland, Spain and Australia, although each of these countries had different housing policies. The Hennessey report aimed to connect the global housing bubble to the global savings glut that emerged in China, the emerging economies and the oil producing countries. The savings glut pushed down borrowing costs which in turn reduced risk. Risk was therefore being underpriced:

> Low-cost capital can but does not necessarily have to lead to an increase in risky investments. Increased capital flows to the United States and Europe cannot alone explain the credit bubble. We still don't know whether the credit bubble was the result of rational or irrational behavior. Investors may have been rational – their preferences may have changed, making them willing to accept lower returns for high-risk investments. They may have collectively been irrational – they may have adopted a bubble mentality and assumed that, while they were paying a higher price for risky assets, they could resell them later for even more. Or they may have mistakenly assumed that the world had gotten safer and that the risk of bad outcomes (especially in U.S. housing markets) had declined. (Hennessey 2011, p. 10)

Hennessey and his group, therefore, opposed the majority report argument that the climate of deregulation contributed to the financial crisis:

> We also reject as too simplistic the hypothesis that too little regulation caused the crisis, as well as its opposite, that too much regulation caused the crisis. We question this metric for determining the effectiveness of regulation. The *amount* of financial regulation should reflect the need to address particular failures in the financial system. The majority says the crisis was avoidable if only the United States had adopted across-the-board more restrictive regulations, in conjunction with more aggressive regulators and supervisors. This conclusion by the majority largely ignores the global nature of the crisis' (Hennessey 2011, p. 8)

The other dissenting report by Commissioner Wallison (2011) attributed the financial crisis to government housing policy, encouraging home ownership and ignoring the fact that 50 per cent of new mortgages were sub-prime. According to Wallison's calculations, therefore, $11 trillion were sub-prime loans. This has to be contrasted with the figure produced by Bernanke, which suggested that between $300 billion and $500 billion were sub-prime (Bernanke 2010):

> I believe that the *sine qua non* of the financial crisis was U.S. government housing policy, which led to the creation of 27 million subprime and other risky loans – half of all mortgages in the United States – which were ready to default as soon as the massive 1997–2007 housing bubble began to deflate. If the U.S. government had not chosen this policy path – fostering the growth of a bubble of unprecedented size and an equally unprecedented number of weak and high-risk residential mortgages – the great financial crisis of 2008 would never have occurred. (Wallison 2011, p. 5)

The hearings of the FCIC reflected the contestability of the financial crisis. Democrats throughout the Inquiry put the emphasis on deregulated markets, the growth of OTC derivatives, the failings of regulators, and on the government having to rescue the financial sector in order to avoid a second Great Depression similar to that of 1929. By contrast, the Republican Commissioners wanted to argue that the financial crisis could be attributed to government. The Republican recurring theme therefore was the issue of moral hazard and that once the government had rescued Bear Stearns there was the assumption that the government would rescue other financial institutions. Secondly, Republicans wanted to show that government policy on housing had encouraged home ownership among a high risk group. Home ownership during the Clinton and Bush Presidencies increased from 64 per cent to 69 per cent. This additional 5 per cent created a climate of high risk. The response of the financial markets was to create a series of derivatives to hedge against high risk.

The following sections deals with three episodes during the Inquiry that reflected the nature of the politics that evolved as the inquiry progressed. The first hearings of 13 January 2010 included receiving testimonies and taking evidence from the CEOs of the major investment banks. This allowed these CEOs to outline their own explanations for the financial crisis. The major controversy to emerge in that first hearing was that Goldman Sachs was selling securities to clients in the knowledge that it was going short on these asset backed securities while selling the long side to their clients. This highlighted a conflict of interest in that investors were being treated by Goldman Sachs as being sophisticated investors who knew the exposure they wanted, while the investors, as clients of Goldman Sachs, assumed that Goldman Sachs would only sell them something that was good. The second hearing on derivatives highlighted the ideological difference between Democrats and Republicans.

FIRST PUBLIC HEARINGS, 13 JANUARY 2010

The FCIC launched the Inquiry by inviting the CEOs of the five major investments to give their own versions for the financial crisis. The FCIC received written testimonies from Lloyd C Blankfein, the CEO of the Goldman Sachs Group, James Dimon CEO and Chairman of JP Morgan Chase, John J Mack, Chairman of Morgan Stanley, and Brian T Moynihan, Chairman of Bank of America. The first hearings polarized on the question of whether the financial crisis was an event that market participants did not anticipate, which was the view taken by the CEOs of

the investment banks. The Democrat Commissioners wanted to empha-
size at the outset that the financial crisis was human made; that there was
asymmetry of information between the investment banks and investors
and that banks were selling securities to investors who were relying on
the triple-A ratings given by the CRA, when it was common knowledge
that the CRAs were dependent for their information on the issuers of the
bonds. Chairman Angelides wanted to show that the investment banks
had a conflict interest in selling bonds to investors. Investors could not
assume that the bank was selling them a 'good' investment. The bank
was assuming that the buyer was a sophisticated investor who knew what
exposure they wanted to take. The bank was not acting as fiduciary or
advisor but as a market maker. The concern of the bank was to unload
securities. The CEO of Goldman Sachs argued that if people wanted to
buy a bond it was assumed they were sophisticated investors who knew
the exposure. The bank was there as a market maker bringing together the
buyer and the seller. Lloyd Blankfein in his testimony identified the global
savings and cheap interest rates in the USA as being major contributory
factors:

> the genesis of the problem wasn't in sub-prime alone. Instead, the roots of
> the damage to our financial system are broad and deep. They coalesced over
> many years to create a sustained period of cheap credit and excess liquidity.
> The resulting under-pricing of risk led to massive leverage. I see at least three
> broad underlying factors: First, there has been enormous growth in the amount
> of foreign capital, much of it held in large pools, and a very significant shift in
> the balance of payments of many emerging markets; Second, and linked to this,
> nearly ten years of low long-term interest rates; and Third, the official policy of
> promoting, supporting and subsidizing homeownership in the United States.
> (Blankfein 2010, p. 7)

Angelides pointed out that Goldman Sachs was selling securities to customers in the knowledge that these securities would soon be downgraded
to below investment grade. Goldman Sachs was taking the short side while
selling the long side to an investor. Angelides compared this to selling
insurance on a car that had faulty brakes. The transcript of the cross
examination between Chairman Angelides and Lloyd Blankfein reads as
follows:

CHAIRMAN ANGELIDES:
. . . And many of the securities that you sold to institutional investors, other
folks went bad within months of issuance. Now, one expert in structured
financing said, 'The simultaneous selling of securities to customers and short-
ing them because they believe they are going to default is the most cynical
use of credit information that I've seen.' Do you believe that was a proper
legal, ethical practice? And would the firm continue to do that practice? Or

do you believe that's the kind of practice that undermines confidence in the marketplace?

BLANKFEIN:

. . . In our market-making function, we are a principal. We represent the other side of what people want to do. We are not a fiduciary. We are not an agent. Of course, we have an obligation to fully disclose what an instrument is and to be honest in our dealings, but we are not managing somebody else's money.

When we sell something as a principal – which is what we are as a market maker . . . In most of these cases, the person who came to us came to us for the exposure that they wanted to have.

. . .

CHAIRMAN ANGELIDES:

Well, I'm just going to be blunt with you. It sounds to me a little bit like selling a car with faulty brakes and then buying an insurance policy on the buyer of those cars. It just – it doesn't seem to me that that's a practice that inspires confidence in the markets. I'm not talking about your own . . . (Angelides et al. 2010a, pp. 27–30)

John Mack, the Chairman and CEO of Morgan Stanley testified:

Morgan Stanley, like many of its peers, experienced significant losses related to the decline in the value of securities and collateralized debt obligations backed by residential mortgage loans. This was a powerful wake-up call for this firm, and we moved quickly and aggressively to adapt our business to the rapidly changing environment . . .

Morgan Stanley moved up its announcement of its strong third-quarter earnings to September the 16th, but our stock remained under heavy pressure. It lost nearly a quarter of its value the following day, falling from 28.7 to 21.75. Despite these strong results, it continued to trade low and, finally, traded as low as $6.71. (Angelides et al. 2010a, pp. 16–17)

The CEO of Morgan Stanley attributed the decline in the value of his bank as being attributable to rumour, speculation and short selling. Dick Fuld, the CEO of Lehman Brothers, and James Cayne, the CEO of Bear Stearns, would make similar arguments at later testimonies to the FCIC. The common theme of their arguments was that once rumours started about the financial condition of a bank it was difficult to push back on that rumour. Any statement made by the bank seems to have increasingly negative feedback; rather than calming the market, the position of the company became further undermined – investors pull out and banks have to meet their liabilities by selling assets. There is a loss of confidence in REPO markets, a reluctance to roll over debt, and a reluctance to unwind debt at the beginning of the day.

DERIVATIVES HEARINGS

The witnesses and testimonies during these hearings proved to be highly controversial, and the questioning of the witness confirmed the fault lines that were developing within the FCIC Inquiry. At this hearing the Democrat Commissioners were led by Commissioner Born who had been Chairman of the Commodities Futures Trading Commission (CFTC) and had campaigned and advised against putting derivatives in unregulated markets. Chairman Angelides recognized the work of Commissioner Born at the beginning of the two-day hearings:

> It's not as if no one warned us. Back in the 1990s, Commissioner Born, then Chair of the Commodities Futures Trading Commission, saw the looming crisis and argued strenuously for transparency and common-sense regulation of derivatives. Her prescience and tenacity earned her the John F. Kennedy Profile in Courage Award. If she had prevailed, I believe we would have had a safer financial system. (Angelides 2010a, p. 7)

Commissioner Born had become highly involved in the debate on the legislation that eventually deregulated OTC derivatives which eventually expanded from $53 trillion in notional amounts in 1999 to $640 trillion in 2007. OTC derivatives were defined as private swap deals between two willing parties which did not need to be traded on official exchanges. Each transaction was seen as individual and unique. What was qualitatively different about the OTC market is that counter-parties did have to post collateral. There was no daily posting of collateral as to what happened on the trading exchanges.

> Congress passed a statute in 2000 called The Commodity Futures Modernization Act . . . Because of that statute, no federal or state regulator currently has oversight responsibilities or regulatory powers over that market. As of December of last year, the reported size of the market was almost $615 trillion . . .
> Lack of transparency, lack of price discovery, excessive leverage, lack of adequate capital and prudential controls, and a web of interconnections among counterparties have made this market dangerous. (Born 2010, p. 51)

This figure was contested by Republican Commissioners Wallison, Hennessey and Holtz-Eakin who argued that notional amounts did not really measure exposures. Professor Greenberger (2010) agreed that it was difficult to come to an accurate measure of the OTC market because these were private contracts and there were notional measures and real exposures measures. However, Greenberger came to the view that the OTC market for credit default swaps was around $60 trillion and had recently fallen to $35 trillion. However, witness Greenberger, using the Federal Reserve discount for measuring risk at 3 per cent of notional value, came to the view that OTC derivatives during the financial crisis amounted to over $50 trillion – equivalent to world GDP.

> In October 2008, the notional value of the unregulated OTC market was estimated to be in excess of $600 trillion. Included within that amount was estimated to somewhere between $35–65 trillion in credit default swaps (CDSs).
>
> While the Federal Reserve has estimated generally that 3% of the notional amount of a swap is the amount at risk in swaps transactions, a credit default swaps' insurance like aspects mean that if a default is triggered, the entire amount of the sum guaranteed is at risk. While the Federal Reserve's 3% figure establishing amount at risk has been deemed by many . . . to be far too low, combining even the *lower* figure for the value of outstanding CDS ($35 trillion) in September 2008 with Fed's 3% of the remaining notional value ($565 trillion), the resulting amount at risk at the time of the meltdown (about $52 trillion) almost equaled the world's GDP. Even using the most conservative figures for the sake of argument, $52 trillion is a very large figure. (Greenberger 2010, p. 11)

Republican Commissioner Hennessey started his questioning of the witnesses that day by questioning the assumption that derivatives in themselves were harmful. His argument was that derivatives were a tool similar to a hammer, and therefore the issues was how these derivatives were being used rather than the instruments themselves:

> I have heard a couple of you say that derivatives or credit default swaps were culprits. And I think that derivatives and credit default swap are things, and things can't be culprits any more than a hammer used in a murder can be a culprit. The person who uses the hammer, or misuses the hammer is the culprit. And I am concerned that in a lot of cases what we may be doing is confusing form, or the instrument, with the actor who is using that instrument. (Hennessey 2010, p. 69)

Witness Michael Masters, Chief Executive of Masters Capital Management had no problem in pointing out that derivatives and the CFMA had contributed to the financial crisis:

> unregulated credit derivatives were largely responsible for creating systemic risk that turned isolated problems into a system-wide crisis. In my view, with the benefit of hindsight, the Commodity Futures Modernization Act was an unmitigated disaster. It is one of the worst pieces of legislation that I've ever seen with regard to the economy. And, you know, today we are trying to fix a big problem, but it's a long battle. (Masters 2010, p. 58)

Republican Commissioner Wallison questioned Masters's thesis that the derivatives market had frozen during the two days of Lehman bankruptcy.

Wallison pointed out that the number of derivatives transactions had remained stable throughout the period of the Lehman default and therefore the markets had not frozen the way Masters had argued:

> COMMISSIONER WALLISON: Okay. Now you said that the credit default swap market ground to a halt. I think there was some question about that by some of my colleagues, but I actually have some numbers here from Market Serve, which now publishes these numbers, and I want to read you the credit default swap market from June of 23 2008 until December of 2008, so that it covers the period where Lehman failed. I think this was the period you were referring to. In June – I'll leave out anything other than just the dimensions – 251,000. In July, 284,000. In August, 188,000. In September, the month that we had the failure of Lehman, 315,000. October, 379,000. November, 305,000. December, 255,000. (Wallison 2010a, p. 94)

Professor Greenberger answered Commissioner Wallison by pointing out that the number of transactions was misleading because it could have been buying peanuts – the issue was not the transactions but the value of the transactions, which did show a major decline in the CDS market. Furthermore, during the two days of Lehman's bankruptcy the government had rescued AIG and introduced TARP funding.

> WITNESS GREENBERGER: First of all, in terms of your numbers, please look at the number of the overall value of credit default swaps. The swaps dealers after Lehman were running around – the swaps dealers were running around, and you can look at DTCC statistics, Bank of International Settlement Statistics, the overall notional value dropped from $65 trillion to $35 trillion. Mr. Masters was right, this market was freezing up. It dropped by half. You can have – I can buy a thousand peanuts for $1. That doesn't tell me the value of whether this market is going down. (Greenberger 2010 p. 107)

The controversy that day was the rescue of AIG. Witness Dinallo, who was the Insurance Superintendent, argued that statutory insurance had been the main business of AIG. Statutory insurance was qualitatively different from the CDS type insurance that AIGFP was selling. AIGFP had exposures of $180 billion worth of insurance. Goldman Sachs had been a major buyer of CDS insurance from AIG. AIG did not post collateral nor did AIGFP sell their exposure. AIG had also agreed to compensate the buyers of CDS as the products were marked to market, so for any decline in these bonds AIGFP had to post collateral. This was very different from statutory insurance which required the posting of collateral and also required an entity to default. AIGFP was insuring against changes in the value of a CDO. Dinallo criticized AIGFP for misusing the triple-A rating that defined the company:

As you already know, the primary source of AIG's problems was AIG's Financial Products Division which had written credit default swaps, derivatives, and futures with a notional amount of about $2.7 trillion. Perhaps most important, AIG's Financial Products was able to make such huge bets with its credit default swaps with little backing up its promise to pay, thanks to deregulation . . . My essential thesis is that these changes permitted AIG and FP and other institutions to sell wildly under-capitalized pseudo-insurance and other core 'financial products' that previously had well-known capital requirements, reserving, and net capital requirements. (Dinallo 2010, p. 275)

Dinallo argued that the bankruptcy of AIG would have had major repercussions on the global economy and that the government had had no choice but to come to its rescue. Dinallo also argued that during the two days of the Lehman bankruptcy and the uncertainty at AIG did freeze the commercial paper market and this would have had a major impact on the real sector of the economy that depended on commercial paper to fund short-term wages and financial needs:

I would like to reiterate that during this crisis one single factor stood out in its potential to destroy the financial system as a whole: The massive interlocking web of over-the-counter derivatives' exposures among the biggest Wall Street swaps dealers. Many financial institutions might have gone bankrupt or suffered severe losses from the crisis, but the system as a whole would not have been imperiled were it not for the propagation of unregulated derivatives' markets. (Dinallo 2010, p. 277)

THE TOO BIG TO FAIL HEARINGS, 11 SEPTEMBER 2010

This was the last of the public hearings and the focus of the testimonies and evidence included the bankruptcy of Lehman Brothers and the takeover of Wachovia by Wells Fargo. The Commission highlighted these two case studies to deal with the question of whether the government had any choice but to seek the rescue of financial institutions; that is, would there have been catastrophic effects on the economy had these institutions been allowed to go into bankruptcy? In the case of Wachovia Bank, the Federal Reserve, the Treasury and the FDIC ensured that Wachovia found a partner in Wells Fargo. By contrast, Lehman Brothers was allowed to declare bankruptcy in September 2008. The Lehman bankruptcy did contribute to the financial crisis in that within a few days of Lehman going bankrupt the government had to rescue AIG, arrange the rescue of Merrill Lynch by Bank of America and allow Goldman Sachs and Morgan Stanley to become bank holding companies.

The witnesses for the 'Too Big to Fail' hearings included Dick Fuld, the CEO of Lehman Brothers, Barry Zubrow, who was the Risk Manager at JP Morgan Chase and responsible for unwinding and winding the REPO transactions at Lehman, Scott Alvarez, counsel to the Federal Reserve Bank and Thomas Baxter from the Federal Reserve of New York. The second day of the hearings focused on the testimonies of Chairman Ben Bernanke of the Federal Reserve and Chairman Sheila Bair of the FDIC.

As for the hearings on derivatives, the hearings on Wachovia and Lehman continued to confirm the different concerns of the Democrat and Republican Commissioners. The Democrat Commissioners wanted to show that the climate of deregulation had created reluctance among regulators to make recommendations or voice their concerns about problems emerging in the deregulated OTC markets – problems of leverage and the reliance of investment banks on short-term repurchase (REPO) agreements which were making the financial system fragile to a traditional run on the banks. Regulators also had many signals about likely fraud in the housing market. State attorneys were barred from any attempts to oversee derivatives:

> derivatives were a mechanism that transmitted shock during the financial crisis. And I would like to explore with you some of the ways that they did so, and their relevance to systemic risk. As you've said today, the potential failure of AIG was caused by AIG Financial Products Division's enormous sale of credit default swaps without sufficient resources to post collateral as required by their contracts. Was AIG considered to be of systemic importance in part because many of the world's largest and most important financial firms were AIG's counterparties on these credit default swaps and thus could have been impacted with AIG's failure? (Born 2010, p. 52)

During the hearings on derivatives Commissioner Born had made the connection between the decision of the government to rescue AIG and the issues of counter-parties involved with AIG. AIG was too interconnected and would have caused turmoil in the global insurance business:

> COMMISSIONER BORN: [to Witness Gary Cohn of Goldman Sachs] Mr. Cohn, you said that you thought the systemic harm could have come from AIG if the government hadn't stepped in to backstop it because of its concentration in certain instruments, and you didn't designate the instruments. Did you mean credit default swaps?
> WITNESS COHN: That was one of them. But they were a huge player in other markets as well. They were a big repo counterparty. They were a big secured lender. They were involved in many different asset classes. They had an enormous amount of paper out being owned by the money market funds.
> COMMISSIONER BORN: They were just such a big player in so many markets.

WITNESS COHN: Yes.
COMMISSIONER BORN: They were too big to fail.
WITNESS COHN: In essence, yes. (Born 2010, p. 297)

The Republican Commissioners wanted to continue to put the focus on the theme of moral hazard and whether there was an underlying assumption that the government would bail out those financial institutions which were defined as being too big to fail. Republican Commissioners wanted to show that the rescue of Wachovia and the bankruptcy of Lehman could be traced to the decision made by the Fed in March 2008 to rescue Bear Stearns. The issue of moral hazard had been raised during the hearings on derivatives in July 2010. At that hearing Republican Commissioner Holtz-Eakin posed the following question to Gary D Cohn. President and Chief Operating Officer at Goldman Sachs:

COMMISSIONER HOLTZ-EAKIN: . . . Professor Kyle from the University of Maryland said very clearly that prior to Bear there was an expectation by large financial institutions that they could shift losses to taxpayers, that too-big-to-fail was a real thing, that the moral hazard was inaction . . .
WITNESS COHN: . . . Prior to Bear I had never once, for one millisecond, thought that there was any backstop in our organization, or business, or in the financial services industry . . . if we made mistakes and did things wrong we would have to suffer . . .
COMMISSIONER HOLTZ-EAKIN: And after Bear Stearns?
WITNESS COHN: After Bear Stearns, there was confusion, to be honest with you. There was confusion to what happened. How it happened. Why did it happen? Was this the new game plan? Which made the Lehman Brothers weekend even more confusing for people. Not only did it make it confusing for financial institutions, it made it confusing for world investors. (Cohn 2010, p. 35)

Republican Commissioner Wallison, in his questioning of Scott Alvarez, General Counsel of the Federal Reserve, returned to the theme raised by Holtz-Eakin and asked Scott Alvarez for the Federal Reserve Bank whether the bankruptcy of Lehman was due to the fact that the CEO of Lehman, Dick Fuld, having looked at the rescue of Bear Stearns felt that he could get a similar deal from the Fed:

[Wallison to Alvarez:] everything changed after Bear Stearns was rescued. Among other things, participants in the market thought that all large firms, at least larger than Bear Stearns, would be rescued. Companies probably did not believe they had to raise as much capital as they might have needed because they probably thought they didn't have to dilute their shareholders because the government would ultimately rescue them, and fewer creditors were going to be worried about their capitalization. (Wallison 2010b, p. 70)

Scott Alvarez disagreed with the assumption and argued instead that the fault lay in the climate of deregulation and the decision by law makers to put handcuffs on the regulators. Regulators were not allowed to look for systematic failure. Each regulator operated in a silo of focusing on the fitness and soundness of a specific institution; the FDIC was responsible for the commercial bank but not for the banking subsidiary involved in dealer brokers' activities. Alvarez praised the Dodd-Frank proposals for allowing for greater systematic overviews:

> . . . I think that there was a strong press for deregulation through the late '90s and most of the 2000 period, and I think that weakened both the resolve of the regulator and the attention paid by institutions to the risk management . . . the regulatory reduction we were doing across the board I think weakened our resolve at larger institutions, which was a mistake. There are things that we just could not do no matter how much we wanted to do them. And that is where I think the Dodd-Frank bill is most important. It plugs a bunch of supervisory gaps. It authorizes the regulators to look at all systemically important institutions . . . It authorizes us to take a systemic approach to supervision. So it takes off some handcuffs that were put on during the period of regulatory burden reduction. (Alvarez 2010, p. 74)

Dick Fuld, who had been the CEO of Lehman Brothers, in his testimony and evidence argued against the case of moral hazard and instead pointed out that the demise of Lehman was caused by the uncontrollable forces of the market and rumours about the health of Lehman's finances. Fuld pointed out that capitalism only worked with a certain range of volatility in the market and once that volatility had reached the outer limits it was up to the government to put a stop to that irrationality:

> Capitalism works within a finite range of standard deviations of volatility. Had the Fed totally ignored everything, Treasury ignored everything, in a pure capitalistic free market 'let it happen as it falls,' not only would you have lost Lehman, Morgan Stanley quickly, and Goldman Sachs thereafter. What other countries did, very quickly, they stepped in. They said, no more. We're guaranteeing. We're going to stop this irrational sense of panic and put confidence back into the marketplace. (Fuld 2010, pp. 167–8)

The debate concentrated on the bankruptcy of Lehman and the question as to why Lehman was allowed to go bankrupt when the government rescued Bear Stearns, AIG, Wachovia and Washington Mutual? What was different about allowing Lehman to go bankrupt? Chairman Angelides pointed to the ideology within the Bush Presidency and the bankruptcy of Lehman being a political decision. Pointing out that the rescue of Bear Stearns had proved to be highly unpopular within Republican circles, the political pressures had made it impossible for Hank Paulson to be seen as bailing out Lehman.

It also looks like there's political considerations at play. Mr. Wilkinson, who is the Treasury Chief of Staff, says on the 9th of September that, quote, he 'can't stomach us bailing out Lehman. It will be horrible in the press.' And there's another e-mail from Mr. Wilkinson saying, on the 14th: Doesn't seem like it's going to end pretty. No way government money is coming in. I'm here writing the USG [US Government] COM's plan for an orderly wind-down. Also just did a call with WH [which I assume is White House], and USG is united behind no money. No way in hell Paulson could blink now. (Angelides 2010b, p. 342)

The issue of a political dimension to the decision was also raised by Colin Thain, the CEO of Merrill Lynch, who was concerned that allowing Lehman to fail would have a major impact on the finance industry and had argued with the Federal Reserve, alongside other CEOs of investment banks, that the Federal had to find ways for a rescue of Lehman. According to the FCIC (FCIC 2011):

> Thain blamed the failure to bail out Lehman on politicians and regulators who feared the political consequences of rescuing the firm. 'There was a tremendous amount of criticism of what was done with Bear Stearns so that JP Morgan would buy them,' Thain told the FCIC. 'There was a criticism of bailing out Wall Street. It was a combination of political unwillingness to bail out Wall Street and a belief that there needed to be a reinforcement of moral hazard. There was never a discussion about the legal ability of the Fed to do this.' Thain also told the FCIC that in his opinion, 'allowing Lehman to go bankrupt was the single biggest mistake of the whole financial crisis'. (FCIC 2011, p. 342)

Scott Alvarez and Thomas Baxter, the Vice President for the Federal Reserve Bank of New York, together with Ben Bernanke, outlined the case that the primary aim of the Federal Reserve had been to rescue Lehman. The Fed was aware that the bankruptcy of Lehman would cause systematic risk because of its high exposures in the derivatives market and the contagion effect this would have on counter-parties. The reason for not being able to rescue Lehman was that the Federal Reserve could not make naked loans. The Federal Reserve had to be satisfied that it would get its money back. Lehman, according to the Federal Reserve, did not have sufficient collateral to go to the Federal Reserve discount window. The Federal Reserve could not therefore provide liquidity for Lehman. Furthermore, there was the problem on the Monday 15 September that when it came to the unwinding of the weekend REPO, JP Morgan would be highly exposed holding Lehman collateral if the REPO market did not wish to lend to Lehman overnight on Monday 15 September. According to this perspective there was therefore no alternative but to get Lehman to declare bankruptcy. The broker dealer subsidiary of Lehman was allowed to go to the discount window because the Federal Reserve was satisfied with their collateral. What was surprising was that the subsidiary felt it was not appropriate for them to lend collateral to the Lehman holding company.

Lehman was not Bear Stearns. In the case of Bear Stearns the government had found a willing partner – JP Morgan – to buy Bear Stearns. In the case of Lehman, Bank of America and Barclays Bank UK had both opted out from a possible rescue of Lehman. Alvarez argued that the Fed had no authority to provide financial assistance to the Lehman holding company unless the Fed was assured that it would get its money back. Lehman did not have sufficient collateral to satisfy the Federal Reserve and therefore the Federal Reserve had no authority to provide funding for the rescue of Lehman. The Chairman, Ben Bernanke, made clear during his testimony and evidence that the Fed was aware that Lehman's bankruptcy would be catastrophic for the US economy but that the Fed could not fund Lehman:

> That being said, let me just state this as unequivocally as I can . . . I believed deeply that if Lehman was allowed to fail, or did fail, that the consequences for the U.S. financial system and the U.S. economy would be catastrophic. And I never, at any time, wavered in my view that we should do absolutely everything possible to prevent the failure of Lehman. Now on Sunday night of that weekend, what was told to me was that there was a run proceeding on Lehman, that Lehman did not have enough collateral to allow the Fed to lend it enough to meet that run; therefore, if we lent the money to Lehman, all that would happen would be that the run would succeed, because it wouldn't be able to meet the demands, the firm would fail, and not only would we be unsuccessful but we would have saddled the taxpayer with tens of billions of dollars of losses. (Bernanke 2010, p. 7)

In the chapter on the Lehman hearings the Commission concluded that the financial crisis reached cataclysmic proportions which in turn confirmed the fragility of the US financial industry and nearly meant the collapse of the other four investment banks. The OTC derivatives market, leveraging and dependency on the short-term report market contributed to Lehman's demise. However the final report also points to political decisions and inconsistency within the decision-making processes of government:

> Federal government officials decided not to rescue Lehman for a variety of reasons, including the lack of a private firm willing and able to acquire it, uncertainty about Lehman's potential losses, concerns about moral hazard and political reaction, and erroneous assumptions that Lehman's failure would have a manageable impact on the financial system because market participants had anticipated it. After the fact, they justified their decision by stating that the Federal Reserve did not have legal authority to rescue Lehman. The inconsistency of federal government decisions in not rescuing Lehman after having

rescued Bear Stearns and the GSEs, and immediately before rescuing AIG, added to uncertainty and panic in the financial markets. (FCIC 2011, p. 343)

THE POLITICS OF THE FCIC

Inevitably the Inquiry was always likely to become politicized and polarize around party lines. The Republican Commissioners wanted from the outset to defend the climate of deregulation in financial markets that had started during the Reagan Presidency. Republicans had been campaigning for two decades to repeal Glass-Steagill, seeing the Banking Act of 1933 as reflecting the vestiges of intervention of the Roosevelt Presidency. Republicans had argued that that legislation was out of date and that the framework was an obstacle to the American financial sector and global competition. The repeal of Glass-Steagill and the CFMA were seen as pillars of the free market. OTC derivatives were described as being a major innovation that was contributing to prosperity and economic growth. The derivatives market had lowered the costs for end users and confirmed that markets could work with little intervention from regulators like the CFTC.

Republicans wanted to make the case that the financial meltdown was attributable to government policy. Republicans therefore focused on moral hazard and the view that once the government rescued Bear Stearns and provided JP Morgan with guarantees of $30 billion to complete the merger, that other banks would get similar treatment from the Federal Reserve. Investment banks therefore continued to rely on short-term borrowing and yet REPO markets were reluctant to raise capital to improve their balance sheets. Alan Greenspan, keeping interest rates low for too long after 2001, was blamed for creating a climate of irrational exuberance that resulted in high borrowing by consumers and investment banks. The increases in house prices reflected an inflationary bubble that was a common theme for a number of countries, including the UK, France, Australia, Ireland and Spain. House prices were rising fast and were outstripping median incomes.

By contrast, the Democrat Commissioners wanted to show that the financial meltdown represented the outcome of deregulated markets. The shift to deregulation had started with the Reagan Presidency in 1980. The President had replaced Paul Volker as Chairman at Federal Reserve by Alan Greenspan, who was well known for his credentials as a market liberal thinker and who was committed to the process of deregulation and had argued that rational agents were better at regulating themselves than government bureaucracies. Greenspan therefore was seen by the Democrats as the architect of deregulation.

During the hearings in April 2010 Alan Greenspan appeared before the FCIC to give evidence. Chairman Angelides in his interactions with Greenspan made it clear that he believed Greenspan was an ideologue committed to free markets and reluctant to regulate the housing market, even when there was clear evidence of predatory lending. Chairman Angelides to Alan Greenspan:

> But here are the facts: The facts are you adopted those rules in 2001. And at the time that they were adopted, they were projected to cover 38 percent of the subprime lending activity in the country.
> When it was all said and done and an evaluation was done of those rules in 2006, not 2009, 2010, what in fact had happened is the rules you adopted covered just 1 percent of the market.
> And so I return to you, again, was there just a reluctance to regulate? . . .
> In 2004 the GAO weighed in again, urging action given, quote, the significant amount of subprime lending among holding company subsidiaries. But, again, no action, no willingness to go in and examine a non-bank subsidiaries . . .
> MR. GREENSPAN: You know, I – when you've been in government for 21 years, as I have been, the issue of retrospective and figuring out what you should have done differently is a really futile activity because you can't, in fact, in the real world, do it . . .
> . . . my experience has been in the business I was in, I was right 70 percent of the time, but I was wrong 30 percent of the time. And there are an awful lot of mistakes in 21 years.
> CHAIRMAN ANGELIDES: Would this be one of them?
> MR. GREENSPAN: I'm not sure – I'm not sure what good it does –
> CHAIRMAN ANGELIDES: Would you put this in the 30 percent category?
> MR. GREENSPAN: I'm sorry?
> CHAIRMAN ANGELIDES: Would you put this in the 30?
> MR. GREENSPAN: I don't know. (Angelides et al. 2010b, pp. 24–9)

While there had been many warnings at Federal Open Market Committee (FOMC) meetings on predatory lendings in the mortgage market, and evidence of fraud, there was a reluctance at the Federal Reserve to set rulings that would allow for better regulation through the CFTC and the SEC. Greenspan was therefore seen as a non-regulating regulator. He had opposed Brooksley Born's suggestions for better supervision of the OTC derivatives market and had hailed derivatives as a major contributor to US economic prosperity.

Democrats also wanted to show that the government had no choice but to rescue the financial sector, since allowing the banks to fail would have been catastrophic for the US economy. Democrats agreed that some institutions had become too big to fail and that the patchwork of regulation had created a climate for regulatory arbitrage that allowed financial entities to choose their principal regulator knowing that very often the chosen regulator did not have the capacity to supervise large entities.

Thirdly, Democrats wanted to make a connection between money in politics and the financial meltdown. Brooksley Born pointed to the influence of lobbyists and the money provided by the finance industry during election campaign for key policy makers. Money in politics had therefore influenced the scope of deregulation in financial markets.

The financial sector had become highly concentrated, with 10 major banks which between them had assets equivalent to 65 per cent of US GDP.

Finally, Democrats wanted to deal with the issue of ideology in economic ideas and how the rational expectations and efficient markets theories had come to dominate economic policy making. There was therefore a monopoly in economic ideas. To achieve this the FCIC had two days of roundtable discussion, where top economists were allowed to produce their own arguments and research that sought to explain the financial crisis. The FCIC invited the prominent economists John Taylor and Joseph Stiglitz to outline their views in an attempt to show that there was a plurality of views of how the economy worked and also a plurality views that helped to explain the financial meltdown. The aim therefore was to make a break with the conventional wisdom of market liberal thinking. There were other ideas that occupied similar spaces and therefore economic modelling was a contestable terrain.

THE FCIC AND THE POLICY PROCESS

In 1931 President Hoover established the Pecora Inquiry to investigate the financial meltdown. Hoover wanted to show that the financial sector because of its excesses had contributed to the financial crisis. Pecora eventually reported after the election of President Roosevelt. A product of the Pecora hearings was the Banking Act of 1933. The hearings chaired by Pecora had shown that banks had mis-sold bonds in the knowledge that these bonds would soon fall to below investment grade. Pecora also looked at the compensation of the top bankers and the gap that had appeared in the expectations of high earners and the majority of people faced with poverty and unemployment. Pecora had therefore made possible the passing of the Glass-Steagil legislation

The FCIC hearing was different since Congress had made it clear that the FCIC would focus on explaining the financial crisis while Congress would be responsible for policy making. The Dodd-Frank bill, which contained 2,000 pages of legislative recommendations, was passed as an Act in July 2010. The FCIC did not produce its final report until January 2011.

CONCLUSIONS

Keynes was more than an economist (Dow 2010; Skidelsky 2010). In developing his narrative of how economies work, Keynes put the emphasis on trust, conventions, confidence, uncertainty and institutions. These concepts could not be mathematically modelled and yet those who model market economies assume that such institutions exist and are therefore taken for granted. Keynes recognized that it was not always appropriate to analyse the social through mathematical models. Since economies needed to be located in the context and landscapes of institutions and conventions, market economies also required a framework of property rights. Markets needed to be located and anchored in contexts, histories and policy processes. Markets did not exist in their own right, obeying laws of supply and demand similar to the laws of gravity; instead, they were socially constructed in the sense that through the legislative process the nature, labour and financial markets were being continuously defined and shaped.

> The Hume/Smith/Keynes approach takes other-regarding behaviour as a starting-point rather than a modification. Indeed according to this approach, market economies could not function without social conventions, the most important of which is trust. Rather than the calculative trust of the game theory approach, this conceptualisation sees trust as an alternative to calculation. (Dow 2010, p. 15)

In labour markets industrial relations legislation, including the trade unions' rights to strike, secret ballots and trade union recognition in collective bargaining, defined the nature of labour markets. Equally, in financial markets the regulation of banks and consumer and investor protection shaped financial markets. The issue of confidence meant trust, and if that trust was abused it was always difficult to retrieve. People have to have trust in institutions – they trusted their banks to give them good advice. They trusted the institutions of government. During the financial crisis there was a breakdown of trust. Investors could no longer trust their banks. Banks were selling bonds on the assumption that their customers were sophisticated investors aware of the risks.

The common theme between the Pecora Commission and FCIC was the breakdown of trust at a number of levels. Investment banks including Goldman Sachs during the recent crisis had sold asset backed securities to investors as long-term investments when Goldman Sachs had decided that it was selling short these same bonds, which indicated that Goldman Sachs wanted to return home and lower their exposure to mortgage backed securities. However, at the same time, the bank was selling these securities to their clients.

The report by Anton Valukas, the Examiner of Lehman Brothers in 2010, was 2,300 pages in length. The Examiner and his team collected a database of emails and documents totalling 5 million that compromised over 40 million pages, and looked at 4.4 million documents. In his conclusions Valukas argued that there was a colourable case against Lehman misusing REPO 105 at the end of each quarter in which they appeared to be selling assets when in fact there was no such sale and Lehman was buying back those securities a few days later. Acccording to Valukas:

> Although Repo 105 transactions may not have been inherently improper, there is a colorable claim that their sole function as employed by Lehman was balance sheet manipulation. Lehman's own accounting personnel described Repo 105 transactions as an 'accounting gimmick' and a 'lazy way of managing the balance sheet as opposed to legitimately meeting balance sheet targets at quarter end.' Lehman used Repo 105 to reduce the balance sheet at the quarter-end. (Valukas 2010, p. 13)

CEO Mitchell of City Banks was also mis-selling bonds in 1931 in the full knowledge that these bonds would collapse.

Secondly, there is the issue of the concentration of power and influence. The finance industry had lobbied Congress during the 1920s for a light touch approach to financial markets, arguing (as during the late 1990s) that banks were better than government at regulating themselves.

Ferdinand Pecora in his memoirs recorded:

> Before the Committee came an imposing succession of the demi gods of Wall Street, men whose names were household words, but whose personalities and affairs were frequently shrouded in deep, aristocratic mystery. Never before in the history of the United States had so much wealth and power been required to give a public accounting. (Perino 2010, p. 274)

In 2010 the FCIC also called the CEO of the major investment banks to explain the crisis. These same banks had received taxpayers' money as part of their rescue and yet still continued to pay compensation packages to their chief executives as if there had been no crisis. The hearings showed that the government had had no choice but to rescue AIG, even though AIGFP had created exposures of $270 billion without providing collateral. The government had to buy out all AIG's contracts for $29 billion. Goldman Sachs received $12 billion to cover its CDS exposure with AIG.

The US Government had no choice but to rescue the financial system: the alternative could have been global financial collapse.

REFERENCES

Alvarez, S. (2010) Financial Crisis Inquiry Commission, Official Transcript Hearing on 'Too Big to Fail: Expectations and Impact of Extraordinary Government Intervention and The Role of Systemic Risk in the Financial Crisis', 1 September, Washington, DC.

Angelides, P. (2010a) Opening Remarks of Chairman Phil Angelides at the Public Hearing of the Financial Crisis Inquiry Commission, 13 January, Washington, DC.

Angelides, P. (2010b) Financial Crisis Inquiry Commission, Official Transcript Hearing on 'Too Big to Fail: Expectations and Impact of Extraordinary Government Intervention and The Role of Systemic Risk in the Financial Crisis', 2 September, Washington, DC.

Angelides, P. et al. (2010a) *First Public Hearing of the Financial Crisis Inquiry Commission*, 13 January. Washington, DC: FCIC. Available at: http://fcic-static.law.stanford.edu/cdn_media/fcic-testimony/2010-0113-Transcript.pdf

Angelides, P. et al. (2010b) The Financial Crisis Inquiry Commission, Official Transcript, Commission Hearing, 7 April, Washington, DC.

Bernanke, B. (2010) Statement by Ben S. Bernanke Chairman Board of Governors of the Federal Reserve System before the Financial Crisis Inquiry Commission, 2 September, Washington, DC.

Blankfein, L.C. (2010) Testimony by Lloyd C. Blankfein, Chairman and CEO, The Goldman Sachs Group, Inc., Financial Crisis Inquiry Commission, 13 January.

Born, B. (2010) Financial Crisis Inquiry Commission, Official Transcript: Hearing on 'The Role of Derivatives in the Financial Crisis', 30 June, Washington, DC.

Cohn, G. (2010) Testimony from Gary D. Cohn, President & Chief Operating Officer, The Goldman Sachs Group, Inc. Before The Financial Crisis Inquiry Commission, Financial Crisis Inquiry Commission Official Transcript Hearing on 'The Role of Derivatives in the Financial Crisis', 30 June, Washington, DC.

Dinallo, E. (2010) Testimony to the Financial Crisis Inquiry Commission Hearing on the Role of Derivatives in the Financial Crisis by Eric Dinallo, Former Superintendent, New York State Insurance Department, Financial Crisis Inquiry Commission Official Transcript Hearing on 'The Role of Derivatives in the Financial Crisis', 1 July, Washington, DC.

Dow, S.C. (2010) 'What Kind of Theory to Guide Reform and Restructuring of the Financial and Non-Financial Sectors? A Focus on Theoretical Approach', paper prepared for the inaugural conference of the Institute for New Economic Thinking, April, Cambridge.

FCIC (2011) *Final Report of the National Commission on the Causes of the Financial and Economic Crisis in the United States*. New York: Public Affairs.

Fuld, R.S. (2010) Financial Crisis Inquiry Commission, Official Transcript Hearing on 'Too Big to Fail: Expectations and Impact of Extraordinary Government Intervention and The Role of Systemic Risk in the Financial Crisis', 1 September, Washington, DC.

Greenberger, M. (2010) Testimony of Michael Greenberger, Law School Professor, University of Maryland School of Law, Financial Crisis Inquiry Commission Hearing on 'The Role of Derivatives in the Financial Crisis', 30 June, Washington, DC.

Greenspan, A. (2010) Testimony of Alan Greenspan, Financial Crisis Inquiry Commission, 7 April, Washington, DC.

Hennessey, K. (2010) Financial Crisis Inquiry Commission, Official Transcript Hearing on 'The Role of Derivatives in the Financial Crisis', 30 June, Washington, DC.

Hennessey, K. (2011) 'Dissenting Statement of Commissioner Keith Hennessey, Commissioner Douglas Holtz-Eakin, and Vice Chairman Bill Thomas', *The Financial Crisis Inquiry Report*. New York: Public Affairs.

Masters, M. (2010) Testimony of Michael W. Masters, Managing Member/ Portfolio Manager, Masters Capital Management, LLC Before the Financial Crisis Inquiry Commission, Financial Crisis Inquiry Commission Official Transcript Hearing on 'The Role of Derivatives in the Financial Crisis', 30 June, Washington, DC.

Paulson, H. (2010) Testimony by Henry M. Paulson, Jr. Before the Financial Crisis Inquiry Commission, Official Transcript Hearing on 'The Shadow Banking System', 6 May, Washington, DC.

Perino, M. (2010) *The Hellhound of Wall Street: How Ferdinand Pecora's Investigations of the Great Crash Forever Changed American Finance*. New York: The Penguin Press.

Skidelsky, R. (2010) 'Interpreting the Great Depression: Hayek versus Keynes', paper prepared for the INET Conference, Cambridge University, 8–11 April.

Valukas, A.R. (2010) Statement by Anton R. Valukas Examiner, Lehman Brothers Bankruptcy Before the Committee on Financial Services, United States House of Representatives Regarding 'Public Policy Issues Raised by the Report of the Lehman Bankruptcy Examiner', 20 April.

Wallison, P. (2010a) Financial Crisis Inquiry Commission Official Transcript: Hearing on 'The Role of Derivatives in the Financial Crisis', 30 June, Washington, DC.

Wallison, P. (2010b) Financial Crisis Inquiry Commission, Official Transcript Hearing on 'Too Big to Fail: Expectations and Impact of Extraordinary Government Intervention and The Role of Systemic Risk in the Financial Crisis', 1 September, Washington, DC.

Wallison, P. (2011) 'Dissenting Statement of Peter J. Wallison', Financial Crisis Inquiry Commission, 24 December 2010, *The Financial Crisis Inquiry Report*. New York: Public Affairs.

10. Conclusions: lessons of the financial crisis

The financial crisis confirmed the absence of the notion of a public interest. Financial institutions and financial markets did not necessarily always manufacture instruments that were good for the wider economy. Indeed, derivatives and credit default swaps amplified the financial crisis. Policy makers have increasingly been influenced and guided by the narrow self-interest of financial institutions so that the policy process has reflected narrow vested interests as opposed to the public interest. Decisions on tax revenues and public expenditure became contestable terrain, resembling the politics of the pig trough with those with big snouts having the bulk share of public goods. Corporate welfare in terms of tax breaks, tax loopholes engineered by lawyers and accountants, and subsidies to industry are the invisible dimensions of public provision. The sudden declines in GDP and the shrinkage in tax revenues resulted in major deteriorations in public finances. Some governments saw the crisis as an opportunity to redefine the balance between public and private provision. The response was therefore not a response to a short-term problem but has become an ideological issue about the role of government and expectations in terms of social provision. Regulators, often assumed to be guardians of the public interest, became involved in conflicts of interests between their organization and the public good. The Credit Rating Agencies (CRAs), entrusted with providing accurate ratings of bonds and securities, found it difficult to walk away from a rating, worried as they were about retaining market share. The CRAs rated some $4.3 trillion worth of mortgage based securities as triple-A and downgraded 87 per cent of those securities to below investment grade in 2007. There was a breakdown of trust in the institutions of government, in financial institutions and regulators.

The central argument of this book has been that any explanation of the financial crisis of 2007 needs to be located within an interdisciplinary framework. The recession needs to be located in social structures in the study of power and influence, dynamics of income inequalities and ideology. The financial meltdown confirmed the presence of social, political and economic fault lines (Rajan 2010). While the housing bubble was an important event in the crisis, sub-prime mortgages defaults were a trigger effect, in contrast to the structural fragilities of global financial markets. While sub-prime mortgages totalled between $500 billion and $1 trillion this sum, while large in itself, was comparatively small in a global economy worth $65 trillion. By contrast, the financial sector manufactured securities in the over-the-counter (OTC) derivatives market that amounted to over $640 trillion, equivalent to 10 times GDP, and even if that notional amount is discounted to measure risk exposure it was still equivalent to global GDP (Greenberger 2010). Some investment banks were involved in daily transactions worth $1 trillion. The financial sector had created an inverse pyramid of $640 trillion on a housing market worth a total of $22 trillion, of which $11 trillion was mortgage debt. In terms of mortgage default 90 per cent of households were still meeting their mortgage repayments after the collapse of 2007. The majority of triple-A mortgage backed securities were still performing in 2010. Sub-prime mortgages did not cause the financial crisis. The downgrading of $4 trillion worth of asset backed securities by the Credit Rating Agencies had more to do with the fall in house prices and therefore the decline in MBAs and CDOs on mortgage based securities. As house prices fell, so did the net worth of the asset based securities and banks had to write down the worth of these assets and mark them to market, even when the mortgages were performing.

A second misconception is that the financial crisis can be attributed to government housing policy and encouraging the increases in home ownership from 64 to 69 per cent. The blame has been put on that additional 5 per cent of new home owners who were all high risk. However 90 per cent of new mortgages after 1999 were to home owners who already owned their own homes and were re-mortgaging their homes. Households in both the UK and the USA exchanged approximately $2.6 trillion worth of equity in their homes, re-mortgaging their homes while they used the borrowed cash to satisfy personal consumption desires. The mortgages they were resold were sub-prime in the sense that they were teaser two-year low cost costs mortgages, and after a two-year period interest rates increased from 7 per cent to 12 per cent. This process rested on the premise that house prices would continue to rise. When house prices then started to decline in early 2006 households found themselves with homes which were underwater. House prices declined by 30 per cent between 2007 and 2009.

Economic explanations of the financial crisis have tended to be focused on a micro-economic analysis of market failure. Authors have pointed to asymmetries of knowledge (Stiglitz 2010), externalities (Kohlhagen 2010) or principal/agent (Haldane 2010) type arguments. It is of course true that there existed asymmetries of knowledge in terms of price fixing for derivatives between dealers and investors and between borrowers and mortgage brokers. Also there was evidence that the process of securitization meant that brokers, lawyers and issuers of bonds were all receiving up-front fees and higher levels of compensation, and that their self-interest, focused on the short term, had long-term consequences. However, defining the recession as a series of market failures creates a comfort zone in that policy can be focused on remedying areas of policy failure so that it can be perceived that the system needs to reformed at the margins and that therefore is nothing fundamental needs to be changed. Essentially, the deregulated environment had worked well, but strengthening reforms in some areas would allow the financial markets to return to normal – normal being the deregulated environment created in 1999. However, this study points to the view that the system needs more than tweaking at the margins.

The issues outlined in this study provide a series of lessons from the financial crisis which can be located in seven clusters. These are:

1. The macro economy and financial markets
2. Too big to fail
3. Changing political landscapes
4. The process of deregulation and re-regulation
5. Financial crisis and income inequalities
6. Influence of ideology in economic policy making
7. Breakdown of trust.

The lessons outlined in the following sections operated at different levels. Ideology is an abstract concept and the presence of an ideology is not necessarily tangible since ideology is not a solid substance and therefore can only be understood when located in social context. Turner (2010) had pointed out that when he was appointed chairman of the FSA he felt he had become the high priest of unfettered financial markets and that the role of the FSA was confined to finding solutions that helped markets work better. The FSA had to assume that increasing liquidity was always good for the economy, and that all financial innovations were contributing to economic growth. Turner felt that these axioms were built into the DNA of the FSA and also other key financial institutions and regulators. Turner (2010) argued that he had caused much controversy when he pointed out that the financial market produced transactions which most of the time were economically and socially useless since they did not generate new products or new investment. Most transactions in financial markets were purely speculative.

Keynes, in presenting his view of how economies worked, was challenging 200 years of classical economic thinking. Keynes, through his approach, sought to kick up a fuss against the conventional wisdom. The re-emergence of the classical model after 1980, although under a different guise, requires a kicking up a new fuss in a Keynesian sense.

Secondly, while it can be shown that financial institutions hire lobbyists and finance election campaigns for key policy makers, it is difficult to show an explicit connection between the policy outcomes and the influence of vested interests in shaping policy. This could be achieved through better transparency and minute taking by impartial civil servants in meetings between policy makers and lobbyists. However, while this could be done on government premises, these networks cannot be recorded when law makers meet with their sponsors on the private golf courses or at pre-arranged dinner parties. However, it would be a good beginning to start recording meetings between policy makers and outside influences and making those meeting transparent to public scrutiny.

Thirdly, the process of deregulation confirmed a shift in the policy process. The policy reforms established by President Roosevelt in response to the Great Depression had provided the stability associated with the Quiet Period in US finance between 1950 and 1998. Paradoxically his Quiet Period was interpreted as being an obstacle to financial institutions that argued that the strictures of Glass-Steagill had become irrelevant in the world of global finance. The repeal of Glass-Steagill, the Commodity Futures Management Act (CFMA) of 2000 and the OTC market were the outcomes of the policy of deregulation.

The issues of growing income inequalities after 1979 are connected to the financial crisis in two ways. The concentration of incomes towards the top 1 per cent and 0.01 per cent of earners after 1979 confirmed the reversal of the narrowing of inequalities experienced between 1950 and 1974. During the years of the Great Compression of 1950 to 1974 full employment, rising wages and increased social spending reduced income inequalities. Tax reductions for high income earners, high levels of unemployment and a new climate that allowed for the appropriation of income by the top earners had resulted in 99 per cent of the population experiencing income increases of 0.6 per cent per year while incomes for the top 1 per cent increased from 8 per cent of GDP to 13 per cent of GDP. While the CEOs were earning 50 times the median wage in 1970 this had increased to 480 times in 2007. The repercussions of growing income inequalities were twofold. First the concentration of income towards top earners has meant that top earners now have more money to spend on political contributions and have more influence on the policy process. For the majority of the population that experienced slow increases in disposable income the increases in house prices after 1997 offered households the opportunity to increase their personal consumption by exchanging their equity for liquid cash.

LESSON 1: THE MACRO ECONOMY AND FINANCIAL MARKETS

The first lesson is that governments in the future should no longer assume that all that happens in financial markets is necessarily good for the economy. Not all financial products are necessarily good for investors. Commercial and investment banks do not necessarily sell bonds that are good for their clients. The primary concern of the investment is the balance sheet and minimizing their own exposures. The repeal of Glass-Steagill and the process that created an environment of deregulation was the product of two decades of continuing and intense lobbying by the financial sector.

The process of deregulation and the shift towards a light touch approach in financial markets started with the elections of Mrs Thatcher in the UK and President Reagan in the USA. The continuing lobbying and financial donations by financial services to policy makers were all aimed at the repeal of Banking Act of 1933 and at creating free competitive markets in finance. The theories of rational expectations and efficient markets produced the intellectual underpinnings to the argument of unfettered markets. Market liberal advocates argued the case that government bureaucracies were inept at regulation and it was always better for market participants to regulate themselves.

The processes of lobbying and making financial contributions to key policy makers during elections are therefore important because through such processes the financial sector has been able to shape and define itself. Finance has also become very important to governments. In the USA the financial sector grew from 3 per cent of GDP in 1980 to 5 per cent of GDP in 2007. The financial sector also grew in terms of making a contribution to corporate profits from 15 per cent in 1970 to 40 per cent in 2007. The financial sector was therefore an important dimension of the economy, generating tax revenues and high paying jobs. This was important in the wider historic context of the long-term decline in manufacturing. The financial sector was seen as being central to the making of the New Economy. Banks and financial institutions concentrated their influence on the policy process through lobbyists and through providing campaign funding for law makers and this needs to be brought under closer scrutiny in future, with law makers declaring an interest when it comes to formulating legislation dealing with the financial sector.

Limits need to be put on financial contributions made to political parties. There has to be greater transparency in meetings between policy makers and lobbyists. Civil servants should be present at meetings that take place in government buildings and the minutes of such meetings should be made transparent so that people are aware of how the policy process is being defined by vested interests.

The process of securitization created the ethics of a disavowal of responsibility. Brokers sold mortgages to borrowers on the basis of fees generated in the transaction. Brokers were paid a fee by both the borrower and the issuer of the mortgage. The broker system was broken because brokers were only interested in fees rather than the longer-term implications for the borrower. The borrower was perceived to be rational, yet the asymmetry of information always put the borrower at a disadvantage. The process of securitization meant that banks moved from an originate and hold model to an originate and distribute model, where again the concern was the generation of front-loaded fees. The CRA rated securities and generated fees. Compensation for chief executives was decided on the present profitability of the company. In each of these steps there was no attempt to create breaks so that the people involved in a transaction paid toward the risk. If brokers had to hold 5 per cent of a mortgage for two years there would have been better due diligence. Equally, if chief executives were told that they had to keep their options for a period of five years then the incentives would have been for these CEOs to think about the long-term consequences of their decisions.

In October 2008, which was about seven months after the take-over of Bear Stearns, Alan Schwartz, who had replaced James Cayne as CEO of Bear Stearns, reflecting on the collapse of Lehman Brothers and the turmoil in the financial markets, made the point that it was normal after such an event for people to look for a specific reason for how that event had happened. However, his main point was that the failure was interconnected and that greed, narrow self-interest, focus on the short term, high compensation, misleading risk management and high leverage had all been factors that contributed to the financial meltdown. The intervention by the Clinton and Bush administrations in housing policy, encouraging the financial sector to lend to risky borrowers, created a context for the growth of securities and derivatives which amplified the crisis:

> you have all these things like FHA and HUD and these people saying 'you better lend to all these poor people.' People at first said 'no we won't' and then said 'Oh this is a good gig . . .' So greed was a factor in all this too. But these things do occur with some regularity and we haven't ever figured out how to stop the next one from happenings . . . Wall Street is always good at fighting the last war. But these things happen and they're big and when they happen everybody tries to look at what happened in the previous six months to find someone or something to blame it on. But in truth it was a team effort. We all fucked up. Government. Rating Agencies. Wall Street. Commercial Banks. Regulators. Investors. Everybody. (Alan Schwartz, quoted in Cohan 2009, p. 430)

LESSON 2: THE ISSUE OF TOO BIG TO FAIL

The second lesson of the crisis was that governments were left with no real choice but to provide a series of policy responses that ensured the stability of the financial sector. While President Hoover during the 1929 Great Depression was advised to liquidate the banks and to liquidate labour so that a new economy would replace the old, the idea of allowing major financial institutions to go bankrupt and creating the possibility of a global financial and economic meltdown was never contemplated in 2007. In a sense, lessons had been learned from the 1929 Depression and governments would not allow unemployment to rise to 25 per cent of the workforce:

> Bear . . . deserved to be allowed to fail, both on the merits and to teach Wall Street not to expect someone else to clean up its messes.
> But the Fed rode to Bear's rescue anyway, fearing that the collapse of a major investment bank would cause panic in the market and wreak havoc with the wider economy. Fed officials knew they were doing a bad thing but believed the alternative would be even worse.
> As Bear goes so will the rest of the financial system. (Krugman 2008)

In January 2007 Bear Stearns's shares were worth $172.69 per share. At the time Bear Stearns was being sold to JP Morgan Treasury Secretary Paulson was encouraging JP Morgan not to pay more than $2 per share. In the end, to conclude the merger, JP Morgan agreed to pay $10 a share for Bear Stearns (Cohan 2009). The headquarters building built by CEO James Cayne was, in the end, worth more than the investment bank. During its hey day in 2005 and 2006 Bear Stearns had been ranked number one in the US MBS market and in the top five for transactions in CDOs. The failure of the two hedge funds meant that Bear Stearns had to take on their losses onto Bears Stearns's books. That episode was the beginning of the end for Bear Stearns.

Those involved in the immediacy of the financial crisis did not have the benefit of hindsight and their responses were, therefore, piecemeal and disjointed, but the financial system had been stabilized by June 2009 and a repeat of the Great Depression had been avoided. The year 2007 could be categorized as a Great Recession but not a Great Depression. Unemployment did climb to 9.8 per cent in the USA while US GDP shrank by 4.5 per cent, while UK GDP also declined by 6 per cent in 2008 and 2009. Those involved in the rescue process soon realized that the deregulatory environment created after 1999 had put handcuffs on regulators and therefore had limited jurisdiction in the rescue process. The Federal Reserve was not the principal regulator of AIG or the investment banks. The Federal Reserve had to depend on principle regulators to give them soundness and fitness reports on institutions. This created turf wars between regulators. The US Treasury, the Federal Reserve and also the FDIC (Federal Deposit Insurance Corporation), in seeking a coherent rescue of Wachovia or Washington Mutual, Bear Stearns or Lehman Brothers, did not have the authorization to seek information directly from these institutions. Such excessive risk-taking should not have been allowed. But it was. Despite regulators in 20 different states being responsible for the primary regulation and supervision of AIG's US insurance subsidiaries, despite AIG's foreign insurance activities being regulated by more than 130 foreign governments, and despite AIG's holding company being subject to supervision by the Office of Thrift Supervision (OTS), no one was adequately aware of what was really going on at AIG. It is important to remember that the Federal Reserve, under the law, had no role in supervising or regulating AIG, investment banks, or a range of other institutions that were at the leading edge of crisis. But Congress gave the Federal Reserve authority to provide liquidity to the financial system in times of severe stress. Given that responsibility, the Federal Reserve had to act. The Federal Reserve was the only fire station in town (Geithner 2010, p. 5).

Paul Volcker, who had been Chairman of the Federal Reserve bank during the period 1976–1984, had tried to sound a warning about the fragility in financial markets and the climate of deregulation that had resulted in the explosion of OTC derivatives:

> I have to tell you my old central banking blood still flows under this placid surface, at least the way I see it, there are really disturbing trends, huge imbalances, disequilibria, risks, call them what you will. Altogether the circumstances seem to be as dangerous and unstable as any as I can remember and I can remember a lot. (Volcker 2005)

LESSON 3: CHANGING POLITICAL LANDSCAPES

The third lesson has been the spill-over onto political expectations. In 2008 Prime Minister Gordon Brown was perceived as having been the main architect in stabilizing the global economy, however, he went on to lose the election of May 2010, with his Government being blamed for the financial crisis and also for the large deficits inherited by the coalition government. The financial crises in Greece, Portugal and Ireland highlighted the tensions of the euro currency, and the question has been asked whether the southern economies have the capacity to be inside the euro zone. President Obama equally rescued the US financial system and through the stimulus packages of early 2010 was able to stabilize unemployment. However, the unemployment rate of 8.8 per cent and the US deficits cost his administration the Democrat majority in the House of Representatives in November 2010, and the health and financial reforms which were seen as the President's major achievements came under pressure from the new Republican majority.

More recently, Alan Greenspan, the former Chairman of the Federal Reserve, has criticized the Dodd-Frank legislation as being too cumbersome, too regulatory and thus likely to undermine competitiveness in financial markets. Greenspan (2011) has repeated his previous argument that government cannot regulate markets and that it is always better for markets to regulate themselves:

> The act may create the largest regulatory-induced market distortion since America's ill-fated imposition of wage and price controls of 1971.
>
> In pressing forward, the regulators are being entrusted with forecasting, and presumably preventing all understandable repercussions that might happen . . . No one has such skills. Regulators are caught flat footed . . ..
>
> The problem is that regulators, and everyone else, can never get more than a glimpse at the internal workings of the simplest of modern financial systems. (Greenspan 2011)

While the Dodd-Frank reforms seek to represent a coherent response to the excesses created by the CFMA and the expansion of derivatives, the reforms do not address the issues of social structure identified in this study. The reforms do not seek to deal with the question of 'too big to fail'. The issue of too big to fail is not necessarily related to the size of the financial entities but rather issues of homogeneity. Breaking a large bank into a hundred smaller homogenous entities does not solve the problem of too big to fail since the hundred newly created entities could collapse at the same time. Financial entities need to be diversified, with different entities providing a series of different and competing products. Financial institutions should not assume that all investors are sophisticated investors. There has to be increase in transparency on products and financial instruments that are sold to clients. The issue of asymmetry of knowledge, confined to a narrow section of broker dealers who set prices, has to be opened to transparency by putting derivatives on clearing platforms and onto exchanges where prices will reflect daily market changes, and sellers and buyers have to post daily collateral. This will increase the cost for market participants, but the crisis has already cost some $14 trillion in global rescue packages, apart from the increases in unemployment, the declines in GDP and people losing their homes and their savings.

LESSON 4: THE PROCESS OF DEREGULATION AND RE-REGULATION

The Banking Act of 1933 (Glass-Steagill) separated commercial banks from investment banks. The FDIC provided guarantees for depositors. Due to these guarantees commercial banks were not allowed to become involved in investment banking. The repeal of Glass-Steagill in 1999, together with the passing of the CFMA in 2000, reflected the influence of lobbying by the finance industry to deregulate financial markets. The Quiet Period of banking had facilitated a process where the finance industry could argue that the legislative framework was acting as a barrier and obstacle to American banking and that there was a danger of losing global market share.

The weaknesses in the OTC derivatives markets were best exemplified during the crisis at AIG. Since derivatives were not being traded on exchanges and therefore there were no daily exchanges of collateral, there was an absence of market prices. Asset backed securities were seen as unique and complex. There were few transactions. This meant that when Goldman Sachs approached AIG with a demand for $1.8 billion to compensate on CDS insurance, AIG disputed that figure. AIG argued that there was no market for these CDOs and that Goldman Sachs were aggressively marking down these bonds. Andrew Forster (Forster 2010), who worked on derivatives for AIG, in a series of interviews with the FCIC and emails he sent to the company made the argument that AIG was using its monopoly position to mark prices to market. Eventually, on that disputed transaction, AIG paid Goldman Sachs $500 million. This episode emphasized the inadequacies of the derivatives market. The market was opaque, there was no price discovery and the complexity of instruments had created increased uncertainty.

Secondly, there was the issue of concentration. The derivatives market was dominated by the five largest banks including, Goldman Sachs, JP Morgan Chase and Barclays. The OTC market therefore was within the narrow bands of a few broker dealers whose priority was to be rid of assets the bank was holding and which were likely to be marked down. Akerlof and Shiller (2009) used the concept of snake oil to argue that the spirit of capitalism is not just about selling what we need, but selling what we think we need. The ABS securities were a form of snake oil since the instruments were too complex, especially when it came to CDOs and synthetic CDOs. Clients did not have full knowledge of what they were buying or their levels of exposure. There was an asymmetry of knowledge between the seller whose primary aim was to offload mortgage backed securities and the buyer who trusted that the institution would sell them something that was good for them. Goldman Sachs had decided to go short on mortgage backed securities in 2006 and yet were still selling ABS to their clients throughout 2007. The investors had the confidence that they, as clients, were being sold a security that was good for them. The investment bank's major concern was to sell off the securities.

> But the bounty of capitalism has at least one downside. It does not automatically produce what people really need; it produces what they *think* they need and are willing to pay for. If they are willing to pay for real medicine, it will produce real medicine. But if they are also willing to pay for snake oil it will produce snake oil . . .
> But when there is false accounting the sale of assets resemble the sale of snake oil. Just as it is possible to hawk a fraudulent medicine by claiming it does something that it will not do, it is also possible to hawk stock, bonds or credit. (Akerlof and Shiller 2009, pp. 26 and 28, original emphasis)

The deregulated environment of 2000 made it possible for AIGFP to take on an exposure of $80 billion; selling CDS for an insurance of $7 billion would not have been possible had AIGFP had to post collateral. The 'grown-ups' at AIG would not have allowed for such an exposure.

> Suppose we had had traditional market controls. We have heard that the management of AIG didn't understand what was happening. If we had had traditional market controls, the subsidiary would have had to go to the holding company and say I've got to put collateral down. $80 billion probably would have been $7 billion in collateral. And when the adults in AIG understood that they were insuring mortgages by non-creditworthy individuals, my confidence is that they would have said: Are you kidding? We're not giving you $7 billion to run the risk of $80 billion. (Greenberger 2010, p. 58)

The celebrated ABACUS CDO manufactured by John Paulson is now part of financial folklore (Lewis 2010). Paulson had arranged with Goldman Sachs to select a number of securities that Paulson bet would default. Paulson took out insurance worth $15 million a year to insure these bonds even though Paulson did not have a direct interest. Goldman Sachs found a buyer for the CDO – IKB, which then took the long side. The CDO defaulted with one year and Paulson made $1.5 billion for his hedge fund company. IKB had to seek a rescue from their government. The Paulson case study became an issue during the FCIC inquiry with proponents arguing that people going short like Paulson were doing a service to the market by slowing done the optimism and the irrational exuberance that existed in the housing market:

> WITNESS KYLE: Well I think the people that went short did have chips on the table. Mr. Paulson I think had a 1.7 billion dollars worth of chips on the table that he turned into a large profit. But the people that bought the – took the long positions –

VICE CHAIRMAN THOMAS: Did you state that accurately? He couldn't have had a billion dollars of chips on the table going short, and then walk away with a billion dollars.

CHAIRMAN ANGELIDES: ... My understanding is, I believe from the work of our staff, is that I think Mr. Paulson paid about a $15 million annual payment, and I assume it was over probably about a two-year period or so, or three-year period, until payoff. So that was the ratio of leverage essentially ...

WITNESS GREENBERGER: ... And just to go back to the AIG example, or the person who took the opposite end of Mr. Paulson's bet – by the way, Mr. Paulson made that bet with $15 million. He got $1 billion. If he had lost the bet, he would have lost $15 million. He had absolutely no risk. (Kyle 2010, p. 34)

The Paulson study confirms the nature of the financial crisis of 2007. Witness Kyle did not know how much Paulson had bet but wanted to make the case that short selling through a CDO had made a positive contribution to the derivatives market. The derivatives market had allowed market participants to buy mortgage backed assets securities with high leverage ratios. The climate of low interest had reduced the risk factor and the asset backed securities were deemed to be as riskless as treasury bills with their triple-A ratings. The selling of CDS type insurance made the asset backed securities more attractive since investors felt that they were buying insurance against possible default. The problem was in that in these transactions no one was putting forward collateral. The ability to buy a naked CDS meant that short sellers could buy a cheap form of insurance without owning the bond and therefore had no exposure compared to the actual investors who had purchased the bond.

The FCIC (2011) had blamed deregulation and the role of Alan Greenspan in encouraging a deregulated environment: 'More than 30 years of deregulation and reliance on self-regulation by financial institutions championed by Former Federal reserve chairman Alan Greenspan and others ... have stripped away key safeguards which could have helped avoid catastrophe' (FCIC 2011, p. xviii).

LESSON 5: FINANCIAL CRISIS AND INCOME INEQUALITIES

Studies of income distribution during the past three decades confirm a major re-distribution of income toward the top 1 per cent of earners, and this is even more skewed when studying the incomes of the top 0.01 per cent. In the USA the pre tax incomes for the top 1 per cent of households had increased from 10 per cent of household income in 1979 to 21 per cent in 2008, while during the same period in the UK this increased from 6 per cent in 1979 to 14 per cent in 2005 (Sachs 2011). The studies of incomes of the top 1 per cent of earners show incomes growing for this group from 13 per cent to 27 per cent. The top 1 per cent had appropriated 65 per cent of total GDP growth during the past three decades (Atkinson et al. 2010; Stiglitz 2010). The concern with growing concentration of income inequality has been the influence this process has created in the policy making process.

> Each government aims to attract globally mobile capital by cutting taxes relative to others . . .
> The rich doubly benefit: by the forces of globalization and by the governmental response. Another reason for tax cuts at the top is the tawdry role of big money in political campaigns . . . US national campaigns costs several billion dollars every two years . . . Big Oil tends to finance the Republicans while Wall Street tends to finance the Democrats. (Sachs 2011)

In both countries there are parallel arguments about enterprise and incentives and the accompanying arguments that a successful economy requires low taxes. However, the erosion of the tax base means that the government has become increasingly dependent on the majority of the population to pay higher rates of tax. In the UK the number paying the 40 per cent tax rate has increased from 15 per cent of the population in 1979 to 47 per cent per cent in 2010.

Falling tax revenues and lower GDP growth created a crisis in public sector finances which meant governments coming under pressure to reduce spending on social provision, including pensions, unemployment benefits, health care and education. The downgrading of trillions of dollars worth of structured products from triple-A ratings to below investment grade resulted in fire sales which in turn reduced the expected incomes of pensions funds. The declines in equities very quickly led to major devaluations in retirement pensions. People who had retired discovered that their retirement incomes had fallen by 18 per cent. It is estimated that the recession resulted in the write-off of $10 trillion worth of households' net worth (Rich 2010). Furthermore the crisis in the financial markets quickly undermined consumer confidence. The response of households was to try and repair savings. Savings ratios showed major increases, from a savings rate of 1 per cent in 2003 to a savings rate of 5.8 per cent in 2009. These increases in savings impacted aggregate demand, which in turn led to increases in unemployment. In the USA unemployment jumped from 4 per cent to 9.8 per cent during 2010. The USA was losing jobs at the rate of 600,000 a month during late 2008 and 2009. The USA has lost 2 million jobs in manufacturing during the present recession.

LESSON 6: THE INFLUENCE OF IDEOLOGY IN ECONOMIC POLICY MAKING

Ideology as a system of beliefs contributed to the financial crisis in the sense that market liberal theories of rational expectations and efficient markets became the conventional wisdom. Institutions are guided by philosophies and a market liberal approach provided decision makers with ready-made toolkits for dealing with the economy. Theorists working in the laboratories of Departments of Economics needed transmission mechanisms for their ideas to become part of the policy process. The problem with the model was the calculative individual – the narrow ethics of weighing the costs and benefits to the person unencumbered by social context. The theory of efficient markets made the possibility of a bubble an impossibility because prices were supposed to move around their intrinsic values. There was no possibility that prices could become volatile and overshoot normal expectations. If bubbles did occur then this was because of irrational participants.

Market liberal economists were so reassured that the axioms of rational expectations and efficient markets had achieved the Kuhnian concept of a scientific paradigm that Michael Jensen was able to proclaim that rational expectations had been the most tested theory and had therefore emerged as the paradigm for future research in economics (Fox 2009). Robert Lucas, who was the founder of rational economics, was so reassured as to ascendance of market liberalism that he was able to proclaim in 1980: 'One cannot find good under-forty economists who identify themselves or their work as Keynesian. At research seminars people don't take Keynesian theorizing seriously anymore, the audience starts to whisper and giggle at one another' (Lucas 1980, pp. 18–19).

The academic world of economics was totally dominated by the thinking of rational expectations and efficient markets theorists after the mid-1980s. Academic journals would only publish papers which were mathematical. Mathematics became economics and economics without mathematics was no longer economics. The elegance of modelling became more important than the usefulness of the models. Engineers and physicist entered the world of economics without any knowledge of economic history or the discipline of economic ideas. The assumption was that economics could become a science equal in status with physics, with its own laws of supply and demand.

The modelling of data and the fitting of data expunged context and reality. The data was de-contextualized, with no attempt to relate changes in data to changes in policy processes. The models had a purpose in that institutions and policy practitioners need a philosophy and a series of readily available tools.

The myth that markets exist in their own right, obeying the laws of supply and demand similar to the laws of gravity, is in itself an ideology. Markets are socially constructed. To treat markets as a concept means that markets are always bigger than nation states and are always bigger than the global economy. Markets in this sense always become the exogenous factor that need to be obeyed. The laws of markets cannot be questioned because they are scientific laws. The use of mathematical models in economics has therefore excluded other forms of interpretation. Engineers, physicists and mathematicians can enter the world of economics without any knowledge of economic history or of economics ideas:

> Three closely related economic ideas transformed political, as well as economic thinking in the thirty year before the crisis. The first idea [was] known as rational expectations . . . the second ideas [was] called efficient markets . . . the third idea was more abstract but equally powerful: It stated that economics . . . must be transformed into a branch of mathematics . . . between them, these three ideas had profound political effects. Rational, efficient and mathematically inexorable economics legitimized a host of highly controversial political outcomes decreed by markets . . . Widening income inequalities, wrenching dislocations of employment and unprecedented riches for bankers and corporate executives could all be presented as the unavoidable, impersonal outcomes of scientific forces. (Kaletsky 2010, p. 158)

In addition, the recession also had spill-over effects on public finances. Declines in GDP also led to declines in government revenues. Lower GDP meant less revenue to the government. Revenues feel by 18 per cent in the UK. These factors created a problem for public finances. A smaller GDP and lower revenues were interpreted as creating structural deficits in public finances. Public sector reforms were focused on reducing social security benefits and increasing the retirement age.

However, some governments saw the crisis as an opportunity to bring about major policy changes that reflected ideologies rather than short-term pragmatic responses for dealing with deficits. Crises produce climates of uncertainty and changed expectations. After 2007, dealing with public sector deficits became a contestable site between pragmatic and ideological responses.

The UK coalition government has pointed out that that there was no alternative to reducing the deficit. Nick Clegg, leader of the Liberal Democrats, stated that he entered the coalition after listening to a presentation given by the Governor of the Bank of England to the potential coalition partners stressing the urgency of reducing the deficit. However, wholesale reforms of the National Health Service, higher education tuition fees, and the issue of retirement pensions and contributions were blueprint policy documents of the Conservative Party prior to the election and certainly prior to the financial crisis. The Conservative Party therefore had a blueprint for reform if they became the government. The financial crisis made the reforms possible.

LESSON 7: THE BREAKDOWN OF TRUST

People have trust in institutions. Confidence represents an implicit belief that when we as clients approach an institution they will behave as advisors, as our fiduciaries, having our best interest at heart, and we believe that something they sell us is going to be good for us because we are their clients. There is an implicit assumption of loyalty. The loyalty of the client who deposits his income and who believes the bank is acting in his best interest. However, the discovery of a conflict of interest shatters that relationship of trust. Investment banks collated bonds, that is, products which they needed to sell. The broker dealer responsibility was to reduce the exposure of the bank to these securities. The financial crisis was a crisis of trust in institutions. The crisis confirmed that clients who went to their banks to buy a bond could no longer assume that the bank was treating them as their client. The investment banks treated their clients as sophisticated investors who knew what they were buying and who wanted the level of exposure they were buying. So, while Goldman Sachs had been going short on mortgage backed securities since December 2006, they continued to sell mortgage backed securities to their clients as long-term investments. The Levin Investigation of April 2010 and the FCIC Inquiry confirmed that these bonds were often described as 'junk' or 'crap' by the analysts, who even celebrated when they managed to sell these junk bonds to their clients:

> Goldman documents make clear that in 2007 it was betting heavily against the housing market while it was selling investments in that market to its clients. It sold those clients high-risk mortgage-backed securities and CDOs that it wanted to get off its books in transactions that created a conflict of interest between Goldman's bottom line and its clients' interests . . . The ultimate harm here is not just to clients poorly served by their investment bank. It's to all of us. The toxic mortgages and related instruments that these firms injected into our financial system have done incalculable harm to people who had never heard of a mortgage-backed security or a CDO. (Levin 2010, p. 6)

The idea that banks looked after their own interests had already been highlighted during the Pecora hearings in January 1933, when Ferdinand Pecora was taking testimony from Charles Mitchell, the CEO of City Bank. During these hearings Mr Mitchell admitted that his bank had issued $50 million worth of bonds to shareholders and had transferred

$25 million to the bank's affiliates which had then used the $25 million to purchase the Sugar Corporation. The Sugar Corporation paid $25 million to City Bank to clear its debt. Pecora's argument was that the bank had not asked their investors whether they would have voted for such a move. Secondly, Pecora also confirmed that Mitchell had taken a salary of $2.5 million in 1929 – the equivalent to half a billion dollars in 2011. Mitchell and his senior managers were using the affiliates' general fund to compensate the senior executives. Finally, Pecora also was able to show that Mitchell had sold over 30,000 bonds at a loss to his wife in order to reduce his tax bill.

> In the space of three days, Pecora showed that City Bank – that paragon of banking virtue, one of the largest and most respected banks in the world – was engaged in the same kind of petty stock promotion as the Bank of the United States, the failure of which helped spark the banking crisis then gripping the country . . . City Bank was speculating in its own stock and selling it to the bank's own depositors. (Perino 2010, p. 186)

CEOs of investment banks in 2007 were taking salaries of $48 million together with stock options. Even when the dust settled and it turned out that the banks concerned had actually made a loss, none of these executives were asked to pay back their compensation packages. As in 1929, the banks sold ABS securities to their clients even as the banks themselves had bet that these same securities would default in the future.

The study of the financial crisis of 2007 confirms the presence of fragmentation of interests. The study confirms the absence of the notion of a public interest and who are the guardians of that public interest.

It cannot always be assumed that what happens in financial markets is always good for the economy. It is not true that all financial innovations contribute to economic prosperity. Daily transactions in financial markets do not translate into increased investment in factories, technology and new employment opportunities. Turner (2009), in his article in *Prospect Magazine*, pointed out that 90 per cent of transactions are socially and economically useless. Financial markets serve their own self-interest in creating new products to sell to potential investors. Large investors, including mutual funds and pension funds, need to invest income streams representing the retirement savings of clients that have to be invested to produce incomes over the long term. This study has confirmed that investors relied too much on the ratings provided by the Credit Rating Agencies without doing their own due diligence. Rating agencies were rating securities to sustain market share.

The gatekeepers of the public interest are the policy makers, while the daily guardians are the regulators who implement on a day-to-day basis the rules and framework created by the law makers. However, when the law makers come under the influence of narrow vested interests then the policy they generate reflects a particular interest as opposed to the public interest.

The skewed distribution of income towards the top 1 per cent of earners contributes to a process where the focus is on who gets what. Policies on taxation and public expenditure become contestable terrain with those on high earnings being able to hire lawyers and accountants that can help shape taxation policy to serve their interest and allows them to avoid paying their share of taxes, as opposed to those who then have to shoulder the tax burden.

Maybe it has always been so. There is no such thing as the public interest but a series of conflicts of interests and the question of who gets what. Conflicts of interest are issues of power and influence which are not static but which ebb and flow as the tide. Trade unions between 1950 and 1974 were in the ascendancy because of full employment and an increased membership who saw tangible results in belonging to trade unions. Trade unions were flourishing between 1950 and 1974. Full employment and Keynesian ideas contributed to low levels of unemployment and wages increased in line with productivity. From 1979 on trade unions have been in retreat. The narrowing of inequalities that characterized the period 1950 to 1974 went into reverse after 1979, so that inequality in Britain today is of a similar magnitude to that of 1884. There have been major shifts of influence to higher income groups. The paradigm of rational individualism and efficient markets enabled a process that resulted in incomes inequalities and higher levels of unemployment, which could be explained as being the natural outcomes of markets

The recent revolutions in the Middle East confirm that autocratic forms of capitalism, the capitalism of elites amidst a sea of poverty with privileges for a few, is not sustainable in the longer term. The multitudes have aspirations for improved quality of life through education, better health care, improved sanitation and a sense of a meritocracy. The advanced economies since the early 1980s have become high unequal with concentrations of incomes towards the top 1 per cent. There has been a moral deficit with high earners appropriating the largest shares of prosperity. The multitudes in the advanced economies have not been sharing in that prosperity.

There is, therefore, even within the advanced economies with a capitalism located in democracy, a series of contradictions that are making the system look less sustainable. The concentration of power and the influence on the policy process of a few political contributions are distorting the democratic process. In the longer term that might prove to be as sustainable as the autocratic capitalism that has dominated the Middle East.

REFERENCES

Akerlof, G. and R. Shiller (2009) *Animal Spirits: How Human Psychology Drives the Economy, and Why it Matters for Global Capitalism*. Oxford and Princeton, NJ: Princeton University Press.

Atkinson, A.B., T. Piketty and E. Saez (2010) 'Top Incomes in the Long-run of History', in A.B. Atkinson and T. Piketty (eds) *Top Incomes: A Global Perspective*. Oxford: Oxford University Press.

Cohan, W.D. (2009) *House of Cards: How Wall Street's Gamblers Broke Capitalism*. London: Allen Lane.

FCIC (2011) *The Financial Crisis Inquiry Final Report*. New York: Public Affairs.

Forster, A. (2010) Testimony of Andrew Forster Before the Financial Crisis Inquiry Commission, 1 July.

Fox, J. (2009) *The Myth of the Rational Market: A History of Risk, Reward, and Delusion on Wall Street*. New York: Harper Collins.

Geithner, T. (2010) Written Testimony by Secretary Timothy F. Geithner, House Committee on Oversight and Government Reform, 27 January, Washington, DC.

Greenberger, E. (2010) Testimony and Evidence Testimony to the Financial Crisis Inquiry Commission Hearing on the Role of Derivatives in the Financial Crisis, 1 July, Washington, DC.

Greenspan, A. (2011) 'Dodd-Frank Fails to Meet the Test of Our Times', *The Financial Times*, 29 March.

Haldane (2010) 'The Debt Overhang', speech given at a Professional Liverpool Dinner, 27 January.

Kaletsky, A. (2010) *Capitalism 4.0: The Birth of a New Economy*. London: Bloomsbury.

Kohlhagen, S. (2010) Testimony and Evidence Testimony to the Financial Crisis Inquiry Commission Hearing on the Role of Derivatives in the Financial Crisis, 1 July, Washington, DC.

Krugman, P. (2008) 'The B Word', *The New York Times*, 18 March. Available at: http://www.nytimes.com/2008/03/17/opinion/17krugman.html

Kyle, P. (2010) Hearing on 'The Role of Derivatives in the Financial Crisis', Financial Crisis Inquiry Commission, Official Transcript, 30 June, Washington, DC.

Levin, C. (2010) Opening Statement of Senator Carl Levin, U.S. Senate Permanent Subcommittee on Investigations Hearing, 'Wall Street and the Financial Crisis: The Role of Investment Banks', 27 April, Washington, DC.

Lewis, M. (2010) *The Big Short: Inside the Doomsday Machine*. London: Allan Lane.

Lucas, R.E. (1980) 'The Death of Keynesian Economics: Issues and Ideas', University of Chicago, Winter. Cited in R. Mankiw 'The Reincarnation of Keynesian Economics', *European Economic Review*, April 1992: 559.

Perino, M. (2010) *The Hellhound of Wall Street: How Ferdinand Pecora's*

Investigations of The Great Crash Forever Changed American Finance. New York: The Penguin Press.

Rajan, R. (2010) *Fault Lines: How Hidden Fractures Still Threaten the World Economy*. Oxford and Princeton, NJ: Princeton University Press.

Rich, F. (2010) 'Who Will Stand Up to the Superrich?', *The New York Times*, 13 November.

Sachs, J. (2011) 'Stop This Race to the Bottom on Corporate Taxation', *The Financial Times*, 29 March.

Stiglitz, J. (2010) *Free Fall: America, Free Markets and the Sinking of the World Economy*. London: W.W. Norton and Company.

Turner, A. (2009) 'How to Tame Global Finance', *Prospect Magazine*, Issue 162, 27 August.

Turner, A. (2010) 'Economics, conventional wisdom and public policy', paper presented at the inaugural conference of the Institute for New Economic Thinking, April, Cambridge.

Volcker, P. (2005) Speech given at Stanford University, 16 February. Available at: http://news.stanford.edu/news/2005/february16/summit-021605.html (accessed 12 July 2011).

Index